Leading Learning and T[...]
Higher Education

Leading Learning and Teaching in Higher Education brings together contemporary ideas on leadership, engagement and student learning into a practical, solutions-based resource designed for those undertaking the challenge of leading a university-level teaching module, programme or suite of programmes, particularly through periods of transformation or change. It encourages both first-time academic leaders and those who have held teaching leadership roles for some time to review and formalise their development in a systematic, simple way and acts as a framework for navigating the opportunities and challenges involved in inspiring shared purpose, strong commitment and innovation in higher education teaching.

With a clear focus on the energy of leadership rather than the practice of management, and with a strong emphasis on collaborative engagement running throughout, this books offers:

- Insightful guidance which is not bound to subject-specific requirements, making it relevant across the spectrum of course offerings at any one institution.
- An enabling, people-focused foundation for leadership.
- Tools and frameworks which can be readily applied or adapted for the reader.
- A focus on core elements of teaching leadership, such as design, delivery, assessment and building a programme team.
- A flexible and pragmatic approach to leadership which avoids a definitive approach, instead encouraging a dynamic method of engaging leadership.
- Values that assert that leadership and learning go hand-in-hand.
- A wide-ranging discussion of leadership theories, ideas and values related to the university context.

This book puts forward a multifaceted model of programme leadership and links this to a scaffolding of key attributes, skills and qualities that fit the environment of leading learning and teaching in the university. Particularly interested readers will be those beginning to lead teaching in a university setting as well as those who have been leading programme teams and the wider provision of teaching for some time wanting to enhance their skills and perspective.

Doug Parkin is Programme Director at the Leadership Foundation for Higher Education (UK), and was previously Head of Staff and Educational Development at the London School of Hygiene and Tropical Medicine (University of London), UK.

Key Guides for Effective Teaching in Higher Education Series

Edited by Kate Exley

This indispensable series is aimed at new lecturers, postgraduate students who have teaching time, Graduate Teaching Assistants, part-time tutors and demonstrators, as well as experienced teaching staff who may feel it's time to review their skills in teaching and learning.

Titles in this series will provide the teacher in higher education with practical, realistic guidance on the various different aspects of their teaching role, which is underpinned not only by current research in the field, but also by the extensive experience of individual authors, and with a keen eye kept on the limitations and opportunities therein. By bridging a gap between academic theory and practice, all titles will provide generic guidance on teaching, learning and assessment issues, which is then brought to life through the use of short, illustrative examples drawn from a range of disciplines. All titles in the series will:

- represent up-to-date thinking and incorporate the use of computing and information technology (C&IT) where appropriate;
- consider methods and approaches for teaching and learning when there is an increasing diversity in learning and a growth in student numbers;
- encourage reflexive practice and self-evaluation, and a means of developing the skills of teaching, learning and assessment;
- provide links and references to other work on the topic and research evidence where appropriate.

Titles in the series will prove invaluable whether they are used for self-study or as part of a formal induction programme on teaching in higher education (HE), and will also be of relevance to teaching staff working in further education (FE) settings.

Other titles in this series:

Assessing Skills and Practice
Sally Brown and Ruth Pickford
Assessing Students' Written Work: Marking essays and reports
Catherine Haines
Designing Learning: From module outline to effective teaching
Chris Butcher, Clara Davies and Melissa Highton
Developing Your Teaching: Ideas, insight and action
Peter Kahn and Lorraine Walsh
Enhancing Learning Through Formative Assessment and Feedback
Alastair Irons
Giving a Lecture: From presenting to teaching
Kate Exley and Reg Dennick
Inclusion and Diversity: Meeting the needs of all students
Sue Grace and Phil Gravestock

Leading Learning and Teaching in Higher Education: The key guide to designing and delivering courses
Doug Parkin
Small Group Teaching: Seminars, tutorials and beyond
Kate Exley and Reg Dennick
Using C&IT to Support Teaching
Paul Chin
Using Technology to Support Learning and Teaching
Andy Fisher, Kate Exley and Dragos Ciobanu
Working One-to-One With Students: Supervising, coaching, mentoring and personal tutoring
Gina Wisker, Kate Exley, Maria Antoniou and Pauline Ridley

Leading Learning and Teaching in Higher Education

The key guide to designing and delivering courses

Doug Parkin

For MAY,

WITH THANKS FOR YOUR SUPPORT
AND INSIGHTS.

APRIL, 2017.

Routledge
Taylor & Francis Group

LONDON AND NEW YORK

First published 2017
by Routledge
2 Park Square, Milton Park, Abingdon, Oxon OX14 4RN

and by Routledge
711 Third Avenue, New York, NY 10017

Routledge is an imprint of the Taylor & Francis Group, an informa business

Every effort has been made to contact the copyright holders for their
permission to reprint selections of this book. The publishers would be grateful
to hear from any copyright holder who is not here acknowledged and we will
undertake to rectify any errors or omissions in future editions of this book.

British Library Cataloguing in Publication Data
A catalogue record for this book is available from the British Library

Library of Congress Cataloging in Publication Data
Names: Parkin, Doug.
Title: Leading learning and teaching in higher education : the key guide to
    designing and delivering courses / Doug Parkin.
Description: New York : Routledge, 2017. | Includes bibliographical
    references.
Identifiers: LCCN 2016004567 (print) | LCCN 2016005182 (ebook) |
    ISBN 9780415598873 (hbk : alk. paper) | ISBN 9780415598880
    (pbk : alk. paper) | ISBN 9780203817599 (ebk)
Subjects: LCSH: College teaching. | Education, Higher.
Classification: LCC LB2331 .P3625 2017 (print) | LCC LB2331 (ebook) |
    DDC 378.1/25—dc23
LC record available at http://lccn.loc.gov/2016004567

ISBN: 978-0-415-59887-3 (hbk)
ISBN: 978-0-415-59888-0 (pbk)
ISBN: 978-0-203-81759-9 (ebk)

Typeset in Galliard
by Swales & Willis Ltd, Exeter, Devon, UK

For
Mary, Jamie and Kate
The leaders of my heart

Contents

List of illustrations   viii

Series preface   x

Preface   xiii

1 Leadership – *there really is another way*   1

2 A model of programme leadership   24

3 Management and leadership   48

4 Leading with influence   70

5 Understanding your brief   88

6 Leading course design   112

7 Leading assessment and feedback   147

8 Leading course delivery   169

9 Leading engagement   205

10 Leading yourself   218

Appendix 1: The Programme Leadership Model: self-assessment
  questionnaire   226

Appendix 2: The change journey: emotional responses to change   230

Bibliography   232

Index   241

Illustrations

FIGURES

1.1 Drivers for change in higher education   5
1.2 The benefits of higher education participation   7
1.3 Winnie-the-Pooh   17
2.1 Action-centred leadership   25
2.2 Managerial grid   27
2.3 Emotional intelligence and leadership   28
2.4 Leadership attributes   29
2.5 Leadership qualities   33
2.6 The Programme Leadership Model   35
2.7 Diamond-nine card arrangement   45
3.1 Leadership in an academic environment   52
3.2 What makes a rectangle a rectangle?   56
3.3 Leadership attributes   64
3.4 Management functions – achieving the task – POMCE   68
4.1 Learning-focused teaching and leadership   76
4.2 Push/pull influencing styles   79
4.3 Open and hidden influence   82
4.4 People Styles at Work   83
4.5 The change journey   85
4.6 The necessary art of persuasion   86
5.1 Stakeholder analysis   100
5.2 The 'what' of change   109
6.1 Engagement, commitment and accountability   115
6.2 The Fully Engaged Curriculum   127
6.3 The Fully Engaged Curriculum – 'doing' domain   128
6.4 The Fully Engaged Curriculum, with details   129
6.5 Divergent and convergent   133

6.6 Example of a six-pointed star   137
6.7 Example of a continuous feedback loop   144
7.1 Verbs are the markers for alignment   159
7.2 Constructive alignment   165
7.3 Bloom's Taxonomy– Cognitive Domain   166
8.1 Leadership and participation   178
8.2 Eight keys to liberating leadership   184
8.3 The Group Development Model   188
8.4 Diffusion of innovations curve   189
8.5 Confidence, competence and commitment   192
8.6 The learning practice spiral   194
8.7 The ingredients of effective feedback   199
9.1 The 3 Es   206
9.2 The student experience: what do students need?   208
9.3 The student experience: what do students need? – elaborated   209
9.4 Cascade of learner motivations   210
9.5 Maslow's Hierarchy of Needs in practice   213
9.6 Ladder of engagement   216
10.1 Three powerful questions   220
10.2 VEEDA   224

TABLES

2.1 Leadership skills   31
3.1 Management versus leadership   58
5.1 Programme Leadership Model – understanding your brief   90
6.1 Programme Leadership Model – leading course design   114
6.2 ART grid   143
7.1 Programme Leadership Model – leading assessment and feedback   149
8.1 Programme Leadership Model – leading course delivery   172
8.2 Facilitation – dimensions and modes   177
9.1 Programme Leadership Model – leading engagement   207

Series preface

THE SERIES

The *Key Guides for Effective Teaching in Higher Education* were initially discussed as an idea in 2002, and the first group of four titles were published in 2004. New titles have continued to be added and the Series now boasts 13 books (with a couple of new editions in the pipeline).

THE SERIES INCLUDES

- *Giving a Lecture: From presenting to teaching*, Exley and Dennick (2004), 2nd edn (2009).
- *Small Group Teaching: Seminars, tutorials and beyond*, Exley and Dennick (2004).
- *Assessing Students' Written Work: Marking essays and reports*, Haines (2004).
- *Using C&IT to Support Teaching*, Chin (2004).
- *Designing Learning: From module outline to effective teaching*, Butcher, Davies and Highton (2006).
- *Assessing Skills and Practice*, Brown and Pickford (2006).
- *Developing Your Teaching: Ideas, insight and action*, Kahn and Walsh (2006).
- *Enhancing Learning through Formative Assessment and Feedback*, Irons (2007).
- *Working One-to-One with Students: Supervising, coaching, mentoring and personal tutoring*, Wisker, Exley, Antoniou and Ridley (2008).
- *Inclusion and Diversity*, Grace and Gravestock (2009).
- *Using Technology to Support Learning and Teaching*, Fisher, Exley and Ciobanu (2014).

It has always been intended that the books would be primarily of use to new teachers in universities and colleges. It has been exciting to see them being used to support postgraduate certificate programmes in teaching and learning for new academic staff and clinical teachers, and also the skills training programmes for postgraduate students who are beginning to teach. A less anticipated, but very valued, readership has been the experienced teachers who have dipped into the books when reviewing their teaching, and have given the authors feedback and made further suggestions on teaching approaches and examples of practice.

In the UK, the work of the Higher Education Academy (HEA) in developing a Professional Standard Framework (UKPSF), on behalf of the sector, has also raised the importance of providing good-quality guidance and support for those beginning their teaching careers. It is therefore intended that the series would also provide a useful set of sources for those seeking to gain professional recognition for their practice against the UKPSF.

THIS BOOK

This book is an exciting addition to the series and I thank colleagues who suggested that the topic of leading learning and teaching should be included in the *Key Guides*. I particularly wish to thank Doug Parkin for researching and developing this aspect of our practice and collating a clear and accessible set of guidance here. He has combined his vast experience of management and leadership development, and educational development, with a clear understanding of the different leadership roles a university/college teacher undertakes when seeking to design and deliver high-quality education programmes and support an excellent student learning experience. Doug has found a very engaging, productive and illuminating way of combining theory and practice to derive a variety of leadership strategies and show their relevance in a range of easily recognisable teaching and learning contexts. One of the central themes of the book is that leadership and learning go hand-in-hand, and this liberating principle is powerfully reflected in the way the book encourages the reader to explore through personal discovery three central questions:

- What sort of leader do I want to be?
- What sort of leader do I need to be?
- And why should others follow me?

KEY THEMES OF THE SERIES

The books in the series are all attempting to combine two things: to be very practical and provide lots of examples of methods and techniques, and also to link to educational theory and underpinning research. Articles are referenced, further readings are suggested, and researchers in the field are quoted. There is also much enthusiasm here to link to the wide range of teaching development activities thriving in the disciplines, supported by the small grant schemes and conferences provided by the HEA. The need to tailor teaching approaches to meet the demands of different subject areas and to provide new teachers with examples of practice that are easily recognisable in their fields of study is seen as being very important by all the series authors. To this end, the books include many examples drawn from a wide range of academic subjects and different kinds of higher education institutions. This theme of diversity is also embraced when considering the heterogeneous groups of students we now teach and the colleagues we work alongside. Students and teachers alike include people of different ages, experience, knowledge, skills, culture, language, etc., and all the books include discussion of the issues and demands this places on teachers and learners in today's universities.

In the series as a whole there is also more than half an eye on trying to peer into the future – what will teaching and learning look like in 10 or 20 years' time? How will student expectations, government policy, funding streams, and new technological advances and legislation affect what happens in our learning spaces of the future? What impact will this have on the way teaching is led and managed in institutions? You will see, therefore, that many of the books do include chapters that aim to look ahead and tap into the thinking of our most innovative and creative teachers and teaching leaders in an attempt to crystal-ball gaze. So these were the original ideas underpinning the series, and my co-authors and I have tried hard to keep them in mind as we researched our topics and typed away. We really hope that you find the books to be useful and interesting, whether you are a new teacher just starting out in your teaching career or you are an experienced teacher reflecting on your practice and reviewing what you do.

Kate Exley
Series Editor

Preface

I would like to preface this book by saying not a single or selective word of gratitude, but rather a flood of thanks to all those I have worked with, learners and learned alike, in the ongoing quest to discover what it means to be a leader. When I look back with a reflective gaze, and the completion of this books seems an excellent opportunity to do so, I see how extraordinarily fortunate I have been. Within the context of higher education there are two institutions that made this possible: firstly the amazing London School of Hygiene and Tropical Medicine (University of London), and secondly and more recently the Leadership Foundation for Higher Education (UK). It does not seem sufficient to try and capture in dull words how special it has been to work with groups and individuals on learning and teaching development and leadership development through my engagement with these institutions and their partners. My thanks to both institutions, of course, and special thanks to all of the wonderful individuals who engaged and go on engaging in the journey of learning, development and discovery.

Amongst many personal highlights in my work as a developer in higher education, I would pick out firstly the Postgraduate Certificate in Learning and Teaching which we developed at the London School, and which perhaps more than anything else sparked my interest and curiosity regarding leading learning and teaching. More recently it has been an extraordinary privilege to be part of the facilitation team for the Leading Transformation in Learning and Teaching programme run as a collaboration for the sector by the Leadership Foundation and the Higher Education Academy (UK). Dipping my toes in the water of running development programmes overseas was another fantastic opportunity that came through my engagement with the London School, and in my current role it has been wonderful to broaden this perspective further facilitating some leadership programmes overseas with the Leadership Foundation.

Whether sculpting a learning experience in a lecture hall, facilitating a seminar or practical, tutoring or supervising students one-to-one, guiding a module team, directing a key programme or suite of programmes, or heading-up the learning and teaching endeavour across a faculty or institution, it is all leadership. And leadership is fundamentally about energy and engagement. As will be discussed in these pages, the difference between management and leadership is energy. Leaders work with their own and other people's energy, and understand that *the land of the possible* is a happier place to be. They liberate potential, harness learning and curiosity, and through collaborative engagement build shared purpose and commitment. Through engagement, they connect people with purpose, and purpose with people.

Finding a joy in serving others is, I believe, the greatest expression of our talents in any situation, whether this is direct service or a contribution that serves the greater good or the wider world. As Albert Schweitzer (1875–1965) said, 'the purpose of human life is to serve, and to show compassion and the will to help others'. So, whilst leaders may need to guide and direct, it is at least equally important that they understand how to serve and facilitate. Sharing inspiration and creating an environment where others can learn and succeed lies at the heart of this.

In the way that a growing child discovers a unique voice through unfolding passages of learning and discovery, so does a leader discover a voice and identity that is their leadership signature through a combination of experience, reflection and development, whether formal or not. Reflecting upon 'who am I?' and 'what sort of leader do I want to be?' is fundamental to this. And whilst empathy, passion and compassion are the essence of leadership, it is true to say that *leaders come in many forms*:

> Leaders come in many forms, with many styles and diverse qualities. There are quiet leaders and leaders one can hear in the next county. Some find strength in eloquence, some in judgment, some in courage.
>
> (Gardner, 1990)

The model of programme leadership presented and explored in this book is a framework for supporting personal discovery, developing increased self-awareness, and planning and structuring development. It also powerfully articulates the key attributes, skills and qualities that frame the challenge of leading learning and teaching in higher education and, indeed, potentially other contexts. It is a framework within which the reader can explore and discover what sort of leader they want to be.

In writing a recent book review, Susan Calvin, the author of *Quiet: The Power of Introverts in a World That Can't Stop Talking* (2012), made the following incisive observation:

> Great leaders aren't measured by their volume but by their ability to be truly heard. To motivate others, leaders must listen and communicate empathetically.
>
> (Susan Calvin, 2016, reviewing Duarte and Sanchez, (2016))

I would underline and emphasise the point that listening comes first in engaging leadership. Leaders must never stop listening. If they do, they stop being leaders.

Chapter 1

Leadership – *there really is another way*

THE CHALLENGE IN THIS CHAPTER

Leadership takes place in a context. It is, or should be, context-sensitive. Being a successful leader in one context, situation or era may involve quite a different set of challenges and opportunities from being successful in another. In this chapter we will set the scene in terms of the leadership of learning and teaching in higher education.

With a subject like leadership, it is very daunting to be definitive and this book won't be. It will, however, put forward a model of programme leadership and, linked to this, a structure of key attributes, skills and qualities that fit the context of leading learning and teaching (Chapter 2 introduces the Programme Leadership Model and an accompanying self-assessment questionnaire). The model and all that surrounds it is intended to act as a gateway and a guide to reflecting on your leadership and developing it further.

This book is aimed at people taking on the challenge of leading a teaching module or course for the first time, and should also be a valuable resource to colleagues with some experience who wish to review and formalise their development in this area or who are leading at higher levels with broader responsibilities. Some colleagues will come to teaching leadership enthusiastically as something that interests them personally and professionally, while others may find themselves persuaded or volunteered, but in either case this book should act as a guide and a framework for navigating what is often something of a neglected subject.

Our focus in this book will be on leadership – leadership in the context of course design, development and delivery, and particularly the leadership of change and transformation. This involves engagement, commitment, direction, alignment, generating energy and interest, and accountability. Our focus is on the leadership of people – teams and individuals – and how to influence, engage and empower.

We will not be looking in detail at management processes, project management or educational administration.

Whilst leadership is in some ways elusive to define, it should not be left to chance as regards personal and professional development. There is nothing greater than great leadership, not for what it is in itself but for what it enables others to achieve, create and become. By serving others, leaders enhance the present and help to shape the future.

In this chapter we will explore some of the issues and tensions in the current higher education landscape and will consider them in relation to leadership and the challenge of 'being' a leader.

To set the scene a little more conceptually, some features and principles you will find throughout this book are as follows:

- the value of collaborative engagement;
- leadership and learning go hand-in-hand;
- a highly student-centred approach, including partnership;
- having a purpose-driven outlook;
- participation helps to connect people with purpose;
- trust as the foundation of relationship for teams and individuals;
- 'being' is as important as 'doing';
- the power of listening;
- understanding others and being kind.

The chapters in this book will use a number of conventions:

- Each will begin with a short summary of 'the challenge in this chapter'.
- Chapters 4–9 all include a section showing links to the Programme Leadership Model (Chapter 2).
- At the end of every chapter (with the exception of Chapter 10), there is a set of questions for action and reflection. These are purely prompts, so pick out and consider those that either interest or, perhaps, challenge you most.

IN AT THE DEEP END OR GRADUAL STEPS?

There is something curious about the way we approach responsibility. Give us a little and we often protest, but give us a lot and we shoulder it with stoic resilience. It is even more curious how we approach giving responsibility to others. Ask someone to write a two-paragraph course description and we will frustrate them mercilessly with feedback on a dozen drafts, but ask someone with no prior experience to take over the leadership of a degree course and we quickly become arch-delegators. 'Just shout if you hit a problem' we chirp over a retreating shoulder or around the edge of a closing door. And what lies at the root of this obvious folly? Well, top of the list is the *knowing-your-stuff* fallacy that is actually the cause of many of the failings in education.

Being an expert or someone who 'knows their stuff' is a qualification – in the case of higher education usually a string of very grand qualifications – that prepares the individual to perform to a high standard, hopefully, within that particular discipline or profession and related areas. However, it does not necessarily prepare the individual to teach others. And it certainly doesn't prepare the individual *to lead others to teach others.*

An interesting comparison between management and teaching comes to light when we consider the answer to the question 'what matters most?' in terms of either leader or teacher attributes. High on many people's list in both cases will often be knowledge, and very often this will be seen as paramount. Many managers are promoted on the basis of their expert knowledge, and many have struggled as a result, not least because of their lack of empathy with those less knowledgeable than themselves. The manager needs to 'know their stuff' and be at least one step ahead of their underlings in the knowledge stakes: knowledge after all is power . . . But what about inspiring others to perform, succeed, achieve or learn? That's fine, many people will answer, but first you've got to *know your stuff.* We are back to that again. As we will discuss further in Chapter 4, knowledge can be one source of power when it comes to leading others, but used in isolation or in an unbalanced way, it can have severe limitations. There are strong parallels between what has been termed the 'expert manager' and the misconception in education that subject expertise is the main prerequisite for teaching others:

With regard to leadership:

> There are dangers in expert power. Research at the London School of Economics suggests that, while leaders who display a powerful 'leader' demeanour may boost their appearance of competence, they may stifle contributions by followers or subordinates in participative decision-making interactions.
>
> (Gill, 2011)

And with regard to teaching:

> One of the commonest errors that lecturers make is trying to present too much material. Slide after slide, overhead after overhead, example after example, the information pours out of the lecturer and the students end up trying to drink from a fire hose . . . One of the reasons why lecturers present too much information is the erroneous belief they have that if they 'cover' an area of knowledge in a lecture the students will automatically learn it. This is simply not true.
>
> (Exley and Dennick, 2009)

This knowledge trap, as we might term it, this 'knowing your stuff' is problematic in both contexts because it is about the difference between directing and facilitating. Does the teacher direct or facilitate student learning; does the leader direct or facilitate the performance of the team? Is it a passive or empowering form of student/team development? Does the teacher wish to fade into the background as students acquire both knowledge and the process of the discovery of knowledge (self-direction); does the leader wish to fade into the background as the team develops both shared commitment and a sense of mutual accountability (distributed leadership)? Since at least the 1970s, we have learnt from Carl Rogers (1983) and others of the humanist school that facilitating learning is more than anything else a human relationship, and as we will move on to discuss in later chapters we have similarly learnt over roughly the same period the same powerful message regarding the centrality of relationship in what has been termed transformational leadership (see Bass, 1985).

Meeting the challenge of moving from being a subject specialist or technical expert to becoming a leader involves a new range of attributes, skills and qualities in just the same way as becoming a facilitator of learning in the classroom:

> As professionals . . . move into leadership roles, their challenges largely arise from the fact that in their previous roles they put a strong emphasis on using data and logical reasoning. Learning the soft skills leaders use to manage people and teamwork – such as showing empathy and listening well – is typically not part of their education or training, and in many cases these skills do not reflect their natural preferences.
>
> (Eiser, 2008)

If a teacher needs to combine content knowledge with pedagogical knowledge linked to the specific challenge of what is being taught (Shulman, 1987), then a leader of learning and teaching needs to acquire an understanding of leadership in just the same way. The models, ideas and frameworks in this book are intended to provide a basis for this development linked to the specific challenge of leading learning and teaching in higher education: *a basis for more gradual steps*. This confluence causes us to focus on something that could be termed *learning-focused teaching and leadership* (see Figure 4.1 in Chapter 4).

'In at the deep end' is an expression that often goes hand-in-hand with the idea of 'sink or swim' and these two together are sometimes used, unfortunately, in relation to both education and leadership/management:

> In my work on accelerating leadership transitions, I still encounter lots of organizations that just don't get it. They persist, against reasoned argument and data, to foster a 'sink-or-swim' approach to leadership development. They hire and promote good people only to let them drown in the deep end of the pool. In the process, they damage the careers of high-potential managers, experience regrettable losses of talent, and weaken their leadership pipelines.
>
> (Watkins, 2007)

The alternative to this would be something like 'gradual steps', which suggests a more considered, better supported, and less brutal and risky approach. It suggests a structured approach to developing leadership capabilities that are specific to the leadership context.

THE WORLD IS CHANGING

The world is changing and learning and leadership change with it. The character of student engagement is evolving and the needs and expectations of students, and those who support them, are moving fast. The character of leadership is similarly evolving and the qualities of collaboration, boundary-spanning, relationship building, emotional intelligence and facilitating engagement required of leaders at all organisational levels reflect today's empowered work environments.

Surrounding higher education, there are currently a wide range of drivers for change, and these will differ depending on the geographical and cultural contexts. Figure 1.1 below provides five broad headings that create the basis for a worthwhile overview, although the shelf-life of any such discussion is inevitably limited:

1 **Funding and competition** The last ten years have seen considerable turbulence in global economies, firstly with austerity economics in the West and then a slowdown of economic powerhouses in the East. Linked to this, the public investment in higher education and university systems has come under pressure, and questions have been asked regarding how the financial burden should be shared between taxpayers, students, graduates and employers to make systems both more sustainable and socially inclusive. In England this was the premise of the Browne Review (Browne, 2010), which was published in October 2010 and made recommendations leading to the cap on student fees controversially being raised to £9,000 in the 2012/13 academic year. There has been much discussion regarding the impact of this, including concerns regarding the debt burden being placed on young people, the further perceived shift in the goal of higher education from a social good to a private good, and also the issue of students

DRIVERS
1. Funding and competition
2. Global – international
3. Quality and fairness
4. Technology
5. Students – students – students

FIGURE 1.1 Drivers for change in higher education

potentially becoming consumers. Alongside these funding reforms, a range of competitive pressures have also entered higher education or have become more apparent or pronounced:

■ competition between existing universities;
■ competition with higher education taking place in other settings (for example, further education in the UK);
■ competition with other forms of adult education;
■ competition with private educational providers and new entrants to the market;
■ competition with other modes of study and learning (mainly through the use of online technology);
■ competition with universities overseas;
■ competition for students;
■ competition for the 'best' students;
■ competition for international students.

Some governmental policies, for example those currently emerging in the UK, regard competition as a basis for innovation and reform.

2   **Global – international**   The growth in student numbers internationally combined with student mobility and the kind of competitive pressures mentioned above have resulted in the emergence of a truly global market-place for higher education. This in turn is transforming many institutions. Some are emerging as a kind of transnational corporation, some are looking to balance attracting international students with having campus operations in other country settings, and others are looking to establish strategic partnerships and collaborations in terms of joint provision and transnational programmes. Others still are using technology to blend traditional forms of education with online offerings and innovative forms of learner engagement. And amidst this it has proved challenging for institutions to remain strategically clear about their purpose, role and distinctiveness as the rapid pace of these changes has created a sense of imperative pressure, an adapt-to-survive mentality. For learning and teaching specifically, remembering the importance of things like community, relationship, place and belonging for deeper and more transformative student development has not always been easy in the face of these pressures. In a horizon scanning paper produced jointly in 2013 by the UK HE International Unit, the Observatory on Borderless Higher Education and the Leadership Foundation for Higher Education (Lawton et al., 2013), the following question was asked: 'What will higher education look like in 2020?' With regard to international student mobility and transnational education, the paper put forward the view that:

> The number of mobile students will grow significantly by 2020, although at a slower pace than in previous years. Transnational

education will also keep expanding, driven by growing demand in Asia, the expansion of international branch campuses in new markets and the spread of distance education, including MOOCs.

3   **Quality and fairness**   The drivers for change relating to quality and fairness take in all aspects of higher education – the inputs, the process and the outputs, to use that basic business model. Three questions predominate:

■   Who is higher education for?
    (The inputs)
■   What should be the quality and standard of the student experience?
    (The process)
■   What should higher education produce and who should benefit?
    (The outputs)

The simple answers to the first two questions might be 'everyone' and 'excellent'. The third question does not have a single facet, or even the pretence of one, and any answer needs to combine well-qualified, capable and prepared graduates with a wide range of private, social and economic benefits. In October 2013 the Department for Business Innovation and Skills in the UK produced a paper (Department for Business Innovation and Skills, 2013) reviewing the benefits of higher education participation for individuals and society. At the core of the report is a four-quadrant table with benefits illustrated through two dimensions: one being individual/society and the other market/non-market. Figure 1.2 below shows a simplified version of this table.

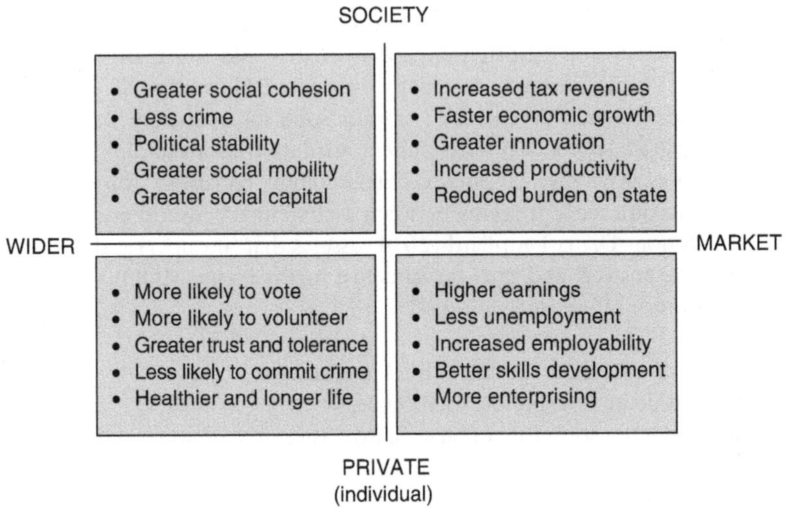

SOCIETY

• Greater social cohesion • Less crime • Political stability • Greater social mobility • Greater social capital	• Increased tax revenues • Faster economic growth • Greater innovation • Increased productivity • Reduced burden on state
• More likely to vote • More likely to volunteer • Greater trust and tolerance • Less likely to commit crime • Healthier and longer life	• Higher earnings • Less unemployment • Increased employability • Better skills development • More enterprising

WIDER   MARKET

PRIVATE
(individual)

FIGURE 1.2   The benefits of higher education participation

In different ways and in different contexts the goal of improving access to higher education is a significant driver. As well as the virtues of social mobility, inclusion and equality, the needs of modern economies in terms of a highly skilled, flexible and sophisticatedly dynamic workforce are growing by the day. This presents exciting challenges for learning and teaching in higher education as widening participation brings with it the need for more engaging and inclusive forms of curriculum design and learner support. Alongside this, a variety of systems, policies and frameworks have emerged, or are emerging, to enhance or safeguard aspects of student life and institutional performance: equality, fairness, transparency, inclusion, academic standards, quality assurance, consistency and transferability. National frameworks and codes of practice are increasingly looking to assure and mediate the performance of institutions able to grant higher education qualifications with quality audits, qualification standards for achievement and subject benchmarks. Enhancing the quality of teaching is another aspect of this, and the question of training and appropriately qualifying or accrediting those who teach and support student learning has become progressively more important and is increasingly in line with student expectations. In a UK student academic experience survey published by the Higher Education Policy Institute and the Higher Education Academy in June 2015 (Buckley et al., 2015), lecturers having formal teaching qualifications was valued more highly by the students surveyed than lecturers being active researchers.

4   **Technology**   A humorous remark I once came across is that 'any lecturer who is afraid s/he might be replaced by technology probably should be . . .' – a little unkind, perhaps, but it makes an important point. When massive open online courses (MOOCs) started to hit the headlines in 2011 and 2012, the fear was that this represented a form of disruptive innovation (Bower and Christensen, 1995) that would cause an avalanche of change. It has not quite materialised that way. However, what the debate around MOOCs has enabled is a more sophisticated appreciation of how to integrate technology with student learning without diminishing either. This is perhaps the real essence of technology 'enhanced' learning. There is a big difference it seems between a content revolution and a learning revolution. Diana Laurillard (2014) asserts that 'unsupervised learning is not the answer' and puts forward five myths about MOOCs which she goes on to refute:

- The idea that 'content is free' in education,
- Students can support each other,
- MOOCs solve the problem of expensive undergraduate education,
- MOOCs solve the problem of educational scarcity in emerging economies,
- Education is a mass customer industry.

Whether working online or not, students are certainly bringing with them new and rapidly evolving expectations of what technology is and what it can do. And this goes beyond the functional, with these digital natives (Prensky, 2001), as they have been termed, regarding communication, for example, as instinctively incorporating various digital channels and formats.

There are exactly 550 years between the invention of the printing press (1439) and the invention of the World Wide Web (1989) – a propitious figure, it would seem. However, even after 550 years, we had still not reached the point where around the world a book was within everyone's reach, but in the 25 or so years since the launch of the World Wide Web, computing and mobile technology has enabled the immense content of the Internet to come within the reach of an extraordinary range of the world's population, including in many low-income settings. Current estimates are that over 40 per cent of the world's population now have Internet access, a sevenfold increase since 2000 according to the International Telecommunication Union (ITU), the United Nations specialised agency for information and communication technologies (ITU, 2015). It is this extraordinary, perhaps exponential, rate of change that makes it so challenging for leaders at all organisational levels to forecast, make decisions and plan in relation to technology and activities involving technology (whether or not this is apparent when plans are made). Leading learning and teaching is no exception and it sometimes feels perilous knowing that the good decisions of today may be looked back upon as the bad decisions of yesterday due to technological advances. There is no single piece of good advice to remedy this, but the mindset of 'supplement not substitute' seems a virtuous starting point for beginning to incorporate technology enhanced learning into many traditional settings (a conservative stance, no doubt . . .).

5   **Students – students – students**   Students are now so central to not only the direction of their own learning but also the future direction of the curriculum and, indeed, the institution itself that they deserve to be trumpeted at least three times in any piece about change in higher education. There are also three important E's that recur again and again in the current narrative about students: student expectations, student experience and student engagement (see Figure 9.1 in Chapter 9). As a starting point, if leaders of learning and teaching keep these three E's alive in all of their thinking, planning and interactions, they will be well placed to respond to the changing world.

Why be a student? Good question! If we started to brainstorm ideas, we would quickly generate a long list. We would also highlight all sorts of variations based on the 'type' of student and various speculations regarding their background, needs and expectations. Are we considering a student living in the local community who is continuing their education at age 18 with a particular vocational calling in mind, or are we speculating upon a mature international student with no recent educational experience? There are big variations and rich diversity. And have the answers changed over time? With massification, with internationalisation, with changes to funding, with the use of technology, and with increasing concerns regarding careers and employability, have the answers changed? Well, some may have changed and some new answers may have entered the list. In the UK recent student academic experience surveys have included questions regarding value for money, for example. One consequence of student tuition fees and a loan system is that consumer-based questions of this kind start to have their relevance. Getting value for money – however 'value' is defined – would not have been a strong consideration in England until relatively recently and it suggests a mindset very different from the open-ended self-discovery that is potentially offered by, for example, a three-year, campus-based honours degree.

The motivation of students as learners and linking this with the nature and quality of the student learning experience brings in a new set of challenges and opportunities for course and module leaders. Being open and clear about the type of engagement, relationship and commitment that a course will entail, and modelling and reinforcing this at the outset of the programme are essential. Student choice should engage with these factors as well as considerations regarding subject, content, reputation and employability. Does the course do what we said it would in the way that we said that it would, and can students enjoy the opportunities for learning and discovery that we claimed were significant aspects of the course experience? Does the offering match the offer? There are then the attributes that exist through and around a subject – sometimes termed transferable skills – that equip students with a broader set of proficiencies and reflect the needs of employers and other stakeholders. Developing these attributes works well when they are integrated with equal emphasis within the programme aim and outcomes rather than being pursued as a parallel track.

Student engagement, the student voice and partnership are themes that we will return to throughout this book, and in Chapter 9 we will develop some specific ideas regarding the challenge of leading engagement.

This changing world brings with it a complexity to leadership that increasingly points towards a shared, inclusive and collaborative approach. It will need many minds (and hearts) working together and a shared commitment to a clear educational vision to continuously enhance a module, programme or suite of programmes in response to factors of this kind, which even the most informed horizon scanning cannot forecast with certainty. And creating a climate that draws inspiration from some of this uncertainty is part of the game (over recent years it has been fashionable to talk about VUCA business environments: volatile, uncertain, complex and ambiguous). A single focused transformation or pedagogic change may serve a particular goal, but could there be an opportunity alongside this to develop the potential and capacity of the team to innovate? Can the skills and capabilities around transformation and innovation be made sustainable so that we do not just reach the next steady-state that quickly becomes stale or outmoded? *Leaders as enablers of leaders* is a way of thinking that distributes responsibility for complex challenges such as curriculum enhancement, improving quality and student engagement throughout the team and which concurrently develops change capacity. From this mindset springs the importance of collaborative engagement for all core aspects of course design, the importance of shared purpose for assessment and feedback, and the importance of collective commitment and mutual accountability for course delivery.

POWER AND RESPONSIBILITY

In the very first Spider-Man story published by Marvel Comics in 1962 (Lee and Ditko, 1962), the narrative voice tells us in a caption that 'with great power there must also come great responsibility' following the death of our eponymous hero's uncle – a death he could have prevented ('with great power comes great responsibility' is a phrase or sentiment with, it seems, uncertain origins ranging from the Bible to Voltaire). Tragically Uncle Ben had no inkling of his nephew's extraordinary powers and therefore the enormous significance of these words. Now, being asked to be a course or module leader is not quite the same as acquiring super-powers, although many course leaders wish they had them, but the point on power and responsibility absolutely applies. The leadership of a formalised learning programme brings with it both power and responsibility, and leaving to chance the development of those new to such roles is both a great risk and a great injustice. Many may suffer as a result: students, academic colleagues, administrators, professional stakeholders and from a reputational perspective the institution itself, not to mention the hard-pressed individuals concerned.

Into whose hands do we place the responsibility for learning? Well, in many important respects, we would like students to take responsibility for themselves and their own learning. We would like them to be empowered regarding the learning process and to develop the skills of enquiry and discovery within and around their subject focus. Unfortunately, though, there seems to be something about enrolling on a course run by an institution that is inherently disempowering, and this may be one of the reasons why it is so hard to get many traditionally focused students to really embrace the idea of their own learning being their own responsibility. This is connected with the directed nature of traditional forms of study and the prevailing model of giving and receiving knowledge, and also the almost transactional goal of achieving and being granted a qualification. But the responsibility for course leadership is not something we can escape or conveniently side-step with worthy notions of self-directed students, because leadership and good course management create the framework, the practical set-up and the work and study culture that enable important principles such as student-centred learning to flourish and a truly collaborative learning environment to become a reality. All of the decisions made, the teamwork, the interplay between colleagues and the attention to detail in course arrangements are critical to supporting and enabling successful student learning. This is not to say that it is a purely administrative challenge, although the value of good administration should never be underestimated, but the art and science of good leadership is fundamental to supporting the 'art and science of helping adults learn' (Knowles, 1980) within institutional settings such as colleges and universities. And with great power does come great responsibility, and when the heat of the managerial battle becomes a little too hot to bear, as sometimes it will, it is worth remembering that it is actually a marvellous privilege to have responsibility for enabling others to learn.

CONTRASTING EXPERIENCES

'The first year was hell' was one individual's opening remark when I asked him how his experience as a module leader had developed. His account of being 'dropped in it' at the last minute, receiving no worthwhile training or support, poor administration, non-cooperative and uncommitted colleagues, shambolic assessments and disaffected students will, unfortunately, ring bells with other, often relatively junior, lecturers. To this individual's credit, he came through the experience, made considerable improvements to the teaching module (both process and product) in subsequent years and is now in a position to offer invaluable guidance and support to others. However, we should not dress this sort of example up as being in any way proof of the merits of trial-and-error development. We should see it for what it is: cruel, unhelpful and potentially very destructive. Huge risks are attached to this 'in at the deep end' approach and without listing them, it should be self-evident that they involve risks to the students and their learning, risks to the staff and their development, and risks to the department/faculty/institution and its reputation. Of course, experiences are highly contrasting, both between individuals and institutions, and some colleagues are well supported both formally and through the friendship and diligence of their peers.

One solution to these contrasting experiences, and the problematic outcomes that can result, might be some form of regulation or a framework of relevant standards. However, regulatory reform is a difficult and contentious area for higher education. Preserving independence – of thought, governance and purpose – is highly valued, and whilst university status, degree-awarding powers and public funding all come with a variety of standards and requirements, including different kinds of scrutiny and accountability, the underlying status of universities as independent institutions in contexts such as that in the UK remains fundamental. A key aspect of regulation concerns ensuring things like quality, consistency and transferability, and giving coherence to a 'university system' that works both within a country and across countries and regions. Linked to this is the notion of preserving or enhancing the reputation of a university

system. Commenting on a report specifically focused on regulating higher education (Norton and King, 2013) produced by the Higher Education Commission
(UK), itself an independent body, the co-chair Lord Norton expressed the
view that 'we need to move now to protect higher education because we have
this global reputation and if something goes wrong it becomes extraordinarily
difficult to regain that reputation' (Swain, 2013).

The narrative of reform and standards in UK higher education, as regards
what might be termed the modern era, has an excellent point of reference in the
report produced by the National Committee of Inquiry into Higher Education in
1997 (Dearing, 1997), also known as the Dearing Report after the Committee's
Chairman and the report's main author, Sir Ronald Dearing. The report makes
a total of 93 recommendations and it is remarkable how much of the higher
education agenda in the UK has been shaped or influenced by them in the years
since the report's publication. In relation to course management and teaching design, one of the recommendations was that all university courses should
have a 'programme specification' giving the intended learning outcomes of the
programme in terms of:

■ The knowledge and understanding that a student will be expected to
have upon completion;
■ Key skills: communication, numeracy, the use of information technology and learning how to learn;
■ Cognitive skills, such as an understanding of methodologies or ability
in critical analysis;
■ Subject specific skills, such as laboratory skills.

(Dearing, 1997: Recommendation 21)

That such a recommendation was necessary perhaps illustrates the variability
in standards and practices that existed in the higher education sector at that
time. That same landmark report also set out an expectation 'that institutions of
higher education begin immediately to develop or seek access to programmes
for teacher training of their staff' and that a professional body be established
'to accredit programmes of training for higher education teachers' (Dearing,
1997: Recommendations 13 and 14). Since Dearing, much has changed in
the UK and on the whole this is to be celebrated, with a Quality Assurance
Framework launched in 2002 which includes independent institutional audits
(conducted by the Quality Assurance Agency for Higher Education (QAA))
and a framework of professional teaching standards launched in 2006 with
independent accreditation for HE teacher training (carried out by the Higher
Education Academy (HEA)). Many university websites now have pages replete
with programme specifications, and a large majority of UK universities now
require new academic staff to engage to some degree with formally accredited
teacher training or continuous professional development. It is interesting to
speculate regarding the UK's apparent success in this area: it could be seen as 'a
reflection of the growing regulatory environment which has become common

13

in Britain in recent years throughout the professions' (Gosling, 2010) or a sign of how the funding environment has created competitive pressures. It may also be linked with student expectations and a more empowered and influential student voice. Interestingly one of the results of a UK Academic Experience Survey published in June 2015 was that students ranked staff 'have received training in how to teach' as more important than staff being 'currently active researchers in their subject' (Buckley et al., 2015). In the USA, by contrast, accreditation and regulation is through authorised regional and subject specific organisations, often federations of professional and technical societies, all of which are non-profit corporations, and the federal government plays a very small role. The current indications are that in the USA, any attempts to similarly centralise quality assurance and teaching standards would be strongly resisted on the grounds of academic freedom. The current position in Australia is different again, particularly following the Bradley Review in 2008 (Bradley et al., 2008), which has led to a raft of governmentally driven and funded measures, including the establishment in 2010 of a new national body for regulation and quality assurance (the Tertiary Education Quality and Standards Agency (TEQSA)). Branded as 'a new era of quality in Australian tertiary education', the TEQSA's remit was ambitiously described originally as follows:

> The Tertiary Education Quality and Standards Agency (TEQSA) will enhance the overall quality of the Australian higher education system. It will accredit providers, evaluate the performance of institutions and programs, encourage best practice, simplify current regulatory arrangements and provide greater national consistency.
>
> (Commonwealth of Australia, 2009: 31)

A key driver behind many of these national initiatives to improve the quality of higher education is the idea of becoming or remaining 'world-class'. The Bradley Report refers to this directly by highlighting the importance of Australia providing 'a clear and unequivocal statement about its intention to maintain a world-class university system' (Bradley et al., 2008: 124). When announcing his intention to develop a framework for higher education in February 2008, the then UK Secretary of State for Innovation, Universities and Skills, John Denham, emphasised that 'we need to decide what a world-class [higher education] system of the future should look like, what it should seek to achieve, and establish the current barriers to its development' (Denham, 2008). Even in the USA, despite the relative reluctance regarding federal intervention, a 2006 report commissioned by the Department of Education into the future of US higher education identified as top of its list of expectations that 'we want a world-class higher-education system that creates new knowledge, contributes to economic prosperity and global competitiveness, and empowers citizens' (US Department of Education, 2006: xi). In all of these cases one could, perhaps, stop the carriage for a moment and ask the drivers concerned exactly what they mean by a world-class university system: as Philip Altbach has poignantly observed, 'everyone wants one, no one knows what it is and no one knows how to get one' (cited in Salmi, 2009). Notwithstanding this clear dilemma, being 'world-class' is a common aspiration for both national university systems and leading universities, but achieving world-class institutional performance requires a grassroots investment in individual staff and leadership: it cannot be imposed, it has to be grown and nurtured.

Having reflected on reform, regulation and standards in higher education, and considered some of the key reports and enquiries, one is left with an impression of both expectancy and tension – tension, for example, between tradition and modernisation, autonomy and regulation, inclusiveness and exclusivity, and, perhaps rather worryingly, research and teaching. And it is interesting to ask where does leadership development feature in all of this, particularly as regards the leadership of learning and teaching? It certainly doesn't leap out as a clearly identified priority. And I'm not talking about what might be termed strategic or organisational leadership, but rather the tactical and operational leadership that turns ideas into action and in the case of teaching enables programmes to flourish. Where amongst all of this 'world-class' reviewing of the sector will you find anything emphatic and empowering regarding perhaps the single most important factor influencing quality, programme leadership? Surely leadership development should feature as a cornerstone of any new quality framework, or are we content to go on with the often cruel practice of throwing colleagues 'in at the deep end'?

In the UK the current version of the UK Professional Standards Framework for Teaching and Supporting Learning in Higher Education (UKPSF) (Higher Education Academy, 2011) sets out four descriptors. Descriptor three includes as regards the typical role profile 'the organisation, leadership and/or management of specific aspects of teaching and learning provision' and descriptor four refers to 'wide-ranging academic or academic-related strategic leadership responsibilities in connection with key aspects of teaching and supporting learning'. As an enabling framework linked to recognition and accreditation, both within institutions and through the Higher Education Academy's national accreditation scheme, the UKPSF can be used to support, frame and structure more formalised approaches to leadership development. It is also valuable for those with experience of leading learning and teaching as an opportunity to reflect on their journey of development, consider their influence and impact, and consolidate their learning through an individual application for recognition. In future versions of the framework there is the potential to integrate leadership, with a broad definition, as a strand throughout all four descriptors to encourage a more explicit developmental focus on the attributes and skills that are increasingly needed at all levels to work collaboratively, engage colleagues and students, and respond to creative challenges and innovations. Many teaching module leaders, for example, or those leading components within a module face these challenges.

More broadly, in the UK there are generic national occupational standards relating to management and leadership at various levels (the latest is the 2012 version: Skills CFA, 2012). These underpin, for example, apprenticeships and vocational and vocationally related qualifications of various kinds. Nationally recognised organisations such as the Chartered Management Institute (CMI) use these standards to structure some of their own awards and also as a bench-mark for providing recognition and accreditation to training providers, including employers. The Institute of Leadership and Management (ILM) uses the national occupational standards in a similar way and both organisations also offer various levels of recognition and membership. Neither organisation has a particular focus on higher education, although many universities in the UK use their qualifica-tion and accreditation structures to some degree, particularly to support relevant aspects of staff development.

Another issue with 'sink-or-swim' development strategies is that they often cause people to perpetuate the only educational paradigms they really know: their own. It is not at all unusual for staff on learning and teaching courses to reflect along the lines that 'I taught the students that way because that was how I was taught myself' or perhaps more problematically 'if it was good enough for me it should be good enough for them'. The same kind of serial neglect, or lack of informed awareness and development, can apply to leadership, such as when a leader leads as they were led, even if sometimes they suffered as a result of that leadership. Better still and a lot more positive are the reflections that highlight revelations, such as my favourite with regard to classroom teaching, 'I never realised you could ask the students questions' (there is again a direct parallel with leadership). This is not a criticism of the teachers concerned – far from it. Without a reasonably well-structured framework of educational ideas and approaches, and the encouragement and support for active reflection, such as should be the basis for any good learning and teaching certificate, it is very dif-ficult to review and change teaching practices. There is a wonderful E. H. Shepard illustration from A. A. Milne's *Winnie-the-Pooh* (1926) that summarises this beautifully: 'there really is another way' (see Figure 1.3 below).

How many of us as teachers bump down the stairs on the back of our heads suspecting that there really must be a better way without ever having the time, space, opportunity and for that matter support to discover it? And how many leaders do the same?

All of the above becomes horribly magnified when it comes to leading courses or modules. The influence of one's outlook and decisions suddenly goes beyond the consequences for student learning of a poorly facilitated session or two, or a misjudged tutorial, to impact upon the character of an entire curriculum, or cur-riculum element, and the effectiveness of the teaching and assessment of which it is comprised. As we will explore throughout this book, leading teaching is much more than an organisational endeavour – it is also about modelling and inspiring the ethos of the learning and teaching experience.

But the bumping can stop, and so can the lack of considered support for leadership development in the area of learning and teaching. It doesn't always have to be that way and it isn't always that way. There are various examples of staff being supported to develop into teaching leadership roles in a reasonably well-considered manner, through 'gradual steps' of at least partially thought-through development. One scenario that is often seen is a growth-from-within approach where a member of the programme team takes on more and more of

Here is Edward Bear, coming downstairs now,
bump, bump, bump, on the back of his head,
behind Christopher Robin.

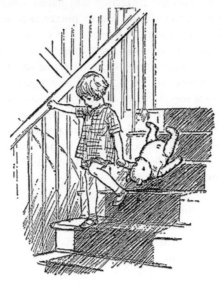

It is, as far as he knows, the only way of
coming downstairs, but sometimes he feels that
there really is another way, if only he could
stop bumping for a moment and think of it.

FIGURE 1.3 Winnie-the-Pooh. Text by A. A. Milne © Trustees of the
Pooh Properties 1926. Published by Egmont UK Limited and used with
permission. Reproduced with permission of Curtis Brown Group Ltd, London
on behalf of The Shepard Trust Copyright © The Shepard Trust. From
WINNIE-THE-POOH by A. A. Milne, illustrated by E. H. Shepard, copyright
1926 by E.P. Dutton, renewed 1954 by A. A. Milne. Used by permission of
Dutton Children's Books, an imprint of Penguin Young Readers Group, a
division of Penguin Random House LLC.

the teaching and assessment as successive cycles of delivery go by. They move on
to leading by virtue of their extensive familiarity with the content of the module
and the learning and teaching strategies involved. The challenge for them is generally twofold: firstly taking a fresh perspective and being receptive to innovation,
and secondly managing and influencing people (often close colleagues). Another
approach is a form of collaborative management, or distributed leadership, where
all staff involved in the course are actively encouraged to have a say in the planning and evaluation stages of the course cycle. This encourages colleagues to
start engaging with key tactical and operational questions regarding course management before they move on to formal leadership roles. A third approach is

co-management, which has the advantage of providing a form of apprentice-ship with staff new to course leadership working alongside more experienced colleagues. This brings in the mentoring skill-set which is a form of 'on-the-job' development, which deserves greater recognition generally in terms of the impact it can have on personal development and its potential to enhance the perfor-mance of teams and organisations. A precursor to co-management might be a shadowing relationship, with one colleague having the opportunity to observe at close quarters another with recognised experience and ability in course manage-ment prior to being mentored to take up the reins themselves. To some, though, this might come across as something of a luxury in resource-constrained environ-ments. There also needs to be a word or two of caution regarding mentoring, a grand term that is often inappropriately applied to any form of ad hoc one-to-one guidance. Careful thought should be given to who mentors, the development of the mentor in terms of both skills and their understanding of adult learning, and the nature of the mentoring relationship:

> A rough-and-ready rule of thumb is that [mentoring] programmes intro-duced without any training, or with a minimalist briefing, rarely result in more than one in three [mentoring] relationships delivering any significant benefits to the participants.
>
> (Clutterbuck, 2001: 82)

We will move on to consider mentoring in more detail later as one of four key leadership attributes that make up the Programme Leadership Model proposed in this book.

So, reassuringly, there are good practices that we can draw on as potential anti-dotes to the 'in at the deep end' approach to leadership development described above. However, being parachuted in to do one's best for a group of hope-fully able students is a mindset that many, unfortunately, have hitherto at least regarded as acceptable. Amongst other factors, this is partly brought about where teaching as an academic activity has a Cinderella status. Institutional contexts differ considerably as regards the perceived status of teaching relative to other activities, particularly research, and where teaching is generally seen as a lesser or secondary academic activity, it is more likely that the challenge of leading learning and teaching will be undervalued.

As observed previously, the growth of higher education and widening par-ticipation brings with it the need for more engaging and inclusive forms of curriculum design and learner support, and this presents exciting challenges for those leading learning and teaching. Commenting on the changing scene in university teaching, Biggs and Tang (2007) observe that 'in the days when university classes contained highly selected students, the lecture and tutorial seemed to work well enough', but now that in many countries more than 40 per cent of school leavers are in higher education, 'cramming students into large lecture halls is no longer good enough'. As student diversity has grown, so has the diversity of their needs, motivations, approaches to learning and capacity for independence, and with this the emphasis on high-quality teaching and student support has increased as never before. It is therefore good to see that across the higher education sector, teaching leadership is starting to feature in role definition documents of various kinds concerned with academic progression, pay structures and career mapping.

We shouldn't in all of this lose sight of the fundamental satisfaction that comes from doing things well. The satisfaction, for example, of giving colleagues the opportunity to learn more about the module they teach on, to have a say in how it could be further developed or improved, to follow the teaching design cycle through from planning learning outcomes to evaluating student performance against those same intended outcomes, to shadow a gifted and experienced course leader, and to enjoy formal development through a combination of tailored leadership workshops and skilful mentoring. All other arguments aside, this nurturing, developmental approach is simply a more satisfying, more life-enriching, and more human and humane way of going about things.

AN UNDERESTIMATED UNDERTAKING

It is now the case in the UK that the large majority of higher education institutions run or provide their staff with access to formally accredited courses in learning and teaching, usually postgraduate certificates or similar, but increasingly wider continuing professional development (CPD) schemes (Harrison, 2014). But leadership? Well, that's another matter. It is great if course leaders have strong insights into the key principles of course design based on educational theory and good practice, but that is only one aspect of programme leadership, as we will explore.

It is easy to take anything that is very well organised for granted. Take the humble letter or parcel that arrives at your home. It may be a surprise or something you were expecting; it may bring you pleasure or be an irritating tax demand. No matter. The often uncelebrated victory is that it arrived there at all. The intricate pathways through a modern, international postal system are extremely complex, and the coordination of human activity, technology and resource management that leads to the successful delivery of not just one but millions of items is a study in organisational management and leadership that is extraordinarily impressive, if only one took the time to appreciate it. The same is true of the modern university degree course. It may have become, in some people's minds, something of a shopped-for commodity, with institutions giving every impression of competing for custom just as much as they compete for scholarly recognition, but when a student graduates, it is just as impressive as the parcel arriving. It is expected to happen, it is part of our raison d'être after all, and even though it is an exceptional moment in the life of the individual, it is a common outcome that is routine business for the university. But if we take the time to look and appreciate everything that went into this underestimated undertaking, it is extraordinarily impressive. And the more apparently smooth the journey, the more consummately well organised the course, and much of this is down to great leadership. Other university activities may attract large amounts of funding, they may be prestigious, they may be well resourced, they may be flexible with changes in direction and emphasis, and they may be able to extend their deadlines if circumstances change (something that's hard to do with a three-year degree course), but if you really want to see effective management and leadership in action, take a look at a well-run course or module with high levels of student satisfaction and good employability credentials.

Coming back to our letter or parcel, one way of appreciating the 'plonk on your doormat' is to stress-test the system. This is basically a fancy way of saying analyse everything that could have gone wrong but didn't. So, when cousin Jack handed the letter to Bill the postie whilst rushing to work one morning in suburban Melbourne, Australia, what were all the potential points of failure or delay between there and its safe arrival five days later at the intended address in Edinburgh, Scotland? Sure, some letters go missing and some students drop out of their degrees, and, to stretch the metaphor a bit further than is really advisable, some packages get a little damaged along the way . . . But when you consider all of the critical points for students, tutors, lecturers, assessors, course leaders and professional support colleagues along the complex journey of a degree course, it really makes no sense at all to underestimate the leadership challenge involved. This underestimated undertaking needs far greater recognition, as do the course leaders who work so hard to try and guarantee safe delivery.

YOU GET WHAT YOU REWARD

There are few careers in modern life as preoccupied with recognition as academia. The nomenclature of grades and titles is wonderfully rich, and manages to combine excitement with mystery and ambiguity in roughly equal measure. For instance, in the UK we can confidently say that the executive head of a higher education institution is called a vice chancellor . . . or a president, or a provost, or a rector, or a director, or a master, or a warden . . . And just as we begin to agree some common ground that most of them are, in fact, called vice chancellors, someone will pipe up that in Scotland the usual term is 'principal'. Some, now, are even termed 'chief executive'. It's rich with history, tradition and generally poorly defined significance. But in case you get the impression that in the liberalised environment of a modern university these titles have the nature of a charming tradition that just happens to persist, think again. Titles such as 'professor' or 'reader' are hard-won markers in an elaborate career structure that is highly aspirational in its nature. Take for example the advice sometimes given to junior administrators: *if in doubt about an academic's title, always use the highest of the likely options.*

But does the current system and structure in higher education give appropriate recognition to teaching and the development of learning and teaching? Well, institutional contexts vary, of course, but in many the emphasis on research performance outweighs other factors. And there is some irony in this because one of the most clearly recognisable titles in academia is that of lecturer. The clue is in the title, you might think. Many would quite naturally associate the noun with its corresponding verb, meaning one who lectures, and would look to the term's derivation in 'reading aloud' to prove their point. However, there are many lecturers who regard teaching as a secondary role to be fitted around what they see as their primary pursuit: research. Rather than highlighting these differences and divergences, a healthier and more holistic approach might be to see research and teaching as intrinsically linked – two sides of the same academic coin, as it were: developing knowledge and sharing it with others. And research-based teaching draws students in as participants in the research process as well as engaging with research content to develop the 'skills of intellectual flexibility, analysis and enquiry' (Jenkins et al., 2007) that the modern world increasingly demands from future graduates.

The context in which we lead teaching, whether as module leader or dean of studies, is strongly influenced by the framework of recognition and reward that surrounds the undertaking. 'You get what you reward', a provocative expression used in management consultancy, says it all. Recognition through formal and informal structures, from pay and grading to simple praise and encouragement, is essential in determining the value we place on teaching activities. If we want dedicated and talented teachers, we must reward their dedication and their talent, and not just in a token way that is an adjunct to other 'grander' undertakings. To some extent this issue of reward and recognition, and the Cinderella status of teaching in some contexts, is beginning to be faced up to by the modern university system. New models for career structures are seen as one solution, such as having separate strands where senior teaching fellows and teaching professors operate alongside their research counterparts. Requiring lecturers to demonstrate their achievement of professional teaching standards as a stepping stone to progression, usually through accredited certificates in learning and teaching or wider CPD schemes, is regarded as another. But perhaps the most profound change is coming from the students themselves. As explored in an earlier section, the influence and impact of the student voice has grown considerably and there is now the potential to work with students as partners in the course design and development process, as well as with regard to wider institutional issues and decisions. We are back to the three E's that recur again and again in the current narrative around teaching in higher education: student expectations, student experience and student engagement.

We must recognise that the landscape of higher education has changed profoundly as what was a system for highly selected students has become a truly mass market, and an international one at that. Writing in 1998, Paul Ramsden observed regarding growing student numbers that 'they are no longer a gifted and motivated academic group, capable of surviving the bleakest of bad teaching, but more like school students in their range of ability' (Ramsden, 1998: 15). This inevitably requires more skilful, flexible and innovative teaching, and much stronger and more diverse systems for student support. However, despite this, it is still unfortunately not unusual for academic staff with a real commitment to teaching to sometimes feel marginalised, and for people leading learning and teaching to experience frustration with colleagues who fail to teach well because they fail to prioritise the teaching element of their wider role.

In later chapters (particularly Chapter 3) we will explore some definitions of both management and leadership, and some conceptions around this. But the key message is that 'there really is another way' when it comes to supporting and developing colleagues at all levels who hold responsibility for leading learning and teaching. *Leaders connect people with purpose . . . and purpose with people.* And this involves having a passion for the purpose and a compassion for the people. It requires the drive of the 'champion' and the emotional intelligence of the 'enabler'. This underestimated undertaking is, perhaps, the hardest of them all.

QUESTIONS FOR ACTION AND REFLECTION

1   What has helped you to know, understand and appreciate all aspects of the module/course(s) that you are involved with?

2   What motivates you to teach and facilitate student learning to a high standard? What would help to strengthen this motivation further?

3   What positive steps are taken in your environment to support colleagues taking on leadership responsibilities in relation to learning and teaching? Identify one or two additional actions that could be taken to support colleagues further (particularly those taking on leadership responsibilities for the first time)?

4   Aside from knowledge of the module/course, what other qualities do you feel are essential for a leader of learning and teaching?

5   Considering your context, how would you say the world is changing in terms of learning and teaching and student support? What do you see as the factors driving these changes (think both internal to your institution and externally)?

6   How well do you feel your department/faculty/institution is responding to reflect the way the world is changing as regards learning and teaching and student support? What would you highlight and applaud, and where do you feel there is scope for further innovation or enhancement?

7   Considering your context, who in your view is responsible for student learning? How could this responsibility be further shared and distributed (or transformed)?

8   What opportunities, structures or frameworks are available, internally or externally, to support your continuing development as a teacher, a facilitator of student learning and (if applicable) a leader of learning and teaching?

To what extent are you using these development opportunities? How could you use them further?

9 How in your context is teaching recognised and rewarded? What more (or different) could be done to strengthen the recognition of teaching and student support?

10 How in your context is the leadership of learning and teaching recognised and rewarded? What more (or different) could be done to strengthen the recognition for leadership?

11 If leadership is about connecting people with purpose, what could you do to strengthen your own and others' sense of connection with the purpose behind learning and teaching in your context?

Chapter 2

A model of programme leadership

THE CHALLENGE IN THIS CHAPTER

This chapter introduces a model of programme leadership and discusses how it can be used to enhance our understanding of the attributes, skills and qualities involved in effectively leading learning and teaching in higher education.

To set the scene, the chapter begins with a short overview of some established leadership models, including more recent developments centred on emotional intelligence. This provides a theoretical backdrop to introduce the Programme Leadership Model itself.

The Programme Leadership Model is described in detail, using a series of figures that capture it diagrammatically. The key features described are:

■ the spectrum of personal characteristics – from passion to compassion;
■ the four key leadership attributes: champion – organiser – enabler – mentor;
■ the five critical skills associated with each of the leadership attributes;
■ six fundamental leadership qualities linked to self-awareness.

A short narrative is provided that introduces and describes each of the four key leadership attributes, and links are made to the other chapters in this book covering specific aspects of learning and teaching leadership. Similarly a short description is given to amplify each of the six leadership qualities.

The second half of this chapter provides a self-assessment questionnaire based on the four key leadership attributes and particularly the associated critical skills. For learning to lead and manage, the Programme Leadership Model needs to be applied as a practical tool, and as a first step this short self-assessment exercise (48 items) provides an opportunity to gain a quick 'snapshot' insight into where the balance of your leadership skills may lie.

The questionnaire includes directions on use, a scoring grid and guidelines on how to interpret results.

The chapter concludes with a set of guidance notes for facilitators using the Programme Leadership Model in a workshop setting, including an introductory exercise to explore: 'What is leadership?' The Model and the self-assessment questionnaire can be used in a variety of ways to support the development of leaders working either individually or in groups. The Model could also be used as the basis for an institutional framework to support and enhance the development of leaders of learning and teaching. It is very scalable and whilst in its application it is focused on the development of the individual leader, it can also be used to stimulate a discursive exploration of leadership with a group.

ANOTHER MODEL OF MANAGEMENT AND LEADERSHIP

'Oh, no, not another model of management' could be one response to this chapter – and with some justification. Currently there are over 300 books published each year on leadership. There have been many, many attempts to capture the skills, qualities and attributes of effective management/leadership into a scheme of terms that will somehow decipher and demystify what some people do very well whilst others struggle significantly. But the management models, despite their proliferation over the last 50 or more years, are extremely valuable. Many are represented diagrammatically, with varying degrees of complexity, and often these visual representations seem to achieve more than the text which accompanies them. There is an impact, clarity and persuasiveness that many find compelling and instructive in these model diagrams. They capture big ideas in simple and manageable ways. As a prime example, look no further than John

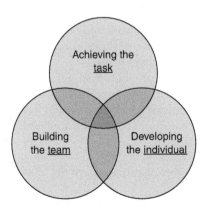

FIGURE 2.1   Action-centred leadership

Adair's model of action-centred leadership (1973): a simple Venn diagram of three intersecting circles, as shown in Figure 2.1, telling us that a manager's attention should take in the needs of the task, the team and the individual.

This model is simple, persuasive and fundamentally coherent. It tells us that successful achievement of the task will only come about through building and maintaining the team and within this supporting the development of individuals appropriately. The three areas interact with each other and the manager's attention shifts dynamically between them as needs demand. Similarly, where teams lack cohesion and individuals underperform, the level of task achievement will fall away or fail.

An earlier model put forward by Blake and Mouton in 1964 called the Managerial Grid used the dimensions of concern for task (originally termed concern for production) and concern for people without differentiating between the team and the individual. Represented as a grid (see Figure 2.2 below) with the horizontal axis representing concern for task and the vertical axis representing concern for people, the model generates five distinct leadership styles:

- *Impoverished* (or indifferent) management – *evade and elude* – a low concern for both people and task: the main driver is likely to be to avoid responsibility and not make mistakes, and as a result there will be few, if any, innovative decisions.
- *Country club* (or accommodating) management – *yield and comply* – a high concern for people but a low concern for task: the main driver is to look after the well-being and security of people in the hope that this will enhance performance, and this may result in a friendly but not necessarily productive work environment.
- *Produce or perish* (or dictatorial) management – *control and dominate* – a high concern for task but a low concern for people: the main driver is to get things done and people are a resource contracted to achieve clear goals (which may be appropriate in some crisis situations), and this may result in a lack of commitment, loyalty and engagement.
- *Team* (or sound) management – *contribute and commit* – a high level of concern is paid to both people and task: the main driver is to achieve high performance through teamwork and constructive participation, and this should result in commitment, strong contributions and a sense of mutual accountability for collective results.
- *Middle-of-the-road* (or status quo) management – *balance and compromise* – some concern is paid to both people and task: the main driver is to strike an even balance between achieving goals and meeting the needs of people without too much disruption, and as a result the risk is that neither goals nor people are satisfied.

Two further styles were subsequently added to the model:

- *Opportunistic* management – *exploit and manipulate* – individuals do not have a preference location on the grid, but rather adopt whichever behaviour offers them the greatest personal benefit.

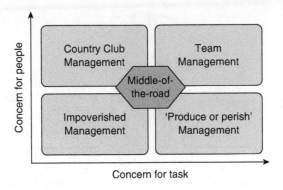

FIGURE 2.2 Managerial grid

- *Paternalistic* management – *prescribe and guide* – individuals using this style praise and support team members, superficially at least, but discourage challenges to their own views and thinking.

The short narrative describing the five/seven styles in the Blake and Mouton model that is given above is valuable, and will appeal to certain learning styles, but it is the grid itself as displayed in Figure 2.2 that has the real impact, combined with the memorable titles originally given to the styles themselves. Whilst it is now over 50 years old, this is a model that still has resonance. It presents both insights into leadership and a powerful way of reflecting on one's own approach and, perhaps, the prevailing leadership climate in the organisation.

Moving away from what a manager does (or does not), which suggests a fairly transactional relationship, more recent models have focused on leadership qualities based on self-awareness and particularly emotional intelligence. The work of Daniel Goleman (1996) identified that for leadership, emotional intelligence was more important than cognitive and technical competency combined, and that at the highest levels of leadership around 90 per cent of the difference between success and failure was attributable to emotional intelligence. He asserted that IQ and technical skills do matter 'but mainly as "threshold capabilities"' and that 'emotional intelligence is the *sine qua non* (essential condition) of leadership'. Similarly, Caruso and Salovey (2004) argue 'that the integration of rational and emotional styles is the key to successful leadership' and that 'decisions must incorporate emotion to be effective'. Goleman's work identified five skills (see Figure 2.3 below), or components, which enable successful leaders to maximise their own and their followers' performance:

- *Self-awareness* – knowing one's strengths, weaknesses, drives, values and impact on others,
- *Self-regulation* [self-management] – controlling or redirecting disruptive impulses and moods,
- *Motivation* – relishing achievement for its own sake,

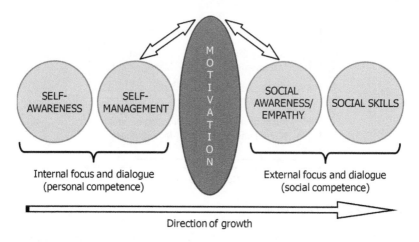

FIGURE 2.3 Emotional intelligence and leadership

- *Empathy* (social awareness) – understanding other people's emotional makeup,
- *Social skill* – building rapport with others to move them in desired directions.

(Chapter 3 provides a more detailed discussion of management and leadership overall, and in Chapter 8 a number of theories regarding leadership and participation are explored.)

THE PROGRAMME LEADERSHIP MODEL

In developing a model of management and leadership to fit the challenge of module or course leadership in higher education, the first feature that emerged was a spectrum of personal characteristics with 'courage' firmly at its centre. Why courage? Well, to lead a course well, to agree, assert and achieve worthwhile learning outcomes with a diverse group of tutors and students, and to reconcile the host of tensions that exist between enabling freedom to learn and meeting administrative goals, including assessment, takes a courageous approach:

> Courage is the first of human qualities because it is the quality which guarantees the others.
>
> (Aristotle, 384–322 BC)

This can be, and often is, a quiet courage – unassuming and seldom outspoken, but nevertheless a firmly grounded courage based on strong convictions regarding the nature and character of worthwhile learning in the subject area concerned. This core characteristic and others that flow from it are underpinned by self-awareness and emotional intelligence: SELF sits at the centre of the model.

The best courses have this courage at their core; the worst become timid tick-lists that perhaps meet administrative requirements but little more and are ultimately unsatisfactory for all concerned.

The two poles of the spectrum were easy to identify because they are things we talk about all the time: passion for the subject at one end and compassion for all those engaged in inspiring others to learn at the other (see Figure 2.4 below). Passion is used because this is what brings a subject to life, and compassion because leaders must care for those that they lead. And here, thinking about these two extremes of the spectrum of personal characteristics, we can see that on one side there are a set of essentially goal/task-focused attributes, and on the other a set of people-focused attributes. The programme leader acts as both leader of the course (the goal/task focus) and leader of the team (the people focus). It is the interaction between these two aspects of the role that will more than anything else determine success. You cannot succeed by being passionate about the course and 'pushing' this along with great energy and not giving attention to the cohesion of the course team, creating a sense of common purpose and caring for the needs and concerns of individuals within the team. Similarly, focusing all of your energies on 'pulling' the team together through consultation and careful persuasion will not succeed if you are not also a champion of the course with a clear sense of vision and direction. An inspired team with its collective energy fully aligned behind a clear course vision is the ideal towards which this model of programme leadership points.

There are four key leadership attributes identified in the model. These can be seen in the four corners of Figure 2.4 and carry the headings 'champion' and 'organiser' on the goal/task-focused side of the spectrum and 'enabler' and 'mentor' on the people-focused side:

- *Champion* – this is the most outward and demonstrative of the four attributes. The skills and behaviours involved are about generating and sustaining energy and interest. There are times when leading learning and teaching involves promoting a vision through a range of influencing channels: powerful communication, cultivating relationships, linking key stakeholders, enthusing the team and institution, modelling

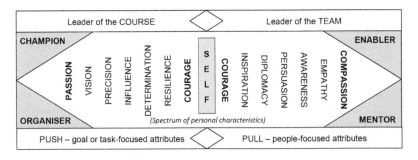

FIGURE 2.4 Leadership attributes

key behaviours and being an advocate of the chosen pedagogy. Being a champion, advocate or campaigner requires passion, vision and precision. It involves modelling a level of commitment, conviction and clarity that will inspire others to follow. It also involves the ability to challenge and negotiate, and the determination and resilience to keep going in the face of discouragement or disinterest. The champion uses vision and narrative to appeal to both the head and the heart of everyone involved, and understands that *people are inspired by a dream not a plan*. (Chapter 5 will expand on the champion attribute and the associated critical skills, but this will also come into play in many other sections of this book.)

- *Organiser* – for a dream to succeed, it must become a plan – something executable that can be managed, monitored and controlled. The leadership of learning and teaching involves very close planning and management. Educational programmes that lead to recognised qualifications linked to standards, national frameworks and other forms of recognition do not happen by accident. A plan essentially links activities, resources and time (the ART of planning) and uses the logic of goals, sequencing and priorities to map what should happen, when and where, and who should be involved. Universities and colleges have detailed and highly developed administrative systems to manage and support many of the core processes relating to programme delivery, assessment, student support and quality assurance. But there is another sort of planning around projects/initiatives to develop, design, transform and enhance teaching programmes, courses and modules. The skills of the organiser are equally important here. None of the four key leadership attributes stand on their own, and the organiser role needs to interact dynamically with the other three so that plans remain flexible and responsive. Transforming learning and teaching will not succeed if it is reduced to purely an administrative process. (The organiser attribute will be touched on in most of the subsequent chapters, but this book is focused on leadership and does not go into detail on either project management or educational administration.)

- *Enabler* – this is the most facilitative and collaborative of the four leadership attributes. It is about bringing people together: staff, students and other stakeholders, where appropriate. It is about creating transformative spaces for collaborative engagement, co-creation and collective learning. Design and development processes involving teams work well when particularly at the early stages there are phases of divergent thinking (creative and expansive): opportunities for exploring, challenging and developing ideas in a well-supported environment. The co-creation of a vision also helps to build and foster team identity, and part of the role of the leader may be to shield the team during this process and represent its needs to the wider organisation. If the champion tends to lead from the front, then the enabler will lead from alongside or behind. The enabler has a strong belief in human potential and looks to work with people in teams to pursue innovation and develop a sense of energy and collective commitment about the way ahead. (Chapters 6 and 7 will expand on the enabler attribute and the associated critical skills, but it will also come into play in many other sections of this book.)

■ *Mentor* – this is the attribute that is most focused on leading individuals. Facilitating student learning in higher education demands a high level of engagement from individual teachers, and guiding and supporting their development is critical not only for the success of courses but also for the institution overall. The leader as mentor operates at the compassionate end of the spectrum of personal characteristics and this involves high levels of empathy and awareness. But passion and compassion do not need to be seen as being poles apart. Passion ignites our interest and stirs the heart; compassion supports us as people and sustains the heart. So, the energy of praise and positive, constructive feedback, possibly linked to the vision, are important aspects of the mentor role. If one skill had to be picked out as being central to the mentor attribute, it would be listening: deep listening that empowers individuals to self-appraise, think for themselves, be creative and find great solutions; and wide-band listening that is not just focused on skills and outputs, but that listens to the whole person, their competence, their confidence and their commitment. The mentor also relates stories about themselves to sometimes share insights regarding facilitating student learning but also to build a relationship of trust. (Chapter 8 will expand on the mentor attribute and the associated critical skills, but it will also come into play in many other sections of this book.)

We will go on to discuss these four key leadership attributes in much more detail and will relate them to various aspects of programme leadership, but in Table 2.1 five clear, critical skills are defined for each. By skills, we are looking at things people actually do and say. They can be developed through practice, rehearsal and experience, hence the term 'skills development'. For the purposes of this model, skills combined with personality give us personal characteristics. So, for

TABLE 2.1 Leadership skills

CHAMPION	ORGANISER	ENABLER	MENTOR
Enthuse	Plan	Encourage	Listen
Promote	Organise	Shield	Invest
Model	Monitor	Support	Praise
Challenge	Control	Share/Convene	Review
Negotiate	Evaluate	Mediate	Relate

31

example, effective persuasion (a characteristic on the people-focused side of the spectrum) results from a combination of various enabling skills linked to the personality of the individual concerned. As a result, different individuals can be equally successful at being persuasive whilst appearing, at least, to approach situations quite differently. A key part of the discussion around leadership, as distinct perhaps from management, is the degree to which it is about enhancing personal traits to match circumstances. This starts to open up a very significant aspect of the literature on leadership concerning what has been termed leadership styles and adaptability – more on this later. The key point to note here is that skills, combined with some strong challenges to individual attitudes, are normally the key focus for leadership development.

It has been noted that running through the centre of the programme leadership model is the word 'self'. Needless to say, this is the most individual aspect of the model. It is fundamentally about the person of the leader and the degree to which they are able to inspire trust and carry respect. The importance of trust for successful and rewarding team management cannot be emphasised enough: 'Trust is the emotional glue that binds followers and leaders together' (Bennis and Nanus, 1985). A survey conducted by the Institute of Leadership and Management and the journal *Management Today* in 2009 used the following six dimensions to establish an index of leadership trust:

1 Ability
2 Understanding
3 Fairness
4 Openness
5 Integrity
6 Consistency.

The findings of this survey of over 5,000 UK employees pointed to one clear conclusion: 'integrity is the foundation of trust and it grows in importance with seniority' (Campbell, 2009). The piece goes on to observe that 'managers who master the management basics – listening to and understanding their teams and treating them fairly – will build trust'. Patrick Lencioni, author of *The Five Dysfunctions of a Team* (2002), takes this even further:

> Teamwork begins by building trust. And the only way to do that is to overcome our need for invulnerability.
> When there is trust, conflict becomes nothing but the pursuit of truth, an attempt to find the best possible answer.

No two 'selves' are the same, and being yourself is fundamental to authentic leadership, as indeed it is to good teaching and facilitation. Knowing yourself is the tricky bit, to enjoy a moment of true understatement, and it is as much about finding out how others see you as it is about introspection (more on this in Chapter 10). But there are some qualities within this business of leading others

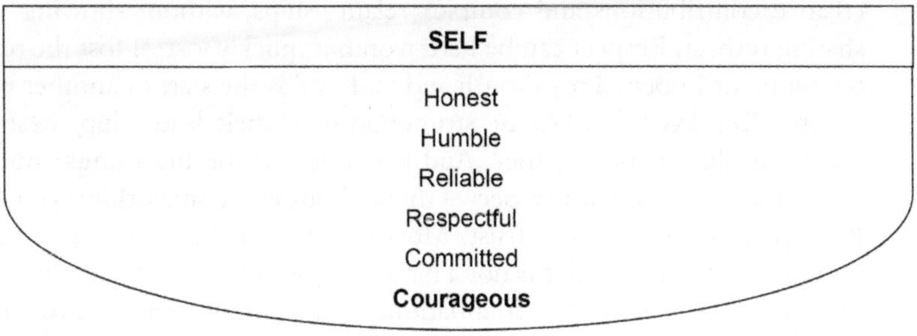

```
┌─────────────────────────────────────────────┐
│                    SELF                       │
├───────────────────────────────────────────────┤
 \                 Honest                       /
  \                Humble                      /
   \               Reliable                   /
    \             Respectful                 /
     \            Committed                 /
      \          Courageous               /
       _____/
```

FIGURE 2.5 Leadership qualities

that we can properly term fundamental leadership qualities, for in their absence trust will quickly evaporate. This can all too easily become an extended list, but Figure 2.5 above captures concisely what could be termed 'the indispensable six', ending with the term that was the starting point for this programme leadership model: courage.

There is an attractive symmetry to this list of qualities: honest and humble, reliable and respectful, and committed and courageous:

- *Honest* – Kouzes and Posner (2002) had at the heart of their enquiry into leadership (a series of surveys repeated since 1982) the following question: 'What do you most look for and admire in a leader, someone whose direction you would willingly follow?' The leadership quality that was ranked consistently top by a very large set of contributors across six continents over more than 20 years was 'honest'. Their work shows this to be 'the single most important ingredient in the leader-constituent relationship' and that 'regardless of what leaders say about their own integrity, people wait to be shown; they observe the behaviour'.
- *Humble* – that others flourish and succeed should be the primary aspiration of any leader, but this requires that leaders should embrace a selfless approach. Whether working with people who are driven by the need to be recognised as unique or with people who are motivated by belonging to a worthwhile group (Prime and Salib, 2014), the leader's role is to enable and empower. This is a far cry from the heroic leader who, standing in the bright light of recognition, wants their legacy to be that of someone indispensable.
- *Reliable* – 'I wouldn't mind what he did so long as he was consistent!' were the memorable words that one frustrated colleague confided in me about her manager. And this is not unusual. A reputation for reliability and consistency goes an awfully long way in leadership, and it is a tremendously important quality to model for others in the team. If you don't deliver on your undertakings and your values, why should others?
- *Respectful* – you will not get far as a leader, particularly a leader of something like learning and teaching, which calls for collaborative engagement,

creative contributions and complex relationships, without showing and sharing respect. Respect can be hard won but quickly lost. 'I lost the team the moment I opened my mouth and said . . .' is the start of another rueful anecdote from a colleague struggling with their leadership. Respect and leadership work together. And it is not just the big things you do or say that show or earn respect – think about every small thing you do. Respect also demonstrates trust. Most people feel they have earned the right to be respected – if it is not a natural right in any event – and mutual respect is often one of the foundations of trust. So be the first to show trust and let others follow your example.

- *Committed* – if you don't care, why should anyone else? And it does not matter what you say, people will judge your commitment by what they see you do and how they see you do it. Your commitment as a leader is an intrinsic part of the collective commitment of the group. Commitment is also contagious, so spread the infection by modelling yourself as a leader of learning (level one modelling – see Chapter 8). Commitment is a combination of clarity about 'what matters now', dedication to a cause or undertaking and a willingness to get involved (usually with some level of personal sacrifice). And the set of behaviours relating to commitment is a powerful and effective way of influencing others. People will sometimes struggle to say why they devoted their energy to project X instead of project Y and will often end up telling you 'well, the leader and the team were so committed'. And commitment that is inspiring needs to be congruent across all critical areas: in the case of learning and teaching, commitment to our vision, commitment to our values, commitment to our chosen pedagogy, commitment to quality and, most importantly, commitment to students.

- *Courageous* – in developing the Programme Leadership Model, the first feature that emerged was a spectrum of personal characteristics with 'courage' firmly at its centre. In its origins the term 'leader' is about *showing the road or path ahead*, or in some definitions 'going first'. It is more than just management, maintaining and delivering what we have already, but leadership, and that means to whatever degree re-shaping the future. Leadership and change are inextricably linked; in fact you could say that change defines leadership, and developing a shared vision, communicating powerfully, overcoming resistance and maintaining momentum are all leadership challenges that require courage. Sometimes this is courage for yourself, sometimes it is courage for the team, and sometimes it is the courage of conviction that what we are doing matters.

To bring all of the above together, Figure 2.6 shows the Programme Leadership Model in full. Whilst focused on the challenge of leadership in higher education, this model could also be applied to programme leadership in other educational settings, both academic and vocational. The first element of the model, entitled 'Leadership attributes', actually represents the whole, and illustrates figuratively how the various elements relate to each other. The second element, 'Leadership skills', expands on the four key leadership attributes that are highlighted in grey in the four corners on either side of the spectrum of personal characteristics. The third element, 'Leadership qualities', develops upon the notion of self which is highlighted in grey at the very heart of the leadership

Leadership attributes

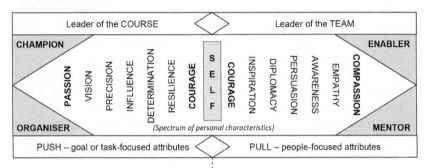

Leadership skills

CHAMPION	ORGANISER	ENABLER	MENTOR
Enthuse	Plan	Encourage	Listen
Promote	Organise	Shield	Invest
Model	Monitor	Support	Praise
Challenge	Control	Share/Convene	Review
Negotiate	Evaluate	Mediate	Relate

Leadership qualities

FIGURE 2.6 The Programme Leadership Model

attributes and flows through the centre of the model overall. Amongst the various other messages and signals this should send regarding engendering trust and respecting colleagues, there is the simple and straightforward lesson that we cannot effectively manage others if we cannot manage ourselves. Why should followers follow? Because the leader acts with integrity based on an authentic and self-aware projection to others of who they really are. This honest belief in the integrity of the leader is the basis for true consent and collaboration and is a stronger and more enduring foundation for leadership than fear, obligation or compulsion:

> Up to a point, I think you can lead out of fear, intimidation, as awful as that sounds. You can make people follow you by scaring them, and you can make people follow by having them feel obligated. You can lead by creating guilt. There is a lot of leadership that comes out of fear, dependence, and guilt. The marine boot camp is famous for it. But the problem is that you're creating obedience with a residue of resentment . . . There're two other qualities that I think are more positive reasons to follow someone. One is an honest belief in the person you're following. The other is selfish. The person following has to believe that following is the best thing to do at the time.
>
> (Sydney Pollack, film director, as quoted in Bennis, 2003)

Different sets and theories of leadership styles abound. Some have aspects and insights that are distinct, while others overlap and complement each other in various ways. The Programme Leadership Model brings together a range of styles, all of which have their place in the leadership of learning and teaching, from the inspirational to the managerial and from the collaborative to the developmental. As an approximate relationship the four key leadership attributes in the model could be associated with broad leadership theories/perspectives as follows:

- *Champion* – inspirational, goal-driven or achievement-focused leadership.
- *Organiser* – task-oriented or direction-focused leadership (or functional management).
- *Enabler* – engagement-focused, collaborative, participative or collective leadership.
- *Mentor* – coaching-focused, developmental or attuned leadership (or a coaching style of leadership).

HOW ARE YOU MANAGING? A MINI SELF-ASSESSMENT EXERCISE

As a behavioural framework for programme leadership, the Programme Leadership Model has many merits. It will also have points that could be debated, contested or challenged, and that is good. That is as much the purpose of a model as anything else. But for learning to lead and manage, it needs to be applied as a practical tool, and as a first step towards this the following short self-assessment exercise provides the opportunity to gain a quick 'snapshot' insight into where the balance of your skills may lie in this area. The main focus of this questionnaire-based exercise is on skills. As mentioned earlier in the chapter, skills can be developed through practice, rehearsal and experience, and are normally the key focus for leadership development. This simple questionnaire is linked to the leadership skills and key attributes in the Programme Leadership Model.

Completing this self-assessment exercise may also provide an initial insight into some of your current preconceptions regarding management and leadership which may well reflect your own experiences of it as a 'follower' in various settings, both formal and informal. This may in turn provide clues regarding your current leadership style, the aspects of leadership that may come most readily to you and other areas you may find more challenging.

There are several ways of using this questionnaire. The first is as an individual exercise for your own reference. The second would be as something to discuss within a personal development planning (PDP) framework with a mentor, supervisor or manager. The third would be within a workshop setting, and following the questionnaire, there is a short set of guidelines for workshop facilitators.

This questionnaire has been designed with speed and simplicity in mind. It is far from being a rigorous psychometric test. There are no tricks or traps within it, nothing designed to validate the consistency of your responses or eliminate irregularities. Your own personal review and development is its only goal, and if it helps to provide some insights, a few ideas and pointers as regards your development and some starting points for discussion, then it has more than served its purpose.

PROGRAMME LEADERSHIP MODEL SELF-ASSESSMENT QUESTIONNAIRE

The questionnaire below is made up of 48 statements. You are invited to consider each in relation to yourself and your own approach to management and leadership. If on balance you agree with the statement and feel it reflects how you would go about either leading a course, or leading a team or an individual within a team, then place a tick in the box alongside it (on balance means you agree more than you disagree). Some of the statements relate particularly to leading a course design/redesign process or the redevelopment of a module or course element, and for these you will need to reflect upon yourself and your approach in those situations (your approach to leading transformation and change). If you disagree and/or feel that it does not reflect your approach, then leave the box blank. In addition, there are some star boxes. Not all of the statements have star boxes, but where they do, you are invited to give them additional consideration. However, you can only consider them if you have already ticked the corresponding statement to show your agreement. You have a total of four stars to award by placing them in four of the star boxes. The star indicates that you feel the statement concerned reflects something essential for achieving excellence in programme leadership. So the challenge is to star your top four. If, however, you have ticked fewer than four of the statements corresponding with the star boxes, then you can only star those that you have ticked: for example, if you have ticked just two of the statements that have star boxes, then you only have the option of awarding one star to each of these.

The following are some guidelines to follow when completing the questionnaire:

- Be honest (the results are, after all, for you).
- Be straightforward.
- Do not over-think your responses – if in doubt, usually go with your first response.
- There is no restriction on the number of boxes you can tick.
- Base your responses on reality. Think about how you do lead and manage rather than how you would ideally like to. However, where you do spot such a distinction in one of your responses, you might want to place a question mark in the margin to remind yourself of the dichotomy. It could then be worthwhile to reflect further upon this point, possibly in discussion with your own manager or mentor. Why is it that in reality you do not lead and manage as you would ideally wish, or as you feel you should? What causes you to behave differently? Are the causes internal to yourself or caused by your environment?
- Where you find it very difficult to come down on one side by either agreeing or disagreeing with a statement (as it relates to you), force yourself to do so, usually going with your first thought/response. Remember the approach to take is 'on balance' agreement – that is, you agree more than you disagree. However, you may also want to make a note in the margin in case it helps to review this point further when considering the overall results. Restrict this, though, to just one or two of your responses, if any.
- If you are very new to management and leadership, then it is fine to speculate a little on how you think you would be in a leadership/management situation. Again, try to be as honest with yourself as possible. There may be other situations and experiences outside of a formal work setting that you can draw on, for example, your role as a family member or in a voluntary group.
- Do not forget to also distribute your four stars by placing them in four of the star boxes that appear additionally alongside some of the statements. A star indicates that you feel the statement concerned reflects something essential for achieving excellence in programme leadership. You must, however, have ticked the corresponding statement to give it a star. So if you have ticked fewer than four of the statements corresponding with the star boxes, then you can only award that number of stars. If you have ticked more than four of the statements corresponding with the star boxes, then you need to select your top four.

SELF-ASSESSMENT QUESTIONNAIRE

As a programme leader or course manager, or someone leading a piece of course design/redesign, do you on balance agree with the following statements (on balance means you agree more than you disagree)? If you agree with the statement and feel it reflects how you would go about either leading a course, or leading a team or an individual within a team, place a tick in the box alongside. If you disagree and/or feel that it does not reflect your approach, leave it blank.

In the statements below:

- 'Project' (or initiative, if you prefer) can be taken to refer to new course or module development/design, the redevelopment of a significant part of a course/module, or refreshing a course/module with, perhaps, a new course team and a fresh sense of purpose.
- The terms 'course', 'programme' and 'module' are used fairly interchangeably and should be interpreted widely to encompass the blocks of curricula that tend to be the focus of design, development and delivery in your institution.

		✓	✱
1	People are likely to lose interest in a project if they are not given full credit for their ideas	☐	
2	Thinking through the pathway of logical steps and their timings is the first real management action in the course development process	☐	☐
3	I am happy to field difficult questions and challenges if it leaves others free to stay focused on the task and make progress	☐	
4	Even if I disagree with someone, I will always work hard to understand their point of view	☐	
5	Spotting the links between apparently diverse ideas and viewpoints is often the key to identifying course design opportunities	☐	
6	Progress should be checked regularly, if not constantly, if a complex course development project is going to succeed	☐	
7	The role of the leader is to create an environment in which others can succeed	☐	☐
8	I believe that it is more important to praise small achievements than it is larger ones	☐	
9	Sticking power counts for more than flair during the early stages of a new project	☐	
10	Deciding who does what is the central role of the leader	☐	
11	Team performance always improves when people are told they are doing well	☐	
12	People don't always realise what they are good at, and it is the leader's role to spend time remedying this	☐	
13	The needs of people with strong influence must be addressed or satisfied	☐	

	✓	✱
14 A gentle hand on the tiller is the answer to keeping a project on course	☐	
15 People need to be free to express different views, but in a climate of respect	☐	
16 Helping people to assess their own performance is generally the key to improved performance in the future	☐	
17 Very outspoken people with strong influence must be kept energetically on-side	☐	
18 We should be learning at every step in the course development process and making adjustments accordingly	☐	☐
19 Getting people to meet can be hard work, but it is always worthwhile	☐	
20 I like to talk about situations I've experienced myself to help colleagues explore their own difficulties and challenges	☐	
21 The most infectious quality in any sales pitch is enthusiasm	☐	
22 Consulting on ideas is fine, but ultimately one person has to take responsibility for deciding what needs to be done, in what order and by when	☐	
23 I always aim to settle differences between people before larger problems arise	☐	
24 The most important thing to do when team members have problems is to listen and understand	☐	☐
25 It is easy to find reasons not to do something, and so negative viewpoints need to be openly explored	☐	
26 Each new module/programme development team should successively learn from the experiences of previous teams	☐	
27 If anyone must take criticism, it should be the leader rather than the follower	☐	
28 In management, providing feedback on individual performance is the key to strengthening outcomes	☐	
29 Highlighting the learning benefits to students is more persuasive when seeking support for a course than talking about design features	☐	
30 Milestones should be created in the project plan for the team to take stock, review progress and make adjustments if necessary	☐	
31 When difficulties arise, the leader needs to go on showing belief in the team	☐	
32 I would rather spend time helping a team member find a solution than give them a ready-made solution	☐	☐
33 Saying what you believe and value about a project creates an important sense of conviction	☐	
34 I enjoy the process of bringing people and resources together to achieve goals	☐	
35 If someone is too self-critical, then the leader's role is to balance this with praise and positive energy	☐	☐
36 When working on a problem, I always work hard to see things from the other person's point of view	☐	
37 Presenting a balanced view of risks and benefits from the outset of a project helps to keep obstacles in perspective	☐	

38 If we don't look back and review progress against the goals we set ourselves, then we will never learn how to make better choices in the future ☐

39 If people are protective of their ideas and materials, then the team will not succeed ☐

40 Supporting a colleague to reflect on their work before making changes is key to personal development ☐

41 If people don't see the project as a priority, then you need to sell it to them again ☐ ☐

42 Whilst I sometimes admire managers who improvise what to do next, this is not the approach for me ☐

43 The most demanding aspect of leadership is showing confidence in a team during periods of uncertainty ☐

44 Management is more about listening than telling ☐

45 During the early stages of the project, you must inject energy into every piece of communication ☐ ☐

46 I'm happy to make bold decisions to change the project plan if new circumstances arise ☐

47 People in a team should not have to wait to learn they are doing a good job ☐

48 It pays off in the end if you spend time building a colleague's confidence ☐

Leader of the COURSE PUSH – goal or task-focused attributes				Leader of the TEAM PULL – people-focused attributes			
CHAMPION		ORGANISER		ENABLER		MENTOR	
1		2		3		4	
5		6		7		8	
9		10		11		12	
13		14		15		16	
17		18		19		20	
21		22		23		24	
25		26		27		28	
29		30		31		32	
33		34		35		36	
37		38		39		40	
41		42		43		44	
45		46		47		48	
★41		★2		★7		★24	
★45		★18		★35		★32	
Total		Total		Total		Total	

SCORING GRID

To transfer your results to the scoring grid above, simply give yourself one point for each statement you ticked. So, in the table above, place a one or a zero in each of the numbered cells.

The star boxes each score two points. So, at the bottom of the table, place a zero or a two in each of the star-numbered cells.

Now, total up the scores at the bottom of the table to obtain your results.

INTERPRETING YOUR RESULTS – HOW ARE YOU MANAGING?

As an outcome of this exercise, you will have a score for each of the four key attributes in the Programme Leadership Model. The score will be between zero and a maximum of 16 under each of the headings. This will provide an insight into which of the key leadership attributes and their associated critical skills you naturally favour in terms of both outlook and approach. This can be captured as a leadership attribute profile such as 10-14-6-9, with the numbers representing each of the key attributes (champion-organiser-enabler-mentor). You may well recognise yourself in the scores that emerge and agree that this reflects your natural preferences in terms of how you work and the aspects of your role you enjoy and find rewarding. Alternatively there may be surprises in the results that could be usefully explored to establish whether you are working to your full potential as a leader in certain areas or whether there are blocks and barriers inhibiting aspects of your performance (whether internal to you or arising from the environment).

One obvious way of considering your results is to think in terms of high and low scores. A high score in this exercise is a score of ten or more with usually at least one of the star boxes included. A low score, on the other hand, would be six or less regardless of the inclusion of the star boxes. This leaves a mid-range of six to ten where the score may be regarded as an enhanced outcome if one or more of the star boxes is included.

As important as the high-low outcome is the relative levels of the scores and the order in which they rank. So, a pattern of 8-12-5-4 could be as valuable as 10-14-7-6 in providing an insight into where your strengths lie. This simply highlights that different individuals are more or less cautious in the way they approach self-assessment questionnaires of this kind and is a reason why they are generally more useful for personal review than they are for anything comparative.

Overall in the model the leadership attributes have equal importance and weighting. This reflects the fact that successful leadership flows from a balanced combination of goal/task-focused and people-focused attributes. Therefore, another consideration when reviewing your results is the degree to which the scores are balanced. Comparing a leadership attribute profile of 8-9-12-10 with 7-4-12-14 immediately highlights that the first set is far more balanced than the second. In the second profile the individual concerned favours the mentoring attribute far more highly then the organiser, and furthermore the results indicate an imbalance towards the people-focused end of the spectrum. This could be characterised as someone who struggles to demonstrate passion and vision in their approach to leadership, but succeeds well when it comes to showing a strong awareness (or compassion) for the needs of team members and showing empathy.

Another way of looking at the results is to consider the distinction between management and leadership. As we will consider in some depth in the next chapter, the role of programme leader is distinctly hybrid in its nature, with elements to do with vision, inspiring change and enabling high performance resonating strongly with ideas of transformational leadership, and other elements concerned with meticulous organisation, getting things done and being target-driven, which are more managerial and transactional. The two leadership attributes featured in the top corners (see Figure 2.4), 'champion' and 'enabler', may be regarded as more transformative in nature and therefore more closely aligned to leadership, and the leadership attributes below, 'organiser' and 'mentor', are focused on those 'negotiated' steps that progressively equip, encourage and reward teams and individuals to meet agreed goals, and that are therefore more managerial in their feel.

Appendix 1 provides a listing of the statements in the questionnaire linked to the four key leadership attributes in the Programme Leadership Model, and also the critical skills associated with each of the attributes. If it would be helpful to explore a particular attribute in more detail, you can use this to consider which of the critical skills you responded to with agreement in the questionnaire and which you did not. Some of the forthcoming chapters will begin with a section showing links to the Programme Leadership Model and this will include a table of the attributes and associated critical skills with areas highlighted in an indicative way.

SOME GUIDANCE NOTES FOR FACILITATORS USING THE PROGRAMME LEADERSHIP MODEL IN A WORKSHOP SETTING

The Programme Leadership Model and the self-assessment questionnaire can be used in a variety of ways to support the development of leaders working either individually or in groups. The model could also be used as the basis for an institutional framework to support and enhance the development of leaders of learning and teaching. It is very scalable and whilst in its application it is focused on the development of the individual leader, it can also be used to stimulate a discursive exploration of leadership with a group.

Before getting into the detail of the model, it can be useful to run a more open group exercise exploring the question: 'What is leadership?' Clearly this question is likely to stimulate a wide range of views and perspectives, and to help balance the discussion, maintain focus and enhance participation, a simple card ordering exercise can work very well. The following provides 12 statements about leadership (or definitions) beginning with the words 'leadership is . . .':

ACHIEVEMENT-FOCUSED – Leadership is . . .

- Leadership is . . . presenting a compelling vision for others to follow.
- Leadership is . . . championing the need for positive change.
- Leadership is . . . getting things done well with the full buy-in from others.

DIRECTION-FOCUSED – Leadership is . . .

- Leadership is . . . providing strong and clear direction.
- Leadership is . . . making clear and swift decisions and sticking by them.
- Leadership is . . . taking control whenever challenges arise.

ENGAGEMENT-FOCUSED – Leadership is . . .

- Leadership is . . . getting alongside people/partners to develop a shared plan.
- Leadership is . . . creating collective commitment by aligning energy and interests.
- Leadership is . . . building trust, confidence and cohesion in the team.

COACHING-FOCUSED – Leadership is . . .

- Leadership is . . . creating an environment where others can flourish and succeed.
- Leadership is . . . developing individuals and teams through coaching/discussion.
- Leadership is . . . distributing real responsibility and resources whilst also developing people.

The facilitator will need to prepare several sets of cards. Each set should consist of 14 cards, 2 blanks and a further 12 with one of the 'leadership is . . .' definitions on each. Do not include the headings (achievement-focused, direction-focused, engagement-focused and coaching-focused) – these can be brought into the discussion at a later stage. Two of the cards are blank and are available if participants wish to add further definitions of leadership of their own.

Working in groups of three to six participants, with one set of randomly shuffled cards per group, the challenge through discussion is to come up with an arrangement of the cards that presents an overall proposition of what leadership is. Arrangements might include a hierarchy of layers, a hub with spokes, a diamond-nine (as shown in Figure 2.7 below), a cycle or wheel, parallel columns or even a single column. It is for the groups to decide. However, it may be useful to show them an illustration of one or two examples, such as the diamond-nine, to stimulate their thinking. A rule to include is that they can discard up to 3 of the 12 cards, if they wish, and add up to two additional cards (using the blanks). It is important to emphasise that the cards belong to them, so if they wish to change or add words to take ownership of one of the 'leadership is . . .' statements, that is fine (the nuances of language can be very important to people).

The working groups then present their propositions to each other, respond to questions and challenges, and are encouraged by the facilitator to discuss similarities, differences and points of interest.

In the plenary discussion following this exercise the statements/definitions on the cards can be presented in the groups of three shown above using the four headings (achievement-focused, direction-focused, engagement-focused and coaching-focused). The facilitator can use the following three questions to explore each of the headings:

- When would this type of leadership be effective or appropriate?
- What is the impact of this type of leadership:
  - in the short term?
  - in the long term?
- What could be the downsides of too much of (or over-use of) this type of leadership?

The next stage is to introduce the Programme Leadership Model. Whilst they are by no means a direct parallel, associations can be made between the four key attributes and the four leadership headings in the previous exercise:

- *Champion* – achievement-focused.
- *Organiser* – direction-focused.

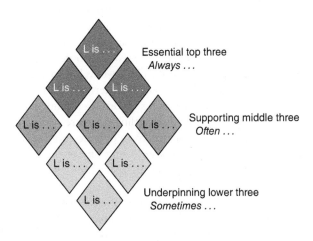

FIGURE 2.7 Diamond-nine card arrangement

- *Enabler* – engagement-focused.
- *Mentor* – coaching-focused.

There are all sort of ways in which sub-groups could be challenged to discuss and explore the Programme Leadership Model. One simple way would be to have four groups each take one of the key leadership attributes and associated critical skills and discuss it in response to a short question set, such as:

- Which aspects of leading learning and teaching most require this attribute and these skills?
- When and where in your department/institution do you see these skills being used? What is the impact?
- How do you use this attribute and these skills in your leadership?
- What opportunities are there for you to develop this attribute further?

The four sub-groups could then present to each other their main ideas and conclusions.

The final phase of the process if you wish to use it is to bring in and consider the self-assessment questionnaire. To save time, this could be completed by participants in advance of the session, with appropriate instructions, and the scoring grid could then be used during the workshop to generate individual results. It will be important for the facilitator to introduce the questionnaire in a sensitive and balanced way using some of the key messages above, such as:

- the questionnaire has been designed with speed and simplicity in mind;
- it is far from being a rigorous psychometric test;
- your own personal review and development is its only goal.

People may be wary of sharing their results in a whole-group discussion, and so as an alternative, colleagues could work in pairs or groups of three. The purpose of this discussion can be twofold: firstly to reflect on insights from the questionnaire results that either challenge or reinforce the participant's current self-perception (how they see themselves as a leader); and secondly to develop a simple action plan of two or three things they would like to develop in their leadership of learning and teaching or otherwise consider further. For these discussions, participants should be encouraged to adopt a supportive coaching style, each taking turn, and the facilitator could provide an outline structure or format for how the discussions should be approached moving from open to more specific questions. The most important thing will be, though, using one of the critical skills from the mentor attribute – that participants create space for each other by listening:

> When you really listen to another person – when you understand them to the best of your ability – something extraordinary happens: the speaker (the coachee) typically arrives at a better understanding of the topic for themselves.
>
> (Downey, 1999)

QUESTIONS FOR ACTION AND REFLECTION

1 Which aspects of your current approach to leading learning and teaching are goal- or task-focused?

2 Which aspects of your current approach to leading learning and teaching are people-focused?

3 Can you think of an example of where as a leader you have used emotional intelligence to control/redirect your own impulses in a positive way for the benefit of the group? Think through the detail of what you did, how you responded and the impact this had on others.

4 What would support you to increase and develop your self-awareness as a leader?

5 Which of the four key attributes in the Programme Leadership Model (champion – organiser – enabler – mentor) appeals to you most and why?

6 Which of the four key attributes in the Programme Leadership Model do you most admire in others and why?

7 In your current leadership role which of the four key leadership attributes occupies most of your time? What could you do to make the picture more balanced? What could others do to help you achieve a more balanced picture?

8 In what order would you rank the six fundamental leadership qualities in the Programme Leadership Model? Which of these is most important to you as a leader?

9 With regard to your current leadership, identify 3 of the 20 leadership skills in the Programme Leadership Model that you would most like to develop?

10 Looking at the next 12 months, what are the leadership attributes and skills that are going to be needed most to move forward your module/course/suite of programmes?

Management and leadership

THE CHALLENGE IN THIS CHAPTER

Building upon the Programme Leadership Model, this chapter provides a broader exploration of ideas regarding the nature of management and leadership, and critically the difference between the two.

Reflecting on the university context, and particularly the challenge of academic leadership, the chapter begins by portraying the issue of how the formal role of manager or leader is sometimes regarded. This illustrates the suspicion or concern that can exist regarding the label 'leader', the problem of 'reluctant managers' and the fact that taking on management responsibility may not be regarded as a positive career move. The discussion includes consideration of the merits and limitations of management/leadership roles being rotational or temporary and the challenge this presents for leading academic talent. Another aspect explored is the different ways in which leadership is conceptualised in an academic environment from intellectual leadership and educational leadership through to administrative leadership.

The chapter moves on to compare and review some contrasting definitions of management: from functional management to the art of leadership. This leads into a more detailed discussion of the differences between management and leadership and a recognition that the two always exist together in combination, and in a complementary way, in all roles that carry responsibility for determining and achieving organisational goals through the collective and individual efforts of people. As part of this, the actions and qualities of management and leadership are looked at side-by-side to develop further conceptual and practical insights into the differences.

Turning more directly towards the focus of this book, the discussion moves on to models that distinguish between transactional and transformational leadership.

The qualities of trust, engagement, inspiration, connectedness and empowerment are highlighted in relation to transformational leadership alongside the psychological mechanisms that are its driving force. This links powerfully to the Programme Leadership Model and the four key attributes needed to effectively lead learning and teaching, particularly through periods of change and transformation.

Leadership and followership is another perspective explored, where the goals come from the followers and the leader becomes simply an enabler, and this points towards new and emergent theories such as collaborative leadership, distributed leadership, inclusive leadership, shared leadership and servant leadership.

The chapter leads through to revisiting the Programme Leadership Model and further positioning it within some of the ideas and theories explored.

Finally, two tools are presented as a structure for reviewing and understanding management (management specifically rather than leadership). The first tool, PRAISE, provides a shorthand for reviewing the responsibilities that make up a management role (*what does a manager manage?*) and the second tool, POMCE, is powerful for understanding the functions of management (*how does a manager manage?*).

TO MANAGE OR NOT TO MANAGE ...

The discussion went something like this:

Academic colleague:	You're talking about management, but I'm not a manager.
Me:	You're not a manager?
Academic colleague:	No, I'm head of a research department.
Me:	Quite a large one.
Academic colleague:	Oh yes, and growing. It's an extremely important area.
Me:	And your team runs two of the core teaching modules?
Academic colleague:	Yes, we fit that in as well.
Me:	Great. So, who is the manager?
Academic colleague:	We expect people to manage themselves. That's part of being an academic. It's not my role to manage people.
Me:	So, who coordinates things? How do you decide who does what and when?
Academic colleague:	We have an administrator.
Me:	And if someone's struggling, not performing as well as they should, who helps and supports them?
Academic colleague:	Well, me, I suppose. But they have a contract, you see. They should know what's expected. My role is academic research. I'm not a manager.

This left me with one of those jaw-dropping moments when as a developer you realise that not only does the person concerned not acknowledge a need for personal development, but they don't even recognise that they occupy a management role with a set of goals and responsibilities. This was new territory for me. Every organisation that employs people to work in teams needs to invest in management development, and there are always a variety of standards in terms of management performance, but line managers and project managers usually at the very least know and accept that they are managers. And where ambiguity exists, this is normally quickly resolved for the benefit of all concerned. Coming to work in a university setting was the first time I had encountered a kind of intellectual resistance or uncertainty amongst some to the very idea of being a manager.

Now the academic colleague characterised above was only one of many, and by no means all held the same view in the same way. But there was at that time, it seemed to me, an underlying suspicion or concern regarding being labelled a manager and how that might impact upon one's status as either a well-recognised or aspiring academic. This concept of 'reluctant managers' (Scase and Goffee, 1989) is a feature within university settings that has been noted previously:

> Many heads of department are reluctant managers in the sense that they see themselves primarily as academics rather than as managers. For many academic staff, being a leader and having managerial responsibilities are not priorities and many do not perceive themselves as prospective managers when they become academics. In the UK, the evidence suggests that becoming a head of department is rarely perceived to be a career move and that in fact it may be viewed as hindering career development.
>
> (Bryman, 2009: 26)

This situation is compounded somewhat by the rotational nature of academic leadership roles in many university settings. The head of an academic department, for example, may step into that role with either energy or reluctance and may occupy it for a period of two, three or five years. In a similar way to Presidents of the United States, a second term may be possible, but after that the Constitution prohibits further engagement. Discussing this with academics who have had experience of occupying leadership roles, a number of points and observations emerge (this list is not intended to be fully representative):

- the virtue of having someone appointed from within;
- the importance of having a respected academic colleague who really understands the context and the culture;
- the credibility needed for effectiveness in the role necessitates academic recognition, an appropriate 'track record' and acceptance;
- the desire for someone who will represent 'us' upwards rather than just drive strategy downwards (or be a 'puppet' of the senior team);

- a concern that the academic leader should be someone who 'won't rock the boat';
- a desire for a more collegial and less ego-driven approach to leadership;
- the possibility of a more selfless approach to leadership as the individual's ambitions may not lie as a leader but elsewhere;
- the concern that research particularly may be inhibited, constrained or corralled if an overly managerial approach is imposed;
- a sense of the leadership being shared and inclusive, and therefore more reflective of the community;
- a sense of taking turns to carry on and conserve the heritage, philosophy and identity of the team;
- a sense that 'what goes around comes around' – leaders who are time-limited and appointed from within are less likely to risk significant conflict (making enemies, etc.);
- there is only time for one cycle of innovation and so a more measured and considered approach is likely (change is also more incremental and less radical);
- if their leadership skills are poor or they are unpopular, the clock is ticking on when someone else will replace them.

Taking turns may be quite an egalitarian approach in one sense, but it is by no means a recipe for effective, inspiring or even consistent leadership. Given the crucial role such leaders now have in leading their institutions through significant change, some are beginning to question the notion that heads of department have to be stars in their field of research:

> Usually they do it because they feel it is their turn. It's a very odd management model – there are not many places where one day you are the line manager and the next you are back with your peers and someone is managing you.
>
> (Interview respondent, cited in Tysome, 2014)

The world is turning, of course, perspectives are changing and views are moving on. A stimulus paper published by the Leadership Foundation for Higher Education (UK) in May 2014 (Tysome, 2014) explored the issue of leading academic talent through a series of interviews with a sample of higher education managers and senior academics. Considering the question of 'who leads?', one vice-chancellor is reported as saying:

> The problem with making a special case for universities in the context of leadership is you start looking for academic leadership rather than just a leader, and that sets you off on a false trail. I don't see why someone from any sector couldn't come in and run a university if they have the right support staff around them and if they understand it.

Unsurprisingly, not everyone in the report shared this view, with others asserting the need for middle managers (deans or departmental heads) in particular to have 'top-notch academic credentials', but there were also concerns expressed about the standard of processes for selecting and training such staff. In the same report an employers' representative observed that:

> Some institutions are starting to unpick this, moving towards a model where senior academic grades are reserved for the best academics, and then finding another way to reward good leaders who take on management responsibilities.

Another issue in this debate is how leadership is conceptualised and the territory it is seen as occupying. If leadership is influence, then who or what is being influenced? John Maxwell asserts that 'the true measure of leadership is influence – nothing more, nothing less' (2007). Well, in an academic environment, there is educational leadership, administrative leadership and academic leadership, and there are also intellectual dimensions to leadership and citizenship. Figure 3.1 below provides a snapshot summary of these four leadership territories and the associated areas of focus and possible accountability.

Our emphasis in these pages will be more on the territory of educational leadership (learning and teaching in higher education), but it would be false to totally partition this from all other aspects of academic leadership. Intellectual leadership, for example, is an important part of the learning relationship with students and the development of what might broadly be termed scholarship.

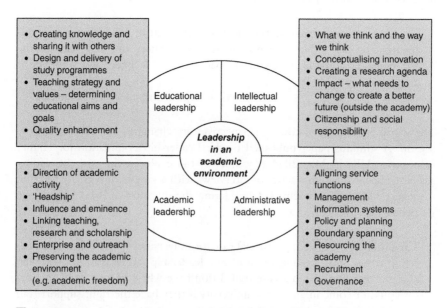

FIGURE 3.1 Leadership in an academic environment

This also links with the Programme Leadership Model and the role of the champion to promote, model, challenge and enthuse. Macfarlane (2012) notes 'a possible link between intellectual leadership and the concept of transformational leadership' (for more on this, see below).

Similar issues, concerns and challenges arise in relation to leading learning and teaching in terms of the rotation of roles and 'taking turns'. Course directors, programme leaders and module coordinators, to pick three likely role titles (there is much variation in the sector), may come into the role for a fixed period in line with, for example, an expectation set in an academic progression framework or a career map. It may be part of the teaching allocation model as applied to a particular academic grade or a stepping stone to some other form of grade-related recognition (for example, sabbaticals may be available). Sometimes it is a subject specialism that determines the appointment, or it may be longevity as a teacher on the course that makes the individual the right (or only) person for the role. There are a wide variety of formal and less formal systems and structures at work within the sector that determine who leads learning and teaching, why and when, and executive roles are largely reserved for more senior positions.

Thinking back to Chapter 1 and the issues raised regarding the Cinderella status of teaching in terms of recognition and reward, this is further compounded if combined with there being shallow regard for the role of leader and also uncertainty of commitment caused by roles being temporary. We are back to that key concept that 'you get what you reward' and the central importance of giving full recognition to the management and leadership of teaching at all levels.

DEFINITIONS OF MANAGEMENT

To start to overcome some of these concerns regarding management and leadership, and to provide clarity regarding the territory we are in, it is useful to have some definitions to work with. As we will go on to explore, there are many standpoints and perspectives that influence how leadership and management are defined. Central questions concern the nature of power and authority, who determines what needs to be done, the work itself and the workplace, whether managers can or should be flexible in how they manage different people, whether managers are also leaders, and the role of the manager in developing team members. Responding to the question 'why study management?', Linstead, Fulop and Lilley (2009: 16) sum things up very well:

> There are many sides to management, no simple and clear answers, and no 'one best way' to do it. Management is a complex field of activity and one that requires enormous effort and will to do well. It is not something that comes naturally to many of us, yet it is something that almost all of us might be called upon to do, not only through involvement in formal organizations, but in our private lives as well.

53

There will never be consensus on a single definition, but there is a lot to be learnt from comparing the different standpoints and drawing upon the merits of each. The following are three definitions of management that work well in this regard. Firstly, there is an enlightened definition that points towards the art involved in empowering others to achieve:

> Managing is the art of getting things done through and with people in formally organised groups. It is the art of creating an environment in which people can perform as individuals and yet co-operate towards attainment of group goals. It is the art of removing blocks to such performance.
>
> (Koontz, 1962)

Secondly, focusing on management in an educational context:

> 'Managing' is about the actual process of moving the organisation along the path towards the identified vision. It involves putting plans, structures and procedures in place and, then, enacting them through the people within the organisation to achieve improvement.
>
> (Anderson, 2003: 14)

And, thirdly, there is a definition of management that despite the passage of 100 years is still regarded, usually with a little bit of tweaking of some of the terms used (as indeed we shall do in this chapter), as classic:

> To manage is to forecast and plan, to organise, to command, to coordinate and to control.
>
> (Fayol, 1916)

What rich contrasts these definitions carry. The French industrialist Henri Fayol put forward a precise system of management that heralded the way for a school of theorists who tried to give us scientific principles of management to work with (Taylor, 1947). Fayol's definition is robust, fiercely organisational, and based on a lifetime's direct experience of successful managerial work. Koontz speaks from the heart by using the term 'art' rather than 'science' and paints a wonderful picture of the manager as an enabler 'removing blocks' to facilitate the attainment of goals through a motivated workforce. And Kydd, Anderson and Newton have us purposefully navigating a path towards an 'identified vision', which for management in an educational environment evokes pictures of colleagues working together in true collaboration to help students discover learning outcomes, both intended and unexpected, and a greater, truer understanding of themselves, society and the world as a result.

All three definitions carry truth. Anyone who has line managed will recognise the 'art' involved in engaging the motivations of very different team members and finding ways to communicate effectively with each (Koontz, 1962). Universities should be purpose-driven environments, with the goal of learning a paramount feature in its vision. Kydd, Anderson and Newton rightly highlight learning as an 'additional dimension' that should influence the character of management in work environments where students are at one and the same time both colleagues, and thereby others to be engaged in a management relationship, and customers (to use that term). And the functional nature of management captured so concisely by Fayol is an ever-present reality with cycles of planning, implementation and review being the focus of so much of a manager's time and energy.

All three definitions, taken in isolation, have faults (the authors of these wonderful definitions all have much more to say to expand and elaborate on the ideas and concepts concerned). The word 'command' leaps out of Fayol's definition to clash with our modern social values regarding healthy workplaces where colleagues should have the opportunity to grow and flourish with some level of self-determination regarding how they define their role and go about their work. Command breeds compliance and raw compliance brings with it resentment. The path-finding aspect of management highlighted by Kydd, Anderson and Newton is only one part of the equation with maintenance, problem-solving and keeping basic operations on track being a large part of what every manager does. And Koontz, whilst elegant in his depiction of the artful manager, perhaps leaves us with a rather passive impression of management that is at odds with the reality that many of us, rightly or wrongly, experience.

MANAGEMENT AND LEADERSHIP

So far we have used the terms 'management' and 'leadership' fairly interchangeably, but it is important to stop and ask whether we are talking about the same thing, different things or two aspects of a single endeavour. Depending on the context, there are a variety of connotations that are connected with these terms and some are quite contradictory – for example, the 'football manager' does a lot that theoretically we would regard as leadership and the 'team leader' in many conventional workplaces is, in many cases, primarily a manager. Perspectives on this dichotomy can raise questions of status, hierarchy, personality, degrees of influence, focus on results, vision and fulfilment of the vision, and even the inspirational versus the mundane. It is certainly worth taking care when picking over these distinctions and focusing in on what actually helps to frame our understanding in a useful way.

As a very broad summary, setting direction and influencing change are key determinants in identifying leadership. By contrast, getting things done and organising resources (including human resources) to achieve objectives would characterise management. Peter Drucker, once beautifully described as the guru's guru, put this better than anyone in his well-known phrase 'management is doing things right; leadership is doing the right things' (Drucker, 1955). But it is a bit like the nature/nurture debate with regard to the development of personality – the truth probably lies in a spectrum where the two are both always present, but to varying degrees. Some roles may be primarily management, but with elements of leadership, and conversely some may predominantly require leadership with a reduced emphasis on management. There will also be transitions as roles move along, with phases where the emphasis on leadership increases and decreases, and very often the factor influencing this will be the prevalence of change. To use an analogy, think of a rectangle. To be a rectangle, the shape needs both height and width. Some rectangles, the tall and thin variety, may have a lot of height whilst being very narrow. Others may be very wide but not high. However, they are all rectangles and to some degree need a combination of both width and height to exist as such. Think of a range of rectangles, with a square being the perfectly balanced mid-point, as illustrated in Figure 3.2.

If the upright edge is leadership and the horizontal edge is management, then clearly the combination of these varies across the spectrum. The point is that management and leadership exist together in combination, and in a complementary way, in all roles that carry responsibility for determining and achieving organisational goals through the collective and individual efforts of people. And all managers are, or should be, involved in achieving organisational goals. It is easy to think that this is the exclusive reserve of senior, strategic managers, but at both the tactical and operational levels, there should be a clear sense of vertical alignment with the goals of the organisation. So, there are at least four factors at work that influence the strength of the leadership dimension: the seniority of the role; the stage of the change lifecycle (when initiating change and gaining acceptance, leadership may be higher than when managing the process); the culture of the work environment (for example, compliance versus participation); and the disposition of the individual. Some have pondered whether it would be useful to have a term sitting above leadership and management that embraces the two, and 'headship' has been one suggestion.

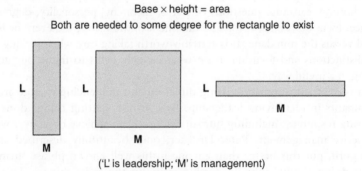

Base × height = area
Both are needed to some degree for the rectangle to exist

('L' is leadership; 'M' is management)

FIGURE 3.2 What makes a rectangle a rectangle?

Writing with regard to management and leadership in schools, Cuban (1988) gives a persuasive distinction between leadership and management whilst prizing the importance of both:

> By leadership, I mean influencing others' action in achieving desirable ends. Leaders are people who shape the goals, motivations and actions of others. Frequently they initiate change to reach existing and new goals . . . Leadership . . . takes . . . much ingenuity, energy and skill.
>
> Managing is maintaining efficiently and effectively current organizational arrangements. While managing well often exhibits leadership skills, the overall function is toward maintenance rather than change. I prize both managing and leading and attach no special value to either since different settings and times call for varied responses.
>
> (Cuban, 1988, as cited in Bush, 2003: 8)

Cuban makes a useful distinction through the emphasis on maintenance with regard to management and change with regard to leadership. But he falls short of categorically saying that there will always be both to some degree. Charles Handy, on the other hand, is unambiguous in this assertion. Drawing on the work of Henry Mintzberg (1973), Handy clearly asserts that managing 'includes leading, administering and fixing' and that 'it is neither a synonym nor the opposite of any one of them':

> The mix of roles varies from job to job. Top jobs have a larger element of 'leading' roles, first line supervisory jobs more 'fixing', while middle-layer jobs are inevitably landed with the administering or informational roles – but every job has some of each.
>
> (Handy, 1993: 322)

We come back to the thinking of Harold Koontz, who reinforces the view that at all levels, and in all occupations, managers have the common goal or challenge of organising and motivating people to get things done:

> Acting in their managerial capacity, presidents, department heads, foremen, supervisors, college deans, bishops and heads of governmental agencies all do the same thing. As managers they are all engaged, in part, in getting things done with and through people.
>
> (Koontz and O'Donnell, 1972: 20)

Koontz could certainly have added course directors and module organisers to his list.

Another useful approach that helps to frame both conceptually and practically the difference between leadership and management is to produce a list of contrasting actions and qualities. This has been done in varying ways by a number of researchers and authors. Table 3.1 below presents such a checklist that links with some of the models and themes explored in this book.

EXERCISE

Reflecting on your current management/leadership role create a table with two columns, management and leadership, and consider which activities, responsibilities and approaches you would place under each heading.

The drawback of this listing method of differentiating management from leadership is that it can almost stigmatise our perception of management as something mundane, workaday and frankly unimaginative, whilst elevating leadership to a sort of divinely inspired and almost unattainable level of

TABLE 3.1 Management versus leadership

Management – *planning, action and stability*	Leadership – *change, energy and direction*
Planning • Identify goals • Set priorities • Create agendas • Link together activities, resources and time (the ART of planning) • Establish a sequence with milestones	**Direction** • Looking outwards and inwards (near, mid and far horizons) • Developing a shared vision • Establishing purpose and values • Setting strategies • Constructing a narrative (with others . . .)
Organising • Activate the plan • Develop a structure • Agree who does what and when • Allocate roles and responsibilities and assign resources • Establish ways of working, procedures and guidelines	**Alignment** • Strategic planning • Communicate change as often and in as many ways as possible • Develop, share and coordinate goals • Work within and across boundaries – develop coalitions and partnerships • Establish, build and support teams
Monitoring and controlling • Track progress and achievements • Link together goals and incentives • Allow appropriate flexibility • Agree solutions, maintain direction and update everyone involved • Bring things back on course or change course	**Commitment** • Create and enable environments for collaborative engagement • Focus on both team climate and individual motivation • Energise and inspire • Empower others to act and perform • Encourage ongoing collective learning
Evaluating • Analysing targets, outcomes and impact • Learning through the process • Supporting team and individual learning • Learning after the process • Feeding results, ideas and insights into future plans	**Accountability** • Remain accessible throughout • Use the language of learning rather than the language of blame • Encourage feedback at all levels • Show that it matters to you – you care • The buck stops with you . . .

insight and inspiration. Neither perception is either true or helpful. A leadership vision can be highly functional in its character with the qualities that make it a reality being simple persistence and consistency. On the other hand, so-called routine management can manifest itself in a highly motivated team of colleagues, working hard, communicating well, displaying a shared sense of purpose, learning together and having fun. This is why whilst it is useful to have an understanding of the differences between management and leadership, the different aspects of one's role that could be regarded as each, and when and why one might need to move towards the leadership end of the spectrum, it is not helpful to demarcate roles as being either one or the other – far better to clearly acknowledge that all management roles involve some degree of leadership.

TRANSACTIONAL AND TRANSFORMATIONAL LEADERSHIP

Another interesting twist in this long-running debate about the differences between management and leadership is a set of ideas that essentially begin to turn the spotlight on different styles of leadership. The American historian James MacGregor Burns (1978) argued that leadership can be either transactional or transformational in its character. The transactional approach is essentially about giving and getting, about achievement and reward. In transactional terms the skill of leadership is concerned with engineering a series of 'negotiated' steps that progressively encourage individuals and teams to meet goals and standards as set by the organisation in return for a selection of rewards ranging from pay and promotion to praise and recognition. Looking back at our earlier discussion, this might be regarded as essentially more managerial in nature, and educationalists may identify it with Skinner's (1968) ideas of behavioural conditioning through sequences of stimulus, response and reinforcement.

Transformational leadership, on the other hand, is about inspiring in individuals a high level of personal engagement with the goals and mission of the team or organisation, and a sense of worthwhile collective effort around these, such that even people with very routine or menial roles feel part of something greater than themselves and are motivated to perform to high levels as a result. The wonderful example of this, often quoted and probably apocryphal, belongs to the J. F. Kennedy years in the early 1960s when he captured the imagination of a generation with his powerful and concise vision for the American space programme: 'this nation should commit itself to achieving the goal, before this decade is out, of landing a man on the moon and returning him safely to the earth' (Kennedy, 1961). As well as inspiring America, which up to that point had been flagging some way behind its Soviet competitors in the space race, to go on and steal the prize of a first Moon landing (20 July 1969), he also created a model of transformational leadership within the US National Aeronautics and Space Administration (NASA). I am not referring to the 'one small step' dialogue between Neil Armstrong and NASA's mission control centre in Houston, but instead to a lesser known and, as I say, probably apocryphal account of a senior NASA executive tripping over a badly placed cleaner's bucket when working late one evening. On admonishing the cleaner by shouting 'what on earth do you think you're doing!', the janitor is said to have replied quite simply 'I'm helping to get a man to the Moon, Sir'. Whether true or not, what a wonderful illustration of an organisational team at all levels having a clear sense of alignment with an inspiring shared vision. This is sometimes referred to as *having a clear line of sight* (see the section on liberating leadership in Chapter 8) – that is, a line of sight from my contribution to the highest goals of the organisation.

Bernard Bass (1985) took the work of Burns further by exploring the psychological mechanisms of transformational leadership (Bass actually used the term 'transformational' in place of the original 'transforming leadership' coined by Burns). He identified four key elements of transformational leadership, known as the four I's (Bass and Avolio, 1994):

- *Individualised Consideration (IC)* – the leader listens actively and attends closely to the needs and concerns of each individual follower, works hard to understand their intrinsic motivation and acts as a mentor.
- *Intellectual Stimulation (IS)* – the leader puts forward challenging new ideas and encourages and enables followers to think and be creative (we noted earlier the links between intellectual leadership and transformational leadership). They look to challenge assumptions and take risks and encourage followers to see difficult situations as learning opportunities.
- *Inspirational Motivation (IM)* – the leader looks to articulate a powerful vision of the future that will be attractive to followers. They project a strong sense of purpose and optimism, they communicate with energy and they look to engage followers at the level of personal meaning and identity.
- *Idealised Influence (II)* (originally termed 'charisma') – the leader models key behaviours and values and 'walks the talk'. Through this they show confidence, instil pride, and develop trust and mutual respect.

Transformational leadership brings with it ideas to do with trusting people, giving them responsibility and accountability, and allowing them to take a personal stake, and possibly personal pride, in the growth and success of the organisational or team endeavour. Transformational leadership is essentially about empowering people. Once again there are clear parallels educationally with theories to do with personal growth and self-actualisation (Maslow, 1943) – encouraging students to take responsibility for their own learning as a gateway to deep learning and self-discovery. In a report published by the UK Leadership Foundation for Higher Education (Gibbs, Knapper and Piccinin, 2009: 8), a striking observation is made regarding the increased likelihood of teachers adopting 'a student focused approach to teaching' when they experience, amongst other factors, transformational leadership. This is an observation that could perhaps have been the headline of the entire report, because if we believe that the learning and teaching environment has a fundamental impact on students' approach to learning, then it follows that the leadership and management environment within the institution will have a profound impact on teachers' approach to teaching. The inextricable link between environment and approach cascades right through the institution, and arguably beyond, and is nowhere more clearly manifested than in the learning outcomes, both intended and unintended, achieved by students. In this report Gibbs, Knapper and Piccinin describe transformational leadership beautifully as:

> where teachers experience leadership driven by values, and engagement through collaboration, inspiration and spontaneity, trust and exemplary practice. The leader helps teachers to think about teaching problems in new ways.
>
> (Gibbs, Knapper and Piccinin, 2009: 8)

As almost a footnote to this, others such as John Kotter (1990) have taken issue with the polarising assertion made by Burns' transactional to transformational spectrum. They argue that transactional strategies can and often do sit alongside transformational leadership. So, a system of targets and rewards can work as an effective system of management in a situation where team members are also motivated and empowered through an emotional engagement with the vision put forward by the leader. There is almost an alchemy at work as the two elements are combined in proportions appropriate to the situation at hand. This reinforces the view that management and leadership exist in union as essential qualities, to varying degrees, in all leadership roles.

Coming back to the dialogue at the start of this chapter, you will remember that my colleague objected to being termed a manager. Would there be the same objection to the term 'leader'? Well, as a generalisation amongst academics, it would appear not. As a small but fascinating research study conducted by Marshall et al. (2003) at an Australian university confirmed, many academics are happy to acknowledge that their work requires them to exercise academic leadership (more than 80 per cent in the Marshall study), but far fewer respond to points concerning areas such as human resource management and budgeting (around 40 per cent in the study). The reasons for this will range from simply being more or less comfortable with the terms used through to perceptions that being an academic and academic leadership are fundamentally interlinked due to the very nature of the academic endeavour – leading thought and knowledge at the forefront of a discipline (Trowler and Taylor, cited in Marshall, Adams and Cameron, 2000: 2), an aspect of intellectual leadership – whilst management can be viewed as an unwelcome administrative addition that does little to move forward an academic career. There may, however, be more scepticism regarding the term 'leadership' as it applies to formal roles (Bolden et al., 2012). These are perceptions that can and will change as the role of the teaching programme

61

leader/manager in universities moves centre stage in the newly emerging, customer-driven, international and professionally focused market for knowledge and skills development.

LEADERSHIP AND FOLLOWERSHIP

Here's a question for you: are followers more important to leaders than leaders are to followers (Kellerman, 2008)? Or, to put it another way, are leaders – good, great or gruesome – made by their followers? And is it always clear who are the leaders and who are the followers, regardless of the titles or salaries they may be granted? These are the sorts of thoughts and questions that lie behind the idea termed 'followership'.

The rather cumbersome term 'followership' is an elusive one to pin down in the literature. Barbara Kellerman writing in 2008 suggests that Robert Earl Kelley 'was the first to bestow on followership a measure of legitimacy' through his work *The Power of Followership* (1992). However, cumbersome or not, it brings home an important point regarding leadership which concerns inspiring others to follow (students, professional staff and academic colleagues). Bennis and Nanus (1985) assert that 'transformative leaders align the energies of others behind an attractive goal' and perhaps that is part of the 'art' that Koontz was alluding to. But followership goes further, because in this the goal *comes from* the followers and the leader becomes simply an enabler of that more or less collective vision. This links with other ideas such as collaborative leadership, distributed leadership, inclusive leadership, shared leadership and servant leadership, which purely as terms conjure up pictures of facilitation and collaboration and the leader essentially being a resource to support the achievement of others:

> In addition to hierarchical or top-down leadership, however, our findings reveal the significance of bottom-up and horizontal leadership. HEIs (Higher Education Institutions) are thus advised to review their leadership strategy to ensure that it facilitates and enables multiple forms of engagement including informal, emergent and horizontal leadership.
>
> (Bolden, Petrov and Gosling, 2008)

Those who have led teaching modules or programmes in higher education may identify quite readily with this notion of followership. Command and control is not a recipe for success when working with independently minded high achievers in any professional environment, but in one where 'freedom' is enshrined as part of the professional fabric to safeguard conceptual exploration and discovery (academic freedom), the approach is almost anathema. However, and in sharp contrast to this, colleagues will often appreciate, for example, a well-thought-through framework in which to efficiently and effectively contribute, and will also value being part of a well-aligned programme with clear aims, well-selected teaching interventions and carefully judged assessments. They will also often respond well to having opportunities to collaboratively engage and contribute creatively during course transformation initiatives.

Back to rectangles. Even the broadest management role has some height in terms of leadership. And even the loftiest leadership role has some breadth in terms of management. The challenge typically faced by the programme leader straddles these two paradigms. A meticulously organised manager focused on planning and delivery takes us towards a broad set of management responsibilities; the art of inspiring a sometimes disparate group of contributors to prepare and facilitate a coherent set of learning activities takes us in the direction of visionary leadership. But perhaps the real art is to capitalise on this notion of followership – enabling others to succeed in sometimes extraordinary ways based on their drive, love of a subject and the infectious joy that can come from supporting others to discover their own potential.

Whenever I think about followers and leaders and the interaction between the two roles, I am reminded of a startling comment that a student once related to me during a session on leadership: 'Either be a good leader, or a good follower, or get out of the way!' It is hard to think of a better observation to round off this section.

THE PROGRAMME LEADERSHIP MODEL

This discussion of how management differs from leadership and how leadership differs from management has high relevance for people involved in running teaching modules and programmes in higher education. Without overstating the matter, there can be few roles at this organisational level that combine elements of inspirational leadership (the learning champion) with elements of target-driven and goal-focused management to such a high degree. Perhaps this stems from the transformational nature of learning, and thus the necessity of adopting transformative styles of leadership to motivate both those who teach and those who study with an energised sense of shared endeavour. A great course or module, seen in action with a group of well-engaged students, always has something of that getting-a-man-to-the-moon, transformative quality that makes it something very exciting to be part of.

The Programme Leadership Model captures this distinction between leadership, which is essentially transformative and linked to enabling change, and management, which is transactional and concerned with getting things done, through the four defined key leadership attributes. The two attributes featured in the top corners (see Figure 3.3 below), champion and enabler, may be regarded as transformative in character and therefore more closely aligned to leadership, and the two attributes below, organiser and mentor, are focused on those 'negotiated' steps that progressively equip, encourage and reward teams and individuals to meet agreed goals, and which are therefore more managerial in their feel. Picking up on the model of transformational leadership put forward by Bass and Avolio (see above) and being a little more analytical, one could suggest the following associations:

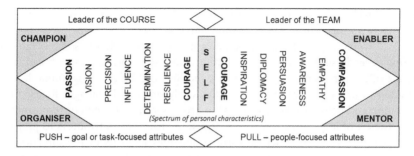

FIGURE 3.3 Leadership attributes

- *Individualised Consideration (IC)* – mentor.
- *Intellectual Stimulation (IS)* – enabler.
- *Inspirational Motivation (IM)* – champion.
- *Idealised Influence (II)* – champion.
- *Transactional leadership* – organiser.

However, it goes against the spirit of a model such as this to draw a hard line through it in an attempt to rather falsely delineate leadership from management. In practice the whole thing is far more fluid than that, with the characteristics of management and leadership overlapping and interweaving in a dynamic way, and so it is important that the model reflects this reality. The attributes, qualities and skills are all termed 'leadership' and that is intended to combat the functional and organisational bias that can all too readily creep into our more mundane perceptions of course management. How far from the truth this should be! A great module or programme, one that inspires learning in all directions, tutor-to-student, student-to-tutor, student-to-student and tutor-to-tutor, has the inspiration of leadership at its heart, whether that's a loud voice that drives the vision forward (the champion) or, equally as validly, whether that's a soft hand that removes blocks to facilitate and enable the performance of a great team of followers (the enabler).

TWO TOOLS FOR UNDERSTANDING MANAGEMENT (MANAGEMENT SPECIFICALLY RATHER THAN LEADERSHIP)

Understanding management, in whatever context, can be done in a haphazard or a structured way. However, one of the barriers that often prevents people from taking a more structured and systematic approach to considering their role as a manager is that it is often seen as a secondary adjunct to their main calling. This can certainly be true of leading learning and teaching in higher education. A module organiser or course director may have taken on this managerial responsibility for no other reason than that they happen to do a large amount of the teaching on the particular course, and teaching delivery itself remains their primary role, and often this too is secondary to their research. Contrast this to, say, a retail manager running a store or a group of stores – they would unambiguously describe themselves as a manager and would think seriously and earnestly about their structured development in that regard. It would also invariably be their sole focus – something that makes working in universities so rich and fascinating is the fact that 'success' is very multi-dimensional.

PRAISE and POMCE, the two tools presented below, can be used as a structure for reviewing and understanding management. They should also help to rationally consider and navigate the various management challenges you may face and plan your personal development. The first tool, PRAISE, will provide a shorthand for reviewing your management role (role is defined by broad areas of responsibility), and the second tool, POMCE, is powerful for understanding the functions of management (the things all managers do – or should do). POMCE also overlaps directly with the 'organiser' attribute in the Programme Leadership Model.

For a complete management framework, we also need to explore influence and leadership styles. We will look at influence, including sources of power and authority (where your authority comes from), separately in the next chapter. And in Chapter 2 we opened up a detailed discussion of leadership styles and introduced the four key leadership attributes relating directly to the leadership of learning and teaching and associated critical skills. In Chapter 8 we will look at a number of theories regarding leadership and participation and consider style from that perspective.

MANAGEMENT ROLE – AREAS OF RESPONSIBILITY

PRAISE is an acronym that usefully identifies the various responsibilities that together make up a manager's role (what the manager manages). The balance and emphasis of these responsibilities will vary between roles, with some, for example, being strongly about the challenge of managing people, whilst others may be more focused on activities and making things happen (project managers, perhaps). Some management roles may have a specialist slant to them such as quality assurance (an emphasis on information and analysis) or health and safety (an emphasis on the environment). The balance will also shift and change as management roles evolve and in some roles (and teaching management is a clear example of this), the emphasis may also change in a cyclical manner depending on set phases in the work programme (for example, the academic year). PRAISE provides a heading for each of the following six broad areas of management responsibility: people – resources – activities – information – self – environment. The following list suggests generically the variety of things that would come under each heading (this is not tailored for learning and teaching):

- *People*

  - Individuals and the team
  - Consultants and advisers
  - Customers and clients
  - Partners, collaborators and supporters
  - Stakeholders and interested parties (internal and external)
  - Upwards management – your boss and senior managers
  - Across boundaries – other teams and key individuals.

(Students could be placed in several of the above categories, interestingly, depending on the ethos and the reality of the relationship.)

- *Resources*

  - Budgets
  - Equipment
  - Technology
  - Office space
  - Facilities and premises (including storage)
  - Materials
  - Online tools, programmes and applications
  - Tools, plant and machinery
  - Vehicles.

- *Activities*

  - Planned tasks
  - Routine tasks
  - Special tasks
  - Individual objectives
  - Team goals
  - Projects and initiatives
  - Production – creating, designing and making
  - Delivery – releasing, presenting and passing on/over
  - Marketing and selling
  - Communication.

- *Information*

  - Performance figures
  - Product or programme specifications
  - Workflow, input and output monitoring
  - Budget forecasts
  - Research results
  - External communications and publicity
  - Quality metrics, surveys and evaluation

- Knowledge creation and management
- Data storage and retrieval.

■ *Self*

- Own objectives (work contribution and development)
- Time and task management
- Image and impact – how you are perceived by others
- Modelling and inspiration – the behaviours and values you model
- Setting standards – your focus, energy and effectiveness
- Personal resilience
- Personal inspiration (what inspires you?)
- Work/life balance – your own well-being
- Outlook and happiness.

■ *Environment*

- The work/study environment
- Health, safety and welfare
- Risk assessment
- Workplace atmosphere – climate and culture (and links to individual motivation, both intrinsic and extrinsic)
- Stress, pressure and well-being
- On-site and off-site
- Social and legal responsibilities
- The responsible use of resources (materials, travel, consumables, etc.)
- Environmental impact
- Sustainability and sustainable development.

EXERCISE

Create a table with the six headings of PRAISE:

- ■ Under each heading, note down the things which you consider to be your main areas of management responsibility (be as specific as you can).
- ■ Reflect on how much time, energy and attention you currently give to each, and allocate points or percentages to record this.
- ■ Now reflect on how much time, energy and attention you should be giving to each. With a different colour, again allocate points or percentages.
- ■ Where are the areas of greatest divergence between what you are currently doing and what you feel you should be doing?
- ■ What might the reasons for this be?
- ■ What simple steps could you (or others) start to take to make a positive change?
- ■ Who could/should you discuss this with?

PRAISE can also be used for considering and reviewing the work of the people you manage, alongside, perhaps, organisational frameworks, and also as a planning tool for setting up new projects and initiatives and understanding the responsibilities involved.

MANAGEMENT FUNCTIONS – WHAT A MANAGER DOES

If PRAISE responded to the question 'what does a manager manage?', then POMCE responds to 'how does a manager manage?' POMCE, our second tool for understanding management, is a key for considering what a manager fundamentally does, in any management capacity, rather than the specifics of a particular role. Adapted from a model originally proposed by Henri Fayol (1949), POMCE helps us to separate out the following fundamental management functions:

- *Plan*: what, how, when and in what order?
- *Organise*: putting the plan into practice – making things happen – action and activity.
- *Monitor*: stepping back from the action – comparing actual and planned performance (and moving into control, responding to the variances with, if necessary, corrective action).
- *Control*: bringing things back on course or changing course (Figure 3.4 below illustrates the way in which plans develop and progress through monitoring and control).
- *Evaluate*: reflecting back and looking forwards – learning from experience and looking to the future.

(Table 3.1 above provides further ideas using a similar list.)

So, as you go about your management role, broadly speaking, everything you do will fall under one of these five headings. These are the classic management

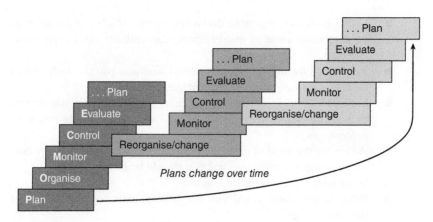

FIGURE 3.4 Management functions – achieving the task – POMCE

functions and this is the management process involved in *achieving the task*. And all of them are needed in some way and to some degree. The absence of any one of them will inevitably lead to some degree of management failure or weakness. These are the series of 'negotiated' steps that progressively move plans into action and deliver results, and this is what sits at the heart of the organiser attribute in the Programme Leadership Model:

Without a plan, there is no commitment, hence no accountability.

(Fayol, 1913)

QUESTIONS FOR ACTION AND REFLECTION

1 How would you define management?
2 How would you define leadership?
3 How would you define leadership and management specifically linked to the context in which you lead and manage?
4 Which aspects of management do you enjoy?
5 Which aspects of leadership appeal to you?
6 In what ways can your current management/leadership role enhance your overall career development?
7 Thinking of someone you admire as a leader, what are the specific attributes and qualities they bring to the role?
8 What is the balance in your role between management and leadership? How could you increase the emphasis on leadership?
9 What sort of follower are you? How would you describe yourself as a follower? What qualities do you most admire in others as followers?
10 If leadership is a relationship with followers, what simple things could you do to enhance or improve the relationship you have with members of your team and other key stakeholders?

Chapter 4

Leading with influence

THE CHALLENGE IN THIS CHAPTER

Building upon the discussions so far regarding management and leadership, this chapter is set out as an important precursor to much that will follow. Can a leader lead without power? The answer is a simple no. Does power only come with conventional authority? Another no. Are leaders powerful and followers powerless? A third very definite no.

In relation to leadership, this chapter invites you to consider where power comes from and how it should be used. This is a very important area of consideration in leadership development generally, but in the context of higher education and other professions involving a lot of what we might term 'smart' people, the challenge is often to lead with influence rather than authority – this is partly about sharing leadership. The expression 'herding cats' (Garrett and Davies, 2010) is an interesting, perhaps over-used simile for academic leadership and one which may be resonant with many principal investigators or heads of department who have attempted to get academic colleagues to work towards or even sometimes acknowledge a common strategy. Cats have a purposeful agenda of their own, or at least are masterful in giving that appearance, and like many academics *they will not be commanded* (Goffee and Jones, 2009).

In this chapter we will explore:

■ definitions of power and influence, and some of the established thinking regarding sources of power and authority in 'organisational life';

■ influencing styles and strategies and what are sometimes termed 'push' and 'pull' behaviours;

■ skills you can exploit, enhance or develop to increase your ability to influence in different contexts and situations – this will include the idea of open and hidden influence;

■ influencing different personality types and speaking the other person's language.

A question no manager should be afraid to ask or consider is quite simply: 'Where does my authority come from?' In fact, the clearer you are on your sources of power and authority, the more capable you are likely to be in terms of achieving your management goals or renegotiating them if necessary. Very simply speaking, power and authority can come from within yourself, from outside of yourself, from relationships and from the resources available to you.

LINKS TO THE PROGRAMME LEADERSHIP MODEL

A powerful central element of the Programme Leadership Model is the distinction between the driving force of passion and the nurturing reflex of compassion. In the model we see on one side, goal/task-focused attributes labelled as 'push' and, on the other, people-focused attributes labelled as 'pull'. All of this is leading with influence, both push and pull, from the open skills of proposing and presenting in formal situations through to the more hidden skills of relationship building and finding hooks into other people's agendas. The nature of impactful influence is that it speaks with a voice that can be both loud and soft, both fast and slow, tuned to my agenda or tuned to yours. The nature of impactful influence is that it speaks to both the head and the heart.

WHERE DOES POWER COME FROM?

There are some people you *have* to say yes to and some people you *want* to say yes to. As one person starts to speak, your instinct is to agree, while as another clears his throat, a 'no' is already on your lips. With hardly any detail, there are projects and programmes you want to be part of; another invitation replete with attractive detail is unappealing to you. Why? Why these differences? Is it the exercise of vague and random preferences or is there something else at work stemming from the leaders involved, their style and the power that they use?

Imagine a father with his son. There is some tension in the air, nothing unusual in a family (or in a workplace for that matter). The situation is this; he simply wants his son to share his sweets with his sister. He is after some fair play, some generosity and probably most of all some peace. What are the father's options? He could wield a mighty stick, if he has one, and compel his son to do as commanded, or at the other extreme he could simply step back and let his son decide, perhaps with no more than a brief moment of eye contact. There are very different kinds of power at work in these two examples, and there are others. Listen to the father's voice in each of these examples:

a I'm your father and I am telling you to give your sister one of your sweets.
b Eating too many sweets is very bad for you. You'll understand why when you get to my age. Now, share some with your sister.

71

c   You'll do it for me, won't you? That's a good lad. Go on, let your sister have one. That's my boy!

d   Sharing is what families do. If we keep things to ourselves, then we all lose out in the end. Now let Lucy have one. It's the right thing to do.

e   You can both have some of my sweets. In fact, you take them and share them between yourselves.

f   We've talked about this before, so I'll let you decide. What do you think you should do?

This simple 'sweet' example shows us several different kinds of power and authority being used. Firstly, the father draws on his positional authority and uses this to command his son: this is a 'telling' voice (a). Next he draws on his greater knowledge and experience and asserts that his son should therefore share his sweets: this is a 'knowing' voice (b). In the third example, personality is the lever as the father calls on love and loyalty by saying 'do it for me': this is a 'charismatic' voice (c). Rightness is exerted by the father in the fourth variation as he makes out a case based on broader principles: this is a 'moral' voice (d). In a neat side-step, the next strategy involves the father sharing with both son and daughter some of his own sweets: this is the voice of 'behaviour' (e). And lastly the father reflects on previous discussions with his son and shows respect for his independence by letting him decide: this is the voice of 'relationship' (f).

This sweet example is a simple way of illustrating the six fundamental sources of personal power and authority in organisational leadership:

- position (the 'telling' voice);
- knowledge and experience (the 'knowing' voice);
- personality (the 'charismatic' voice);
- moral authority (the 'moral' voice);
- behaviour (the voice of 'behaviour');
- relationship (the voice of 'relationship').

This list has had many variations and can be traced back at least as far as the study published by John French and Bertram Raven in 1959. Their list also included notions of reward, coercion and legitimacy.

Coming back to an organisational context, and particularly a context such as learning and teaching in higher education where, as we have already noted, the hierarchy of relationships can be 'hazy', where management lines are often curvy or dotted rather than straight, if I can put it that way, how do these various sources of power hold up? Let's again think them through one at a time.

Position. Well, rank has its privileges, as they say, and one of those historically has been to command and control (this takes us back to Henri Fayol's (1949) original definition of management). There is usually something in the title of a management role that conveys seniority and, were one to look, there is probably also something in the contract. The power of position is a bit like a drum – people should jump when it is beaten. And so they will, initially. But beat it too often, or if beating it is the only thing you do, and people will stop listening. They will shrug their shoulders, look away and start to do what they want to do. Like the inexperienced teacher at the front of a class who shouts to get the pupils to listen, it works to begin with, but if you have no other way of holding their attention, then shouting loses its effect and the crueller children may even start to lampoon you as you get ever redder in the face. Positional authority can be important, but if you keep falling back on it, it will quickly lose its bite – it is not enduring. Besides, in *hazier* organisations such as the academic territories in a university, we may find leadership going on that is not aligned with position, and this is often the case with the director of a teaching programme. Fortunately position is not the only kind of power we can use to influence others:

> Getting obedience on the basis of your formal authority and job position alone is not an effective influence approach . . . If you rely exclusively on your formal authority to get things done, then you cannot be said to be influencing others. You are ordering them what to do, and in the long run, you will end up alienating people.
>
> (Brent and Dent, 2010)

Knowledge and experience. Knowing more than other people can certainly be a powerful thing. It is a competitive advantage and a clear basis for getting ahead of the pack. It could be said that in quite a particular and specialised way, knowing more than others, and finding clever ways to develop new knowledge, is what academic endeavour is all about (although that would be to negate many other aspects of academic life, such as the learning community). There is a cynical perception that goes alongside this that succeeding in academia is about ever-increasing specialisation: *knowing more and more about less and less until you know all there is about almost nothing at all.* That aside, it is a common thing for someone knowledgeable and experienced to be promoted into a leadership role. This is flattering in many ways and is underpinned by the logic that someone very good at something ought to be equally successful at leading others to do the same. The problem is that this is a change of craft. The individual concerned is going from being an expert at one thing (their specialism) to being a novice at another (management and leadership). So, in a sense, the organisation may have lost an asset (for example, a great salesperson) and gained a liability (a poor and inexperienced sales manager, to continue the example). Dissatisfaction, distress and dissent can often result. One of the initial tripwires can ironically be precisely the thing which got them earmarked for leadership: their knowledge. Knowing what you would do can quickly turn into telling others what they should do, and too much of this will quickly frustrate, stifle, demotivate or even anger able and creative colleagues. Reasonable competence and credibility in the role is important, of course, but trying to have all the answers will stifle creativity and breed dependency. Having greater knowledge and experience can also be a terrible strain – it does not endure. People grow and develop, and if they did not start ahead of you, they can quickly catch you up. People's development

73

should be something to celebrate, something to foster with innovation welcomed rather than spurned, but this can be challenging if a leader feels insecure. In an academic teaching environment, this fostering of other people's potential should certainly be the case, and a natural inversion of the 'knowledge stakes' regarded as inevitable. The director of a teaching programme needs to be skilled at engaging a wide range of talented colleagues with levels of scholarship and expertise that surpass their own in a variety of inter-related specialisms and disciplines. The leadership skill is to guide and channel innovation rather than to restrain it, and to serve and facilitate the achievement of others. This links with the enabler attribute in the Programme Leadership Model.

Personality. Perhaps the most fickle form of authority is that which flows from the sparkle or effervescence of our character. The charm of this can be inspirational, with novelty often being the key basis of appeal, but with familiarity the sense of wonder can start to wane and love can turn to disinterest or even contempt. Many politicians would certainly recognise this dilemma. For some of us, the notion of having to sparkle is in itself an offputting thought or even a burden, and others would challenge such a superficial idea of personality straight away. True charisma can take many forms, from the great rhetorician to the quiet but thoughtful guide, from the warrior who steps first into the breach to the compassionate healer. This authentic individuality is crucial to a true understanding of leadership, with the critical issue being a form of emotional intelligence (Goleman, 1996) that enables the leader to be both self-aware and also attuned to the needs of their environment. But the 'do it for me' exhortation is a fragile foundation for leadership, and the basis for love or loyalty which inspired people one day can become a cause of irritation or dissent the next. You can end up in the tired situation where 'people would follow him anywhere, but only out of morbid curiosity'. Personality, whatever we may mean by that, is a hard thing to sustain if we are to lead others on an ongoing basis – it is seldom enduring. We may also find it divisive, appealing to our friends, the ones in the faculty with a 'yes' on their lips (on most occasions anyway), but alienating to those others who may be the very people we most need to engage:

> Charismatic leaders influence by charm rather than reason and when they run out of charm they tend to revert to force.
>
> (Chamorro-Premuzic, 2012)

Moral. Defining moral authority, in relation to leadership, would take more than just a few words here. Interestingly, however, learning and teaching is itself a kind of moral proposition. In all of our various disciplines, we look to develop in students a critical faculty, an ability to debate, evaluate, critique, argue and make judgements – and, if taken further, the ability to create, make breakthroughs, discover unique solutions and enlighten. If, as Gandhi (1957) asserted, 'truth is the substance of all morality', then the calling to teach, to facilitate the learning of others, is in a very real sense a moral quest. There are principles involved that most of us, in one way or another, cherish. Some of these are plain old fundamentals, like the importance of sharing knowledge and the desire to see human potential recognised and supported, but other principles are bound up with social, cultural and even political values like self-directed learning, social constructivism and individual empowerment. And so without necessarily labelling it as such, the leader of learning may assert the 'rightness' of certain approaches, ways of doing things and even the character of relationships (in Chapter 6 we ask the question 'what is your educational philosophy?'). This again can be fragile stuff, not because the rightness isn't there, but because principles as a guiding light can lack the fluent energy of the everyday. It is also a source of authority that can be readily contested in any professional community, not least academia, and if people don't buy into your morality, then the leadership hill will become a veritable mountain to climb:

> Morality is simply the attitude we adopt towards people whom we personally dislike.
>
> (Mrs Cheveley in *An Ideal Husband* by Oscar Wilde (1893))

Behaviour. Within organisations, what we do is the easy bit. 'How' is the game-changer – *how* we do things. Look no further than the lecture hall to see the truth in this – the difference between 'covering' the material and 'uncovering' the learning, as one might express it. Leaders who focus on behaviour, who look to identify and inspire the behaviours needed for success are the ones capable of leading agile teams and organisations. And where does this behaviour come from? Well, from a kind of abstract consensus, sometimes explicit, often not, but the behaviours that the leader models in their own work, approach and interactions are a very key part of this. Why do something a particular way? 'Because this is the way we've agreed to do it and this is the way I do it myself.' That is a very strong basis for leadership. It is strong, consistent and enduring, and it attracts rather than demands respect. It is not about mimicry or clones, because the behaviours are seeded rather than enforced. And it is more than 'leading by example'. Although 'example' can be part of it, the problem with this popular phrase is that it implies the leader being out in front and, in fact, one of the key leadership behaviours may involve sharing responsibility and devolving some of that positional authority we were talking about earlier. 'Leaders as enablers of leaders' is one of the ideas we will explore in Chapter 8 as we look in depth at both team level leadership modelling (values and behaviour) and leading individuals. The power derived from behaviour is the one that ultimately sets the pace, tone and character of a team, work area or organisation. It cannot be talked about, it has to be seen and experienced, and if the words and behaviour do not match, people will always believe the behaviour. The upside and downside of leadership is that everything you do sends a message. The following lines from Chapter 54 of Lao Tzu's Tao Te Ching (*Book of the Way* – sixth century BC) remind us that modelling values and behaviours is not the exclusive domain of the formal leader – many others can also show this leadership:

Your behaviour influences others through a ripple effect. A ripple effect works because everyone influences everyone else . . . Remember that your influence begins with you and ripples outward. So be sure that your influence is both potent and wholesome.

(John Heider's adaptation, 1985)

Relationship. In one sense, every interaction is a relationship. If someone walks past you in a corridor and ignores your presence, either deliberately or inadvertently, but perhaps driven by self-importance, that is a relationship. But it is a relationship based on an impoverished connection. Emotionally intelligent leaders look to connect with people as individuals in ways that are transformational. They realise that the time to build a relationship is not when you need something and look to invest in relationships all the time. Writing about transforming leaders, Burns (1978) identified that power occurs through relationships as leaders and followers forge connections around goals to which they are collectively committed – this is true engagement. If as teachers we see learning as a collaborative process based on relationship, then the same must apply to leadership. If with students we believe in adopting a facilitative approach that is about releasing and realising potential, and not about telling and directing, then for our approach to be congruent, the same values should show through in the relationship between leaders and followers in learning and teaching teams. This could be called learning-focused teaching and leadership (see Figure 4.1).

In Chapter 8 we will look at an approach called liberating leadership, which is focused on removing blocks and interference so that the potential of teams and individuals can thrive. A liberating leader will look to set the tone in terms of creating relationships based on empathy, compassion and passion. These relationships are energising, inspiring and fulfilling, and go beyond the difficulties of today. They are based on trust, respect, warmth and a desire to understand the emotional needs of others. Leadership influence based on relationship, vision and behaviour is not just likely to be more effective and enduring, it is also a more fundamentally fulfilling way of being.

What gives a leader the power to lead is a question that goes back a long way. From the divine right of kings to ideas of servant leadership re-cast in the late

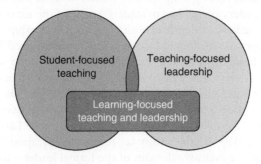

FIGURE 4.1 Learning-focused teaching and leadership

twentieth century. The 'right to rule', if we can call it that, has changed to reflect the values of the society in which leaders and followers interact. Contrast the following:

■ 'To be a king is half to be a god' – *Tamburlaine the Great, Part I* (Act II, Scene V) by Christopher Marlowe (1588).
■ 'The servant leader is servant first . . . It begins with the natural feeling that one wants to serve, to serve first. Then conscious choice brings one to aspire to lead' (Greenleaf, 1970).

If the values of a society support the notion that their leaders are divinely appointed, then that is a very strong basis for positional authority. If, however, society regards all citizens as equal with a strong sense of individual rights, then Greenleaf's proposition that 'good leaders must first become good servants' may, perhaps, be the ultimate expression of power based on, or derived from, behaviour and relationship. (This modern version of servant leadership clearly has its roots in much earlier philosophies and belief systems – 'whoever would be first among you must be slave of all' – Mark 10:44.) Moving through the twentieth century, ideas regarding leadership evolved rapidly, beginning with great man theory (note the gender), which was based on the belief that a select few were marked out from birth with the unique abilities needed to be leaders. A lecture given at St Andrew's University in Scotland in 1934 exemplified this view:

It is a fact that some men possess an inbred superiority which gives them a dominating influence over their contemporaries, and marks them out unmistakably for leadership. This phenomenon is as certain as it is mysterious.

(Cited in Adair, 1983: 7)

Moving on from this widely held (at the time) notion of inborn superiority, ideas then turned to trying to identify, distil and express the traits that great leaders either had innately or were able to develop – trait theory, as it has become known. A large number of trait studies were conducted up to the 1940s, when Ralph Stogdill (1948) conducted an extensive review of the literature. Amongst Stogdill's conclusions was the key observation that leadership status is acquired through active participation involving a working relationship that supports a group in completing a task or purpose. Leadership is not passive in nature or about 'the mere possession of some combination of traits'. This proved pivotal in redirecting ideas regarding leadership away from trait theory and towards situational and behavioural analysis. Leading into the 1950s and the 1960s, a range of leadership theories emerged based around different ways of framing the leadership situation or challenge, taking account variously of the level of development of individuals and teams, the disposition of the leader towards achieving the task or towards supporting people, and the contingent requirements of particular tasks in different team or organisational contexts.

77

We explored some of these theories at the beginning of Chapter 2 and will look at others in terms of leadership style and participation in Chapter 8. As we have seen, in the 1970s, the leadership discourse turned to servant leadership and also significantly the distinction between transactional and transformational leadership, and the emphasis on values and relationship. This combined with work on emotional intelligence which really culminated in Daniel Goleman's contributions in the 1990s, which opened up the ground for many of the new and emergent ideas such as shared leadership, collaborative leadership, authentic leadership, adaptive leadership, followership and many others. A landmark amongst all of this was the clear articulation by Warren Bennis and Burt Nanus (1985) of five myths about leadership:

- 'Myth 1 – Leadership is a rare skill' – it is not.
- 'Myth 2 – Leaders are born, not made' – they are not.
- 'Myth 3 – Leaders are charismatic' – most are ordinary.
- 'Myth 4 – Leadership exists only at the top of an organisation' – it is relevant at all levels.
- 'Myth 5 – The leader controls, directs, prods, manipulates' – they do not. Rather than directing, 'transformative leaders align the energies of others behind an attractive goal'.

Let us go back a few centuries and leave the last word in this section to the Immortal Bard:

Some men are born to greatness, some achieve greatness, and some have greatness thrust upon them.

Twelfth Night (Act II, Scene V) by
William Shakespeare (1601)

'PUSH' AND 'PULL' INFLUENCING STYLES

The author and poet Joan Walsh Anglund described influence as 'what you think you have until you try to use it'. The truth is that is how it often feels. You are pushing with all your energy and all you are meeting is resistance. It is funny when you realise, though, that the door actually opens the other way. Something that has happened to us all, I'm sure: 'I didn't see the sign, and I was pushing when I should have been pulling.' And this is in essence what the push/pull model of interpersonal influence is all about: knowing when to push and knowing when to pull; knowing when to use your energy to move a situation and knowing when to use the other person's energy. When two wrestlers clash, possibly physical specimens of quite different size and body mass, it is not always the largest and strongest opponent who wins; it is about both strength and skill, and the successful wrestler will know how to use the force and energy of his adversary to triumph. This is not to suggest an adversarial approach to leadership influence, but rather to highlight the power and motivation that may result if we can use the other person's energy as much as our own.

Push and pull is an idea, or an image, used in a variety of settings and contexts, not just leadership and interpersonal influence. It can be found in marketing, logistics, migration theory, systems theory and even in relation to how colour and shape can be used to create the illusion of space and depth in a painting (Hans Hofmann, 1880–1966, the pioneering abstract expressionist painter and teacher, used the terms in this way). Common to all is the recognition that, when combined, different energies or demands produce different results.

In Figure 4.2 below the four influencing styles in the push/pull model are illustrated: two are push (mainly about your energy) and two are pull (mainly about the energy of the other person/people):

- *Asserting* – this **push** style is about driving your solution, stating your expectations and needs, and evaluating other people's contributions in relation to these. It is an energetic and challenging style that demonstrates both confidence and clarity. This style can work well when there is something urgent or critical about the situation, where speed and assurance matters, where you 'know' your solution is 'the solution' and when you are working with less ready or experienced people.
- *Persuading* – this **push** style is about *winning minds*. It is about using logic, reason, evidence and precedent to rationally persuade others. This style focuses on presenting a clear case, without emotion, backed up with clear and factual arguments. Proposals are often presented in such a way as

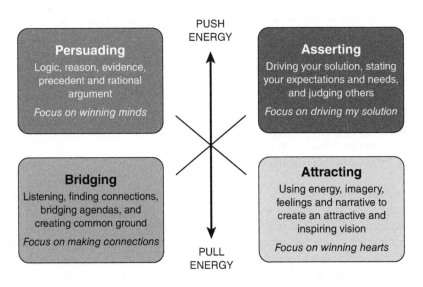

FIGURE 4.2 Push/pull influencing styles

to weigh up all sides of an argument before making a clear recommendation. Leaders sometimes feel that this is the style and approach demanded by their organisation, but the danger is that it does not generate a real depth of engagement if the other styles are absent.

- *Attracting* – this **pull** style is about *winning hearts*. It *stirs the blood*, as it were, with a vision that is attractive and aspirational. Imagery and narrative are used to both cherish the past and also excite people about future directions and potential. This style of influence realises that people are inspired by a dream, not a plan, and appeals to both feelings and values. The approach to communication is energetic and the goal is to enhance and engage the energy of others.

- *Bridging* – this **pull** style is about participation and making connections. Through listening and questioning, the leader gets to understand the range of ideas, opinions and agendas in a situation and how to create connections and compromises (bridging agendas). Finding common ground and building a community is what matters to this leader, and they may not necessarily have an agenda of their own. The bridging style is an investment in relationship, the development of the team and is a longer game than just immediate problem solving. It looks to develop other people's energy through building both a group identity and a common purpose with commitment.

- *Moving away* – this fifth style, not shown in Figure 4.2 but often included in the model, is really a tactic rather than a style. Essentially the leader influences by not engaging. This may amount to a postponement of the issue or it may be about minimising differences by not confronting them. By holding off, it is possible that the differences may diminish or dissipate without the need for confrontation or conflict. It may also be about creating time to reflect on an issue for the longer-term benefit of the group or task.

So, to sum up the push/pull model in its simplest terms, the four influencing styles are that:

- you can *assert* a direction;
- you can *persuade* with reason;
- you can *attract* with a vision;
- you can *bridge* divides and build a community.

Or you can simply move away . . . It would be unusual, and probably foolish, for a leader to use one of these styles in isolation or to the exclusion of the others. The energies of push and pull are always in tension as in different situations and with different teams and individuals, the leader either instinctively or deliberately moves between them. And then there is the matter of preference. Based on a combination of personality and learned behaviour, we each have styles that we are more predisposed to use than others, and an awareness of this can be

80

tremendously valuable in leadership development (feedback from others can help us to build our self-awareness).

We also live with a management heritage that favours 'push'. Managers *get things done* and that involves pushing for results. In the context of leading learning and teaching, however, which is far more about participation than compliance, it is very important to realise that 'too much force will back-fire' (Heider, 1985). Freedom, autonomy and self-direction are fostered and inspired by the 'pull' behaviours. Heider's adaptation of Lao Tzu's Tao Te Ching's *Book of the Way* (sixth century BC), Chapter 29, 'The Paradox of Pushing' goes on to say:

> Too much force will backfire. Constant interventions and instigations will not make a good group. They will spoil a group. The best group process is delicate. It cannot be pushed around. It cannot be argued over or won in a fight.
>   The leader who tries to control the group through force does not under-stand group process. Force will cost you the support of the members.
>
> (John Heider's adaptation, 1985)

There are overlaps between push/pull and the four key leadership attributes in the Programme Leadership Model, although by no means a direct alignment. The champion and organiser attributes are more 'push' in their nature and sit on the goal or task-focused side of the spectrum. The enabler and mentor attributes are more 'pull' in their nature and sit on the people-focused side of the spectrum. In the context of learning and teaching, 'push' could be seen as leader of the course and 'pull' as leader of the team. We will consider more about this task and people distinction when we look at *people styles* below.

OPEN AND HIDDEN INFLUENCE

Another facet to consider in relation to interpersonal influence is open and hid-den influence (see Figure 4.3 below). Within the push/pull model, there are some behaviours that are very open and visible to all, such as presenting a report to a committee with a lot of detailed data and analysis which logically and ration-ally supports a recommendation or proposal (persuading). This is very different from the leader who speaks one-to-one with a range of committee members before a key meeting to build relationships, listening to and exploring the range of opinions (bridging), so as to ensure their proposal reflects and combines the variety of views. This would be termed hidden influence, not because it is clan-destine or underhand, but because it is less visible and is more about behaviour and relationship.

The skills of 'open' influence are more visible and can be more readily iden-tified as areas where an individual either excels or, perhaps, has the potential to improve. They are more overtly 'trainable' and can be identified and pur-sued as part of professional development. 'That was a great presentation' is

Open influence can be seen in:	**Hidden influence** arises through:
• Meetings	• Changing image or behaviour
• Presentations	• Altering attitude
• Debates and discussions	• Networking
• Reports and proposals	• Non-verbal communication
• Negotiations	• Nurturing relationships
• Performance management	• Counselling or mentoring
• Process management	• Using story, metaphor and analogy

FIGURE 4.3 Open and hidden influence

an easier thing to praise and recognise than somebody's informal networking skills or ability to listen to others with empathy and compassion. But it is these softer skills, as they are often termed, that actually make the greatest difference. Going back to the example above, it will invariably be those one-to-one discussions prior to a committee meeting that make the real impact, not the polished performance in the committee room. Petra Wilton, Director of Strategy and External Affairs at the Chartered Management Institute, made the following comment in an article regarding the vital importance of soft skills to the UK economy:

> So-called 'soft skills' are absolutely vital to business success – not least since many of them are in fact the basics of good management and leadership. It's just not possible to be a successful manager without these core people and team-leading skills. We have to get better at helping people develop these abilities. We can only do this by explicitly recognising the value of professional management skills. As such, there's far more that we can do to embed management and leadership into the heart of our education system.
>
> (Haughton, 2015)

The 'hidden' skills are an extension of our authentic selves. For this reason, leadership development is a continuous process of self-discovery, reflection, personal commitment and experience. As J. F. Kennedy famously included in the speech he was due to deliver on the day he was assassinated, 'leadership and learning are indispensable to each other' (1963).

PEOPLE STYLES

Have you ever been baffled by someone's response or reaction? If so, welcome to the human race – it happens to us all. We go in with one style and the other person responds with a different style (or not at all). So, approaching someone slowly, with rational arguments and lots of carefully prepared information and precedents may seem to you the right thing to do because that's your style (persuading). But if their style is big concepts, lots of excitement and creative impulses (attracting), then you may get a response that you find unexpected or baffling. The chances are in any event that you may struggle to reach agreement.

We can overlay onto the push/pull model an additional consideration of personality types and preferences. In significant ways we are more like some people than others and this comes through in our interpersonal styles. Robert and Dorothy Bolton developed the People Styles at Work model (1996) to provide a practical and proven tool for considering how different styles respond to each other in work environments. Their model is based on the work of industrial psychologist David Merrill (Merrill and Reid, 1981), which in turn has its roots in Jung's psychological types (1921). Their approach 'is distinguished from many others in that it focuses on behaviour rather than personality' (Bolton and Bolton, 2009). This means that it is focused on what a person does, what you see and hear in their behaviour. Figure 4.4 below shows Bolton and Bolton's People Styles at Work model.

The four styles relate broadly across to the influencing behaviours in the push/pull model: the driver that asserts, the analytical that persuades, the expressive that attracts and the amiable that bridges. The two dimensions of behaviour in the People Styles at Work model are termed 'assertiveness' and 'responsiveness', and they are defined as follows:

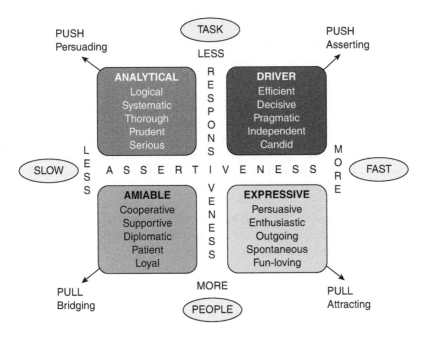

FIGURE 4.4 People Styles at Work

■ Assertiveness is the degree to which one's behaviours are seen by others as being forceful or directive.

. . .

■ Responsiveness is the degree to which one is seen by others as showing his or her emotions or demonstrating awareness of the feelings of others.

(Bolton and Bolton, 1996: 16, 20)

So, the horizontal axis (assertiveness) has a faster-paced, more outward and directive end (driver and expressive), and a slower-paced, more inward and reflective end (analytical and amiable): this dimension can also be termed 'extraversion' and 'introversion'. This is combined with a vertical axis, (responsiveness), which has a people focus at the lower end (amiable and expressive) and a task or goal focus at the top (analytical and driver). The two dimensions taken together determine one's style. Bolton and Bolton's work also provides a very useful behavioural inventory as a tool for developing self-awareness in this area and also potentially considering the behaviour of others.

The People Styles at Work model is a practical tool for firstly reading different styles and then responding based on an awareness of your own style. This interpersonal versatility is the key to reducing style-based tensions or conflicts. Bolton and Bolton refer to 'getting in sync with the style-based behaviours of the person you are with' so as to 'reduce interpersonal tension, thereby fostering well-functioning and productive relationships'. If we can reduce the interpersonal tension, it will put us in a better position to influence the situation without details and distractions becoming obstacles. This is what we really mean when we talk about *getting alongside people*.

THE CHANGE JOURNEY

Another very significant way in which leaders influence people is concerned with how they support them on the journey through a transformation process or initiative: this is sometimes termed the change journey. For a wide range of reasons, people have varying responses to change, with very different levels of interest, enthusiasm and engagement. People experience change in different ways and at different rates, and need to be supported as individuals as well as at a team level, particularly if the change is radical, difficult or disruptive. How change is perceived is a very individual thing, but as Norman Jackson (2002) highlights in the context of learning and teaching quality enhancement and whether change is seen as an improvement, it is also bound up with a range of factors relating to the change process itself:

■ Reasons for change (imposed of self-determined);
■ Scale (quantity/amount of difference);
■ Quality (characteristics of difference);
■ Time (rate at which a difference is created, e.g. slow incremental or rapid radical);

- Whether the benefits outweigh the investment made in terms of personal time and costs;
- Whether change is a solitary or collaborative activity;
- Whether it is supported/unsupported;
- Whether it is valued by students, colleagues and managers.

A model initially developed by the psychiatrist Elisabeth Kübler-Ross (1969) in her work on the grieving process helps to chart and understand the stages of emotional response that may be experienced at the level of personal transition. These stages are shown on a curve as in Figure 4.5 below.

The seven stages in the change journey can briefly be described as follows:

- Immobilisation – caused by shock, surprise or disorientation.
- Denial – disbelief, ignoring the change, looking for ways to reject it.
- Anger – frustration, hurt, a sense of injustice or loss.
- Bargaining – looking to minimise the impact or manoeuvre for position.
- Depression – a low mood, lack of energy, a sense of helplessness.
- Testing – initial engagement, experimenting, checking the boundaries.
- Acceptance – engagement, positivity and discovering a new orientation.

In Appendix 2 a table is provided with some possible leadership actions suggested for each of the seven stages.

The change curve helps to identify where people are on their individual journey through the transformation process (this is termed an emotional model of change). The leader can then work to support and influence them appropriately and encourage the community to understand and support one another. The speed with which people move along the curve will vary, as will the amplitude of the curve (the strength of the emotional responses). Above all, it is important for

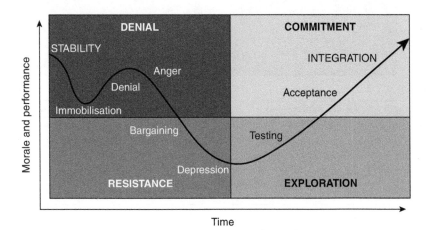

FIGURE 4.5 The change journey

leaders to go on listening and to *be kind*, even if they have to confront or contain certain behaviours, and to remember that 'it may just be the change talking' when difficult situations or encounters arise.

A NECESSARY ART . . .

Like leadership itself, influencing others is as much an art as it is a science. Nowhere has this art been brought to life more powerfully, and dare I say persuasively, than in Jay Conger's 1998 article 'The Necessary Art of Persuasion'. In this article Conger recognises that today's organisations are populated by 'authority-averse baby boomers and Generation Xers' for whom persuasion needs to be seen as a 'learning and negotiation process' involving phases of 'discovery, preparation and dialogue'. Conger gives us four essential steps to persuasion that match this contemporary environment. He also puts forward four common mistakes that people make (four ways not to persuade):

- They attempt to make their case with an up-front, hard sell.
- They resist compromise.
- They think the secret to persuasion lies in presenting great arguments.
- They assume persuasion is a one-shot effort.

As an antidote to this, Figure 4.6 below presents a snapshot summary of Conger's four distinct and essential steps to effective persuasion, all of which resonate strongly with the challenge of influencing in the context of learning and teaching.

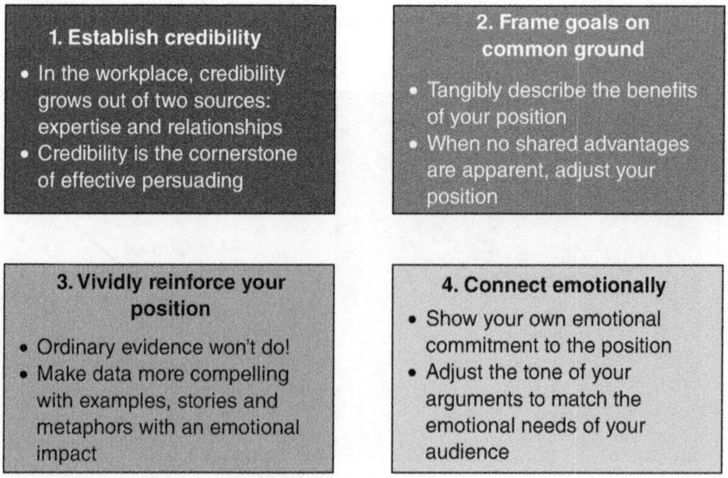

1. Establish credibility	2. Frame goals on common ground
• In the workplace, credibility grows out of two sources: expertise and relationships • Credibility is the cornerstone of effective persuading	• Tangibly describe the benefits of your position • When no shared advantages are apparent, adjust your position
3. Vividly reinforce your position	4. Connect emotionally
• Ordinary evidence won't do! • Make data more compelling with examples, stories and metaphors with an emotional impact	• Show your own emotional commitment to the position • Adjust the tone of your arguments to match the emotional needs of your audience

FIGURE 4.6 The necessary art of persuasion

QUESTIONS FOR ACTION AND REFLECTION

1   What sources of power are available to you in your leadership role? Which do you over-use? Which do you under-use?
2   Which key behaviours do you find it most important to model in your leadership role?
3   What are the key relationships that help you to influence effectively? Which relationships could/should you invest more in?
4   How do you 'serve others' in your role as a leader?
5   What do you currently see as your main influencing challenge? What are you doing well? What could/should you do differently?
6   What approaches to influence do you see in other leaders that you could learn from?
7   Which of the push/pull styles do you feel you use the most?
8   Which of the push/pull styles would you like to do more of? Who could support your development in this area?
9   Which areas of 'open' influence would you most like to develop? What would be a *first step* towards this?
10 Which areas of 'hidden' influence would you most like to develop? What would be a *first step* towards this?
11 Which of the 'people styles' sounds most like you? What could you do to develop further your *interpersonal versatility*?
12 Where on the change journey do you feel most comfortable supporting people as a leader? How can you challenge yourself to support people at every stage of the change journey?

Chapter 5

Understanding your brief

THE CHALLENGE IN THIS CHAPTER

The challenge in this chapter is how to define your brief for leading a course design process.

Working to a brief simply means having reasonable clarity regarding the goals others wish you to achieve. Your own voice is in there, of course, and this may be a prominent or leading voice, but the key thing is pinning down an agreed understanding of what you are going to do and why. It needs to be reasonably clear, with latitude within it for development and discovery, and might in other contexts be termed an initial project brief. Some colleagues will support the clarity that defining a brief brings, and the reference point it creates, while others may regard it as unnecessary or resist the formality of such an approach at what they may see as a very provisional stage in the process. It may also suit them to have some *wriggle room* should the idea not prove as desirable or as creditworthy as they first expected.

How do you define your brief? Well, essentially through drawing together the thoughts, expressions of support and interests of those that might fall under one of three headings:

- *Originators*
- *Stakeholders*
- *Activists.*

In different ways, these people could all be regarded as sponsors of the initiative.

And what should a brief look like? It should be written down, short and concise, and encapsulate in broad terms the vision for the initiative/project. The elements within it are likely to include a note of what triggered the initiative, a reasonably focused goal, a short set of specific objectives, a suggestion of values regarding particularly learning and student engagement, and a list of people and organisations likely to be involved. The brief is not a detailed project plan and so accurate brevity is the key. It should also stimulate rather than restrain people's creative interest and should be a platform for collaborative engagement.

And what do you do with the brief? Well, what you don't do is keep it a secret. It should be circulated to all of the originators, stakeholders and activists for comment and hopefully support, it should be shared readily with others as they become involved or contribute, and it should be the opening section of any document that is subsequently written. It should change and become amended, and when it does, it should be recirculated with the changes highlighted and explained. It should be a working document and become 'dog-eared through use'.

The chapter concludes with a section on understanding and articulating change. This introduces models for exploring and presenting 'the *what* of change', the factors driving change and the context in which the need for change has arisen. It also encourages a systematic approach to identifying and gathering the evidence needed to make the case for your learning and teaching design or transformation initiative.

LINKS TO THE PROGRAMME LEADERSHIP MODEL

At this very early stage in the course development process, the critical leadership skills that are in play come under the 'champion attribute' heading. This is a goal-focused stage and the skills required of the leader clearly reflect this. The ability to inspire others or build on their enthusiasm will be critical, as will the ability to promote the vision with stakeholders in a variety of settings. The role of personal characteristics such as passion, influence and determination are all likely to have a part to play and resilience may well be needed to keep going when the reception may seem either a little lukewarm or even hostile. Competing agendas, both professional and personal, may threaten to diminish the brief or take its focus away from the central questions, in which case it may be necessary to challenge some people and negotiate with others.

Alongside the champion attribute, the critical skills of listening and investing in relationships, from the mentor attribute, will also be important. To influence effectively, the enduring qualities of well-modelled behaviours and creating relationships are essential, as we saw in the last chapter.

In Table 5.1 below the key leadership skills and attributes associated with defining and understanding your brief are highlighted (note: this is purely indicative – none of the leadership skills should be regarded as exclusive or restricted to just one area).

If all of this seems a little intimidating, keep in mind that you need not be a lone champion; in fact, you will seldom succeed if you are. Whilst you may have

TABLE 5.1 Programme Leadership Model – understanding your brief

Leadership skills

CHAMPION	ORGANISER	ENABLER	MENTOR
Enthuse	Plan	Encourage	Listen
Promote	Organise	Shield	Invest
Model	Monitor	Support	Praise
Challenge	Control	Share/Convene	Review
Negotiate	Evaluate	Mediate	Relate

a leadership role, there will be others amongst the originators and particularly the activists who may be able to project a stronger voice than your own based on their position, influence or authority. Getting them to contribute to the brief and how it is expressed will give them a sense of investment and ownership that will carry through into the later stages of the course development process. Never underestimate how persuasive it can be to use other people's words in a key document or piece of communication, even if you feel there might be slightly better words, because it draws them in to feeling a strong sense of personal association which in turn generates a will to succeed:

> Organizational champions are enlightened change makers who are personally committed to mutual values, rather than self-centred ones, and relentlessly driven by possibilities.

> (Thompson, 2009)

HAVING A CLEAR BRIEF MATTERS

It is a remarkable aspect of human folly that so often we agree to do something or accept a new responsibility without having an anywhere near adequate understanding of what it is we are actually being asked to take on. There is a terrific (although probably apocryphal) example of this from the world of banking. An up-and-coming account executive was summoned, presented with the file for a new and important client, and as an opportunity to *prove himself* was given the task of 'closing the deal'. Now, the senior manager knew what he meant, and being so familiar with the world of investment banking assumed that everyone else knew what 'closing the deal' meant, but alas the young executive did not. With all the groundwork done and all the important negotiations finalised, the senior executive just wanted someone to pull together the final agreement, pin down the hard figures and get everything signed off. What the young executive proceeded to do, however, was contact everyone involved to inform them that the bank was pulling out and no longer wanted any involvement. He thought 'closing the deal' meant drawing a halt to everything and *closing down* the deal. The story ends there, and so one can only speculate regarding the consequences, but being kind, we can hope that some important lessons were learnt by all concerned . . .

Understanding your brief is not just about preventing mistakes arising from misunderstandings, although that is one extremely important aspect, as the story above illustrates. It is also about achieving clarity regarding expectations, knowing what choices are 'ruled in' and 'ruled out', having clear goals or at least a strong basis for determining them, and being properly informed and empowered overall. The brief may come from one person, from several people or from one person primarily but involving others. No matter: the challenge of this key step remains the same, and we will explore a range of questions you should be considering as you work to determine your brief and techniques for achieving the clarity and support you need.

The world of client relationships, public relations and communications is one which takes the need for a brief very seriously. Here is a sample of the advice found on various websites:

- If you start working without a clear brief, it's like driving with broken headlights at night.
- A clear agency brief is a ray of sunshine.
- How to make a copywriter happy? Give them a clear brief.
- A bad brief can lead to bad work – it's the old 'rubbish in – rubbish out' scenario.
- Creative briefs are like snowflakes – no two are the same.

MANDATING YOURSELF

Achieving a mandate in political terms involves firstly campaigning to do something and then through various expressions of support becoming authorised to go ahead. It implies both authority and responsibility in response to a need that has been identified collectively. And whilst 'mandating yourself' may sound a contradiction in terms, it is essentially the process of reaching a point where you feel properly empowered to commence a design or development initiative/ project. In colloquial terms we might talk about 'having a green light'. But there is more to this than just a piece of downward delegation with checkpoints and milestones – this is also about personal exposure and levels of comfort as regards both taking responsibility and managing ambiguity.

With regard to commencing the development of a new course or module, or significantly reviewing an existing course to obtain revalidation, there are formal processes within universities for gaining both academic and administrative approval. These tend to be approval processes of the heavily minuted variety, and navigating these patiently and successfully is an important aspect of organisational life. However, by contrast, this idea of mandating yourself leads to a sense of support of a more visceral variety, along the lines of 'I know I've got the backing of the people that matter to the degree I need'. It leads to a sense of assurance that can be the basis for productive activity and may come before any formalised support is crystallised.

This idea of 'self-empowerment' or being a 'self-empowered individual' in different situations is a highly individual thing. It links with ideas to do with tolerance for ambiguity and risk aversion. For some, fairly slender support and encouragement can be enough to propel them into quite confident action, whilst for others, a very stable, firmly based and carefully recorded body of support is needed before the risk of positive activity can be comfortably considered. Personality traits most certainly feature in these differences. In a review of the relationship between the 'big five' personality traits (openness, conscientiousness, extraversion, agreeableness, and neuroticism: McCrae and Costa (1996)) and the performance of financial fund managers, for example, Camgoz, Mehmet and Ergeneli (2011), with reference to an earlier study, observed that:

> Risk propensity was greater for subjects with higher extraversion and openness to experience scores and less for subjects with higher neuroticism, agreeableness and conscientiousness scores.

So, I plant this idea of 'mandating yourself' to make the point that the early stages of contemplating a new course can feel tentative and uncertain, and it can take quite a high degree of drive and personal focus to break through to the firmer ground where formal steps can be contemplated. Sometimes this can be down to the determined effort of a single individual with a strong personal vision, but more often it is one individual with the close support of a core group of activists who sow the seeds for a new and worthwhile initiative.

DON'T FORGET THE LEARNERS

We work in a system known as 'outcomes-based education' (Dearing, 1997: Recommendation 21) or 'outcomes-based learning and teaching'. This is an enormously positive thing because it invites us to design and approach our courses not on the basis of the content we would like to pack into them, but rather on the basis of the essential learning students should achieve as a result of their active participation. Fundamentally it is the structural model that currently underpins a learner-centred approach to formal education. As the term suggests, the challenge at the outset is to think in terms of how the learning will be represented in the student at the end of the defined period of learning, what they will be able to do and say, the cognitive, practical and professional levels they will be able to demonstrate, and how they will be able to interpret, understand and interact with the world. It places the emphasis on purposeful change and is essentially aspirational in nature – the learning outcomes should be worthwhile and desirable and should link with the student's own motivation to learn:

In outcome-based education product defines process. Outcome-based education can be summed up as *results-oriented thinking* and is the opposite of *input-based education* where the emphasis is on the educational process and where we are happy to accept whatever is the result.

(Harden, Crosby and Davis, 1999: 8)

So, coming back to the challenge we have set ourselves in this chapter, how to define our brief for leading a course design process, the first and most central question should be establishing the brief from the perspective of the student. However, this is often something we try to second-guess in a variety of ways. We consider the needs of employers and professional bodies, we become aware of new knowledge domains as scientific advances and new technologies move forward, we get a sense of 'popular subjects', particularly if we see competitors moving ahead successfully, and we even tiptoe around the edges of what previous students might have wished for or preferred on the basis of student feedback and evaluations. But student demand is a difficult thing to pin down and is often represented by their collective response to what is actually on offer. This in turn shifts with social and economic trends and pressures. In times of relative affluence and high employment, the virtue of learning for personal development and as a social good will achieve more traction with policy makers than during times of austerity measures and high graduate unemployment.

The danger with all of this is that we end up back in the trap of *doing learning* to people. We form the view, by whatever means, that there is a need for a new module on integrated transport systems, to give a completely random example, we state our teaching intention and then we *do the learning* to the students who sign up. Well, we are back to that image of Edward Bear once again (see Figure 1.3 on page 17) and the nagging suspicion that there really must be a better way.

So, how can we establish our brief, taking into account the perspective of students as learners? Well, some direct engagement and consultation might be feasible – possibly running focus groups with existing students or by targeting known sources of students for particular courses or subjects. But whilst useful, this could be rather hit and miss in terms of reliability. Another approach would be to keep uppermost the idea of students having choice, flexibility and self-determination in the way they engage with the course. The image that works well here is of a marrying together of a well-crafted curriculum framework with the evolving needs and expectations of individual students. Rather than a course moulding the students through the progressive conditioning of their thoughts and behaviour, how about the students being able to mould the course? And how about this being a key part of your brief from the outset – that whatever else influences the shape, level and emphasis of this course, a key consideration running throughout it will be how the individual student will be able to make it uniquely match their own needs, interests and aspirations? This is active student engagement, a partnership that develops the curriculum

93

within the curriculum through participation in a community rather than being a voice 'before the fact' or 'after the fact' that might benefit *other students*, but falls short of being a piece of co-creation:

> We argue that partnership represents a sophisticated and effective approach to student engagement for two connected reasons. First, it foregrounds qualities that put reciprocal learning at the heart of the relationship – such as trust, risk, difference, empowerment, inter-dependence and agency – allowing us to go beyond a consumerist relationship, and its critique, in meaningful and relevant ways. And second, partnership is different to other, more traditional relationships of power in higher education, which means that it is often experienced as an unfamiliar way of working, learning and thinking. Through this difference, partnership raises awareness of the implicit assumptions – about each other, and about the nature of learning and teaching – which would otherwise remain below the surface.
>
> (Healey, Flint and Harrington, 2014: 17)

This leads us to question the equation we typically apply to creating courses in terms of our conception of learning:

Learning = content + activity

Even in our outcomes-based framework, the degree to which we truly put the learner at the centre of things can be limited. We perhaps go as far as placing the focus on learner activity as it relates to specified packages of content, which are usually presented in a modularised format. The intended learning outcomes are there, and the content and activity may be well aligned to these (see the discussion on constructive alignment described in Chapter 7), but the overall format is largely prescriptive. A more emergent way of conceptualising learning when creating a new course might look like this:

Learning = potential + opportunity

This change of emphasis makes the student rather than the content the central figure in the equation: it places students at the heart of the curriculum. It is their potential that we work with and the curriculum framework becomes a structured set of choices and opportunities that firstly help to raise their own awareness of their potential and then, based on that awareness, supports them to plan and develop their own journey through the course. This allows for both intended and 'unintended but desirable' (Biggs and Tang, 2007) learning outcomes to be achieved on terms that the individual student plays a meaningful part in setting. As Rogers (1983) told us so powerfully over 30 years ago, the teacher becomes 'a facilitator of learning'. There is a simple and very empowering principle as work here – *the best way to find out what students want is to ask them.*

Whatever else, though, aim to avoid the retrofit approach. This is where we place the student at the centre of the learning process, but only after we have decided what they are going to learn and how. When running workshops with colleagues on course or curriculum design, it makes sense to invite participants to bring along a module or course they are currently working on (this usually takes the form of a mass of paper). You can then ask them a simple but rather devious question: 'What are you trying to achieve?' This usually provokes a range of more or less honest responses. Some participants conjure some inventive phrases which when scrutinised really boil down to 'coverage': we are going to cover these areas so that the students will *hopefully* end up understanding them. And then comes the retrofit – we encourage or cajole them into making a change or two, something like turning a small element of the course into a list of options or adding a project-type approach to part of the course assessment, and we call that 'self-directed'. Occasionally we get a different sort of answer to the 'what are you trying to achieve?' question which is about students moving from 'doing' to 'being'. The incredibly important assumption that underpins such an answer is that the students are motivated to become in some way practitioners in the field, discipline or subject. And this idea of 'becoming' is crucial and is really the only aspect of student-centredness that matters. The course design philosophy is then very simple: it is about getting students to 'do' the subject to the point that they 'become' people to whom that subject, conceptual framework or set of skills belongs. The learning is situated in practice (Lave and Wenger, 1991), authentic and personally meaningful. The learning is not an abstract precursor to 'doing', but is about 'doing'. As John Holt wonderfully illustrates (1991), there is no segregation between someone 'learning to play' a musical instrument and the musician who 'can' play an instrument ('I am a violinist' – a 'being' statement) – they are both practitioners continuously learning through doing and being (see also the discussion on the Fully Engaged Curriculum in Chapter 6). And this sense of doing and becoming, of learning how to learn should be captured in your brief very clearly as regards the student's perspective.

> What we can best learn from good teachers is how to teach ourselves better.
>
> (Holt, 1991: 2)

ORIGINATORS, STAKEHOLDERS AND ACTIVISTS

Who is going to support your brief and help you define it? What needs and interests must it reflect if it is going to form the basis for success? And who should own the brief aside from you? These are three good questions that lead us to identify three groups of people: originators, stakeholders and activists. The third of these, activists, is a bit of a cheat, because the people in this group will inevitably be drawn from the other two. The terms are also not exclusive because someone might be both a stakeholder and an originator. However, working with these three terms provides a simple framework for classifying the people involved and therefore how they might be approached, persuaded, engaged and involved.

Originators

The originator group are those people you might point at, notionally rather than literally, when asked the question: 'Where is all this coming from?' In one way or another, these are the people giving you the impetus, formally or informally, to begin the process. As the name suggests, these are essentially the people there at the start of things. One simple example might be a head of faculty drawing you in to discuss a gap that has been identified in either an existing piece of curriculum or in the curriculum offering overall. In this instance there may be a clear strategy in place, out of which the need is arising and this can be cited as a strong foundation for your brief: for example, the faculty is acknowledged as strong on industrial engineering, but needs to make up ground as regards civil engineering. Having a clear strategic driver as part of your brief is *a very big carrot to hit people with*, to misuse the crude carrot and stick model of motivation. It is also the sort of strategic driver which you can leverage to help move people's thinking from 'we can't afford to . . .' to 'we can't afford not to . . .'.

In other cases, the originators may be made up of a series of individuals with ideas that more or less converge on a single point. The art here is spotting the convergence and then acting as a catalyst to draw things together, usually by making the links that are unseen or unspoken explicit. So, one colleague may have the idea that it is timely to start teaching students a new skill or methodology, perhaps based on an emerging technology, while another may have become vocal that an important discipline is being taught too peripherally, and a third may be advocating closer links to professional practice and, alongside this, may be expressing concerns that competing institutions have already started to emphasise this in their courses. And after listening to these voices, in different meetings and at different times, a map starts to emerge in your mind, perhaps hazy in terms of detail, but sharp enough to start a conversation of your own. And then there is your voice, the thing that has sparked your interest and perhaps caused you to listen in and pick up on these signals from others. There can often be one of those *this was meant to be* moments when such a convergence of concerns and interests is spotted for the first time, and this can be both energising and rewarding. The next step is to get the various parties to see the connections and buy into the idea of joining forces to create something new. Helping the originators see themselves as originators with something important to invest is a key part of this.

The following is a short list of approaches to consider as you work to get the originators to firstly contribute to defining your brief and secondly sign up to supporting it:

- *Begin informally* – an informal discussion which begins with something like 'I was really interested in what you were saying about . . .' is the way to begin the awareness raising. There may be a bit of flattery here, a bit of professional interest, but the most important thing is simple acknowledgement: you have an interest in 'x' and there may be some links with 'y' and 'z'. Awareness-raising is a good term to keep in mind because it is very much about bringing to the surface ideas that may not have had much conscious consideration previously. It is not quite sowing seeds, because the seeds are already there – the better metaphor might be helping them to germinate.

■ *Put something in writing* – something quick, something fresh and something that engagingly highlights potential. There is no point raising awareness in someone's mind, and often someone's busy mind, if you simply let it fall away again. To capitalise on this moment of increased awareness, give them something written down to ponder (typically, these days, a well-put-together email). The essence here is really to create something simple for people to respond to. It also needs to start making connections, both conceptually and interpersonally. Using assumptive or trigger-type language can help to prompt reactions and responses, such as:

> Dr Kelly, if I can be bold here and attempt a quick summary of what I understand to be your position and ideas. The term 'global health' has become ill-defined through popular use and unfocused debate, and a new module exploring definitions in relation to a distinct set of health policy issues will encourage students to really challenge their own and others' thinking. Have I got that right?

The next statement would be the one making your first connection: for example, how listening to Dr Kelly articulate these thoughts made you reflect on a related set of questions being voiced by another colleague. And on, hopefully, it goes . . . It is amazing that once someone's awareness and interest has been raised to a certain threshold level, they will suddenly become reluctant to let the matter go. It could be that at this point your originator, in one sense at least, becomes a stakeholder.

■ *Promote a spirit of productive compromise* – this is how all of the best deals in the world are done. The term 'win-win' will be familiar to many and essentially looks to find a fit between usually the most important elements of two or more people's positions, but at the sacrifice of other lesser wants and wishes. Stephen Covey (1992) tells us that to 'think Win-Win isn't about being nice, nor is it a quick-fix technique. It is a character-based code for human interaction and collaboration'. This is the spirit of compromise and respect that you will need to promote as you bring parties together to acknowledge that the outcome of working cooperatively with each other would be to fulfil a significant part of what they want to achieve and more than they could accomplish alone. Better still, however, would be if in some synergistic way they can come to realise that actually the ideas combined have the

97

potential to produce something even greater – something neither party had perhaps contemplated or expected prior to the links being made.

■ *Acknowledge the bigger picture* – this is when the originators begin to really commit to the possibility of a course design and development project, based around their ideas, and all that this would involve. The course itself will eventually need to be placed and positioned within the wider curriculum offering, and so early consideration of the context in which it will operate is essential. It is within the framework of these wider considerations that the originators can contribute to defining your brief. They will want to ensure that the brief contains the essence of their ideas, as negotiated with others, within a structure that begins to acknowledge the practical considerations that will help to make the initiative/project achievable. Their investment in the discussions so far, and the sense of potential and even excitement that has been built up, will hopefully carry through into an enduring commitment. However, one pitfall to avoid is when the 'bigger picture' diminishes the ambitions of the new course you and the other originators are contemplating. Expedient or pragmatic thinking may set in. Creating something new is difficult and daunting, and so it can be very tempting to reduce the challenge by begging and borrowing modules and components that already exist. This is partly a pitfall of modularisation. The right way forward, particularly at this initial stage of the process, may very well be to stick with the vision and remain focused on creating something fresh, new and unique.

■ *Passive or active* – it is very likely to be the case that the activists who will help to champion the project and make substantial contributions towards its fulfilment will emerge from your group of originators. Be wary of making early judgements, though, about who these will be, as for a wide variety of reasons, those displaying early reluctance can gradually become energised and end up showing strong commitment, while conversely the initial enthusiasts can sometimes lose their steam. This may be to do with personality or other reasons. Be patient and gradually try to develop a mental map of the individuals concerned: those who will potentially see the initiative as a priority and take an active role; those who will give it strong support, but will essentially want to be hands-off; those who are happy for others to carry forward the agenda for them, but will express support when required; and those who now that their ideas have been acknowledged will observe progress, but do little more. This mental map will be useful to you, but do not make your ideas fixed because as circumstances change and priorities shift, the players can become more or less close and remote in their involvement and support. There is a political dimension to the roles people play in project teams of all kinds, but during the early stages and before a piece of work becomes certain, this 'politicking' can be particularly volatile and can make people's relationships with the work hard to predict.

■ *Take forward or hand over* – as suggested above, you are yourself one of the originators, although you are also acting as a catalyst in drawing ideas together and starting to articulate the links and connections. A point will come where you will need to decide whether it should be your role to take things further or if handing over would make better sense. This links with the idea of 'mandating yourself' covered earlier. You may, alternatively, develop a sense that the mandate belongs to others. Very often this will be matched with a growing energy regarding the initiative/project from the parties concerned, and stepping back can take the form of a productive acknowledgement of their growing engagement.

As we will go on to discuss in Chapter 6, being an originator in the context of organisational change also relates to personal disposition and personality type (Change Style Indicator, n.d.).

Stakeholders

We began with three questions: who is going to support your brief and help you define it? What needs and interests must it reflect if it is going to form the basis for success? And who should own the brief aside from you? The process of stakeholder analysis draws us into a detailed consideration of the second question.

Taking a stake in something means, quite simply, making an investment. Conceptually, in a framework of business analysis, the term has been broadened to include more than just financial investments. A stakeholder may be someone you look to for input, for endorsement, for resources, for collaboration or for approval. Understanding who these stakeholders are as well as their interests, needs and motivations is a critical part of the background planning for a design and development initiative/project. The support of some stakeholders will be essential and, without it, the project cannot really begin, while others will be regarded as key contributors. Some stakeholders will have less influence, but you may undertake to keep them as fully informed as possible. Like actors on a stage, the stakeholders will have various parts to play, some more prominent than others, and having a clear list of the *dramatis personae* at the outset will help ensure the initiative/project unfolds as it should.

Considering your stakeholders also helps to ensure that you take a strategic approach at this critical early stage. A brief that does not attempt to take proper account of the various needs and interests present in the stakeholder group is unlikely to firstly gain the initial support that you will need and secondly have much of a 'shelf life'. You will find yourself having to adjust direction frequently as different interests emerge, and this makes even the most worthwhile project a turbulent process. Being strategic means looking out as well as looking in, and stakeholder analysis is a powerful way of considering the interests of external and internal 'actors' side by side.

99

STAKEHOLDER ANALYSIS (POWER AND INTEREST)

There are various forms and approaches to stakeholder analysis that have emerged since the stakeholder concept originated in the business literature in the 1930s. The following is one approach that is popularly used.

Stakeholder analysis begins with creating a graphical representation of all of the parties with an actual or potential 'stake' or interest in the initiative/project. There are various approaches to this, but one which works well is to position the people, groups, constituencies and organisations concerned on a graph on the basis of power and interest:

- Power (or influence) – describes a stakeholder's level of influence in or around the initiative/project, particularly the ability to direct, coerce or influence others.
- Interest (or attitude) – this describes the degree to which a stakeholder will be affected by the project and how invested they are in the outcome(s) of the initiative/project. It also considers the degree to which they may be 'for' or 'against' it.

This is a snapshot exercise and catches the position as it is perceived at one moment in time.

The scale for interest is partly determined on the basis of how positive, negative or indifferent the stakeholder is likely to be. It is not just about positive interest. This is their current position, but if you gain an insight which suggests how this might change in the future, then you can add an arrow to the mark on the graph. To ensure that points such as this are clearly captured, you should consider creating a key to enable some brief explanatory footnotes to be added.

The scale for power runs from low to high or from weak to strong. This does not allow for much subtlety, so again it can be useful to have a system to

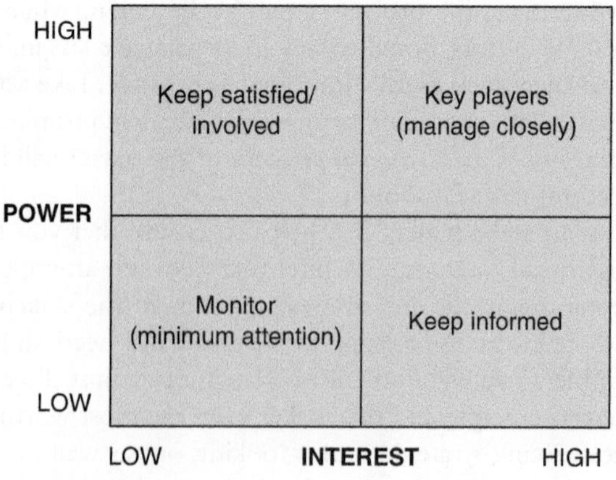

FIGURE 5.1 Stakeholder analysis

capture footnotes. 'What is the basis for the influence?' is the kind of consideration these footnotes should address. There are many facets to this, from position
in the hierarchy to financial influence, to regulatory, to reputation-based or to
someone simply having a strong voice on a particular committee. Which sort of
influence will matter most will differ depending on the type of course or module
initiative you are contemplating.

Depending on the scale of the challenge involved, you may decide to attempt
a single stakeholder analysis or you may prefer to split it. One obvious split is
to consider internal and external stakeholders separately. Another split could
be between supporters and active contributors (contributors being those who
will to some degree be involved in the design or delivery of materials, providing facilities or resources, facilitating assessments, etc.). The most workable
approach will usually become apparent when you begin the exercise.

Another consideration is whether to do the stakeholder analysis as a solitary
activity or in a group. This is partly down to personal preference – do you work
best with a closed door and a furrowed brow? – and partly circumstances. You
may find that one or two of the originators would be very interested to work
with you and this could be a valuable first phase of collaborative engagement –
in the manner of a brainstorm, some unexpected ideas and perspectives can
come out of piggybacking on the contributions made by others in a group. A
likely and useful compromise is to ask the originators informally for their views
on stakeholders and then to write up a formal analysis based on their views plus
your own. It can be very intriguing to compare perspectives on both perceived
attitudes and levels of influence as regards different stakeholders.

Stakeholder analysis is all well and good as an exercise, but what does it tell
you and what should you do with it? The following are five key questions for
reviewing the results:

1   *Who occupies the prime quadrant? Your key players.* These are the stake-
    holders with both a high level of interest and also a high level of power
    and influence. These stakeholders will hopefully be at the heart of your
    guiding coalition. Their interest is high, but is that energy positive and
    supportive? If not, they could be people with the power to block or
    disrupt the initiative. Your aim should be to turn their energy around
    and get them onside. One of the best ways to do this is to get them into
    conversation with other senior stakeholders with a positive and powerful
    interest. By contrast, your positive and supportive key players are likely
    to be the real enablers of the initiative. You should focus your energy
    on these people or groups from a very early stage and look to build fur-
    ther their support, or at the very least ensure that it does not diminish.
    You may seek to draw upon them as activists as the design and devel-
    opment stage of the project gets under way. Within this group of key
    players will be your senior institutional sponsor. This is the person who
    may chair your project board (if the scale of your initiative is such that
    you will have one) and who will represent your interests in senior-level

discussions and on formal committees. The senior institutional sponsor will act in many ways as a figurehead for the initiative and may well be the person to open doors and ensure that busy people find time to contribute. However, the problem with senior sponsors is that sometimes they move on, within the institution or beyond, and it is therefore prudent to cultivate at least one other senior key player who can step into this role if necessary.

2 *Who holds 'red and green light' authority?* There may be people or organisations that have a power of approval of some description, sometimes absolute and sometimes having a bearing on key aspects of a project. They may be internal to your faculty or institution or they may be external, such as professional accrediting bodies. Make sure that these are clearly highlighted. An early indication from them as to whether a green light can be expected will make a big difference to both yourself and others.

3 *Who are the powerful doubters? Keep them satisfied.* Are there any people or organisations with strong influence that are likely to have a negative attitude? Considering these parties is part of the strategic nature of the stakeholder analysis process. Rather than just keeping your fingers crossed that no such negativity will arise, you can actually plan in advance how to either lobby for their support or address their likely objections. Looking at the stakeholder analysis, consider the people or groups who currently fall in the 'keep satisfied' quadrant. Their power is high, but at the moment their level of interest is low. One approach, of course, is to nurture their interest so that by degrees they move across to become positive and supportive key players. But another strategy is to – as it were – maintain their indifference (or tacit support). What you do not want to do is to upset them so that they decide to use their power to disrupt the initiative. You also need to watch for anyone lobbying against the project who may decide to target these individuals/groups.

4 *Who can shout loudly when needed? Keep them informed.* How can you increase the influence of other parties who are likely to have a positive attitude towards the project? Influence is a fascinating thing as it can be both actual and perceived. As many politicians know, sometimes it is the person with the best or most novel rhetoric who wins support rather than the person with the strongest set of facts or arguments. So, encouraging people to express their support in the right way at the right time can be hugely beneficial even if their objective level of influence is actually quite low. These may be people or groups in the 'keep informed' quadrant who have other qualities to bring, or specialist contributions to make, and so maintaining their interest by keeping them informed and to some extent involved is a wise strategy.

5 *Where are the strong combinations?* Can you combine stakeholders to increase their power and influence? This may be possible in a variety of ways. For example, knowing that local employers are very interested

in the course you are proposing may start to persuade a professional accrediting body towards the 'green light' that you need, and setting up a dialogue between the two at an appropriate level may drastically change the stakeholder analysis overall in a positive direction. Another type of strong combination, but not a favourable one, can come from the monitor quadrant (low power and low interest). Whilst the tactic to employ is minimum attention, simply to enable you to focus your time and attention where it will have the greatest impact, be aware that a large group of slightly dissatisfied or uncertain people coming together can sometimes become magnified into a powerful voice of dissent, particularly if someone with a powerful interest against the initiative engages with them. *Misery loves company*, so the saying goes, and thus positive ongoing communication about the project will be vital for *all* stakeholders.

And what should you do with the stakeholder analysis? Well, firstly do not treat it as sacred. However conscientious you may have been, you will not have got it all right and furthermore things will change. Keep in mind that it is a snapshot exercise reflecting one moment in time. It may become necessary to revise it to see how the landscape surrounding the initiative/project has changed or progressed. It is also a working document that should be handled with some discretion. Your assessment of various attitudes and levels of influence may be flattering to some and far less so to others, and so this may be best kept as something primarily for you own reference:

> One thing to watch with stakeholder analysis is that you do not make fixed and rigid assumptions about stakeholders' attitudes. Using the grid over many years leads us to believe that often managers have a pessimistic bias – assuming that certain stakeholders will be against. In fact, they are often in neutral due to overload of existing agendas or due to perceived resource constraints.
>
> (Grundy and Brown, 2002: 146–7)

Stakeholder analysis is one of many tools that can help you to develop an engagement plan. If implementation planning is the management side of the project, then engagement planning is the leadership side. For each individual, group or organisation that has been identified as a stakeholder, what is your plan for engaging them and also keeping them engaged? DICE can be a useful acronym for thinking through your initial engagement plan (*how will you dice with your stakeholders?*):

- **D** – *Discussion* – what discussions will you or others have with them, and where and when?
- **I** – *Involvement* – what type and level of involvement do you need them to have and how will this be initiated and supported?

103

- *C – Communication* – what type, style and frequency of communication will work best with this stakeholder?
- *E – Endorsement and approval* – if some form of endorsement or approval is required from this stakeholder, when will you ask for it and how will this be followed up and formalised?

The engagement plans for different stakeholders will, of course, overlap because, for example, it would not be efficient to send a unique piece of communication to each stakeholder on every occasion, but it is nevertheless useful to think through DICE for individual stakeholders before drawing together a more integrated engagement plan for the initiative/project as a whole.

Now, let's get back to defining your brief. Remember, this is about achieving clarity regarding expectations, knowing what choices are 'ruled in' and 'ruled out', having clear goals or at least a strong basis for determining them, and being properly informed and empowered overall. So, this raises two questions: does the brief you have drafted acknowledge the needs and expectations of the key stakeholders, particularly the key players in the prime quadrant, and have you consulted with the stakeholders who are likely to contribute actively to the initiative/project? The brief, as a short draft document, should be circulated to all of the stakeholders for comment and hopefully support, and so it is important that your first version has no fundamental omissions as regards stakeholder interests. The fact that you have undertaken a process of stakeholder analysis, as described above, will help to prevent such omissions from arising. But keep in mind that this is a very initial and very flexible stage, and so do not be defensive if you receive forceful or strongly expressed responses. Instead, welcome them as a further opportunity to sharpen up the brief in order to really capture the interests of those who will be involved in supporting the initiative/project. Make is clear, too, in the brief that you and others will lead and facilitate the development of the initiative/project using processes for collaborative engagement (the enabler attribute) and that the brief is the start point, not the end point.

Activists

As the name suggests, activists are essentially people who are going to join in and do something. As mentioned before, this third heading is a bit of a cheat, because the people in this group will inevitably be drawn from the other two. Some will be originators involved in the initial drafting of your brief, and others may be stakeholders, people who once contacted embrace the idea and express a clear interest in contributing. Labelled as activists at this initial stage, these people may go on to have a significant role in the design and delivery of the course itself (see the following chapters). Others, though, may play a fundamental role in helping you to champion the project, but will largely regard their input as over once the various approval processes are complete, aside from perhaps in an oversight capacity.

Mike Thompson makes the following connection between organisational champions and transformational leadership:

> Transformational leadership requires envisioning possibilities that aren't clearly defined. It requires an ability to move beyond what's established to what's possible. Leaders aren't bound by transactions. Many strong leaders are, in fact, transformational. The old leadership philosophy, however, allows transactional behavior without ever demanding the transformational . . .
>
> Organizational champions don't have such luxury. The transaction is the easy part for them. They are constantly breaking transactional boundaries to transform their businesses into something better.
>
> (Thompson, 2009: 22)

Thompson also identifies the following key steps in the empowering process taken by organisational champions:

- build connection and trust through mutually beneficial initiatives;
- radiate personal energy;
- enlist others in transformational change efforts;
- imagine possibilities;
- inspire your company's culture.

In the Programme Leadership Model, two of the leadership skills that come under the champion attribute heading are enthuse and model. In order to engage an activist, enthusiasm will be essential, although you may also be grateful for, and sustained by, the enthusiasm with which they respond. An idea starts to become a reality when others show enthusiasm for it. It is a wonderful feeling, combining excitement and relief, when someone simply says 'I think that's a great idea'. But such enthusiasm is far more likely to rebound back to you if you have projected it in the first place. This requires some self-belief and personal energy, and this is part of the second skill: modelling. If you project a sense of assurance and conviction about what you are proposing, whilst remaining open-minded in terms of feedback, you will inspire in others a response which in some ways mirrors the behaviour you have demonstrated. Behaviour breeds behaviour, and this is particularly true when it comes to projecting belief in a project or piece of work. As Henry Ford (1863–1947), the founder of the Ford Motor Company, famously observed: 'whether you believe you can or whether you believe you can't, you're probably right'. So, what tactics and tricks are there for projecting this kind of conviction, whilst keeping the tone of conversation fairly informal at this early stage? Well, here are four:

1   *Rehearse a few key phrases* – Whilst you may have conviction for your idea or the ideas you have drawn together from others (the originators), it is not an easy thing to express conviction fluently and in the moment. So why not identify three key phrases that capture the essence of the argument and

rehearse saying these out loud? Taking an arts management example, you might come up with:

- great art needs great management;
- 90 per cent of performing arts companies that fail do so because of poor administration rather than bad productions;
- no other UK institution offers a course specifically targeted at aspiring arts administrators.

Short and punchy, they can be used at will to excite the interest of others.

2   *Plan a point or two of agreement* – As people in the world of sales will tell you, it is far easier to get a 'yes' from someone who agrees with you. This is also a problem-solving form of argumentation following a *yes-yes-so* format:

- Can we agree that *x* is a problem? *Yes.*
- And that any solution would have to involve *a* and *b*? *Yes.*
- *So*, the new module that we are proposing is focused on . . .

This is partly about establishing common ground, but also building a sense of momentum regarding the value of the ideas set out in your brief.

3   *Ask and listen* – Too much coming in a one-way direction from you is as likely to alienate as it is to inspire. So, plan some questions to elicit their position, even if you think you already know what the responses to these will be. Questions focused on experience work particularly well, partly because of the richness of the answer, but also because of the psychological investment that results from linking past experiences with proposed future actions. A carefully prepared, open question along the lines of 'what has been your experience of business administration in small arts organisations?' or 'how varied have you found the skills and experience of arts managers you have worked with?' should work well. If you can then link your conviction with needs and interests coming from their responses, you will have a strong basis for inspiring them as a potential activist.

4   *Appeal to the head and the heart* – Engagement is not merely an intellectual process – and where it is, it is likely to be short-lived. People engage through their heart and spirit as much as they do for intellectual or rational reasons. And whilst information and data may appeal to the head, and critical arguments may appeal to the mind, it is stories, images and narrative that appeal to the heart. In their influential book *The Heart of Change*, Kotter and Cohen (2002: 1) talk about engaging the heart:

> People change what they do less because they are given *analysis* that shifts their *thinking* than because they are *shown* a truth that influences their *feelings*.

So, what are the stories you can tell and the images you can use to make this sort of impact? As you develop the brief, your leadership antennae need to be on the alert for stories and images that capture the need, highlight the demand/gap or express the potential. And the principle of rehearsal applies again – try your stories out a few times to sharpen them up in the telling. Another aspect of this is using emotional intelligence. The biggest challenge to a negotiation may be people's feelings. If they are unaddressed, interpersonal tension is likely to be high, and when tension is high, details can very quickly become obstacles. So:

■   say what you feel; and
■   feel what you say.

To take forward the initial brief for the initiative/project, a core group of activists prepared to join you in championing the proposal will be almost essential. You will not always be the best person to speak to certain groups, but one of your activists may be. Your role will be to lead them to become activists for the project in the first place. In some cases they will require little persuasion, while in others you will need to be well prepared to inspire them through a combination of enthusiasm, sound arguments and well-modelled behaviours. In all cases the activists will need to buy into the brief as it has been defined at this initial stage.

With the originators, stakeholders and activists carefully identified, contacted and consulted as appropriate, and your initial brief for the initiative/project drafted and circulated, and re-drafted and re-circulated as often as required, you are reaching the point where you can feel truly empowered to proceed.

UNDERSTANDING AND ARTICULATING CHANGE

So far in this chapter, we have said a lot about 'the *who* of change', but we also need to give our attention to understanding 'the *what* of change' and articulating it in ways that will be relevant, meaningful and persuasive.

A vision for change has many elements and dimensions, from drivers perceived in the external environment to new needs arising in the client/customer group, and from enhancements and efficiencies offered by new technologies to concerns about standards relating to quality assurance. In an Ernst & Young paper on academic leadership published in 2000 (Moore and Diamond, 2000), the authors presented a compelling analysis of the competitive intensity in the higher education sector based on Michael Porter's (1979) five forces model:

■   the threat of new entrants;
■   the bargaining power of customers (buyers);
■   the bargaining power of suppliers;
■   the threat of substitutes;
■   rivalry among universities.

107

As a sector-level piece of analysis, this comes across as a powerful way of evidencing the need for change. This and similar models could be adapted to explore and present the forces driving change or transformation at a programme level. Another tool for exploring widely and presenting the context for change is a PESTLE analysis (probably currently the most popular of a number of similar mnemonics used as part of strategy review since at least the 1960s):

- *P* – Political – what are the key political drivers of relevance?
- *E* – Economic – what are the important economic factors?
- *S* – Social – what are the main societal and cultural aspects?
- *T* – Technological – what are current technology imperatives, changes and innovations?
- *L* – Legal – what is the current and impending legislation affecting the university and/or sector?
- *E* – Environmental – what are the environmental considerations, both locally and further afield? (Another 'E' can be added to highlight ethical considerations, if useful.)

Both the five forces analysis and the PESTLE analysis are tools that could be used with a group to collaboratively engage them in a discussion to explore and identify the factors driving or shaping change.

Springing from the world of evidence-based medicine (the conscientious use of current best evidence in making decisions about patient care), there has been a movement towards something termed evidence-based management.

Pfeffer and Sutton (2006) define evidence-based management as 'first and foremost, a way of seeing the world and thinking about the craft of management; it proceeds from the premise that using better, deeper logic and employing facts, to the extent possible, permits leaders to do their jobs more effectively'. They also draw a striking and humorous comparison with the world of medicine:

> If doctors practiced medicine like many companies practice management, there would be more unnecessarily sick or dead patients and many more doctors in jail or suffering other penalties for malpractice.

In relation to learning and teaching in universities or colleges, it would seem a fairly natural expectation, given the academic culture, that transformation initiatives or proposals for change should be supported by relevant evidence. The model in Figure 5.2 has been designed as a framework to help analyse the 'what' of change in a learning and teaching context:

- *Student/subject* – the first diagonal axis running from the bottom left to the top right invites you to consider whether the change stems from the student or the subject:
  - if the student, then what is your evidence?:
    - performance
    - results

- o   feedback (formal and informal)
- o   attendance
- o   retention
- o   option and choice trends
- o   destinations
- o   employability
- o   survey data and league tables
- o   quality audits
- o   application and enrolment numbers/trends
- o   direct student input (through partnership);

- •   if the subject, then what is your evidence?:

  - o   new research
  - o   new knowledge
  - o   new methods overtaking old methods
  - o   new disciplines or sub-disciplines
  - o   disciplines combining or becoming more multi-disciplinary
  - o   new or changing employer expectations
  - o   changes to technology (and ways of using technology)
  - o   external examination

Internal   **SUBJECT**

Strategy/policy/ standards (including external quality assurance)	Faculty and/or administration **People**	Discipline/ syllabus
Learning environment/ resources **Place**	Curriculum alignment -Aim -ILOs -LTAs -ATs -Evaluation	Professional and transferable **Skills**
Appeal/fit (link to needs and aspirations)	Mode of study/ assessment **Approach**	Employability/ careers/ destinations

STUDENT   **External**

KEY:
ILOs – intended learning outcomes
LTAs – learning and teaching activities
ATs – assessment tasks

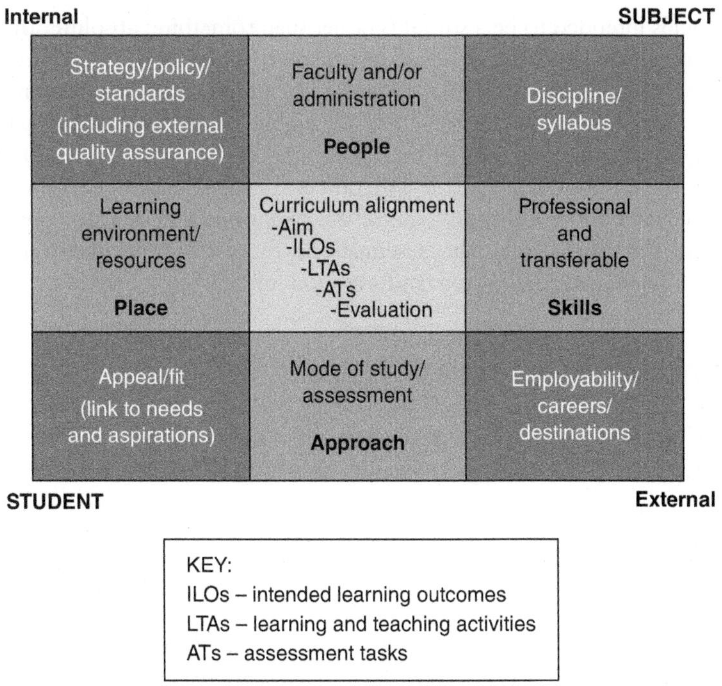

FIGURE 5.2   The 'what' of change

109

- o re-validation feedback
- o professional accreditation (revised standards)
- o competition (new entrants taking new approaches)
- o league tables.

- *Internal/external* – the second diagonal axis running from the top left to the bottom right encourages you to reflect on whether the change is internally or externally focused. Is it to do with internal requirements and expectations (for example, policies or standards) or is it driven mainly by external pressures and developments (for example, careers and employability)?
- *Sitting between student and internal* – this may be a change to do with the learning environment or resources (place).
- *Sitting between student and external* – this may be a change to do with modes of study or methods of assessment (approach).
- *Sitting between subject and internal* – this may be a change to do with the faculty or administration (people).
- *Sitting between subject and external* – this may be a change to do with professional and transferable qualities or attributes (skills).
- *Curriculum alignment* – in the centre of the model sits a well-aligned curriculum that should be the product of the eight factors which surround it. Through the transformation process, the curriculum should become a structural and thematic encapsulation of the issues raised and addressed.

This model is intended to be a stimulus rather than something absolute. In many instances there will be a balance of factors that make up the 'what' of your change initiative. There may, for example, be changing student expectations combined with new methods and techniques that are highly pertinent to practice in the discipline and strongly related to the evolving needs of employers. Using the model, however, should help you and others to consider the nature of your change challenge more holistically (all of the symptoms together, to come back to the medical analogy) and gather systematically the evidence needed to support, inform and shape your design or transformation initiative.

QUESTIONS FOR ACTION AND REFLECTION

1 What are some of the formal approval processes for developing or changing learning and teaching courses or modules in your department/faculty/institution?

2 In your department/faculty/institution, what would you say are some of the informal ways in which people gain support for developing or changing learning and teaching courses or modules?

3 What would you say is your attitude to risk? How carefully prepared and how sure of support do you need to be before commencing a new initiative?

4   On your module/course/suite of programmes, in what ways do students have a voice in shaping or influencing:

  a   the current curriculum?;
  b   the future curriculum?

5   What could you do to move from consulting students regarding curriculum development to empowering them to actively participate in curriculum development?

6   Who are the most powerful stakeholders with an interest in your module/course/suite of programmes?

7   What do you currently do to maintain or enhance the engagement of these stakeholders? What more could you do?

8   If/when you embark on a change initiative in relation to your module/course/suite of programmes, who do you think would/will engage with you most closely and give you active support (your activists)?

9   What is the most effective technique or approach you have used for influencing or persuading a senior colleague? What made it so effective?

10 At the current time, what aspects of your module/course/suite of programmes would you most like to change or transform? What is the evidence to support the need for change?

Chapter 6

Leading course design

It is very important to understand that emotional intelligence is not the opposite of intelligence, it is not the triumph of heart over head – it is the unique intersection of both.

(David Caruso, quoted in Freedman, 2002)

THE CHALLENGE IN THIS CHAPTER

The primary focus in this chapter will be on how to achieve collaborative engagement in the leadership of course design or transformation. Leadership rather than project management or educational design will be in the foreground of our narrative. This wide-ranging chapter will take us from considering 'what are you trying to achieve?' through to how to keep the plan on track.

The chapter begins by exploring three key questions:

- Intention – what are you trying to achieve?
- Inspiration – what are the starting points? Engaging with this question will include considering the drivers for change, valuing what is currently good or great and identifying challenges and opportunities.
- Innovation – what is this? And how does innovation differ from, or overlap with, ideas to do with renovation or enhancement?

Another key consideration is who needs to be involved. The discussion here will explore the qualities of both collaborators and collaborative leaders before turning to look specifically at engaging professional service colleagues and, perhaps most significantly, students as partners. Developing a shared vision in which all of the key stakeholders are fully invested holds the answer to unleashing the energy that will be needed to motivate a significant transformation initiative and maintain the momentum to see it through.

Opening up the major theme of collaborative engagement, and to stimulate some big picture (or divergent) thinking, we will introduce the idea of facilitating a group dialogue around the educational philosophy that needs to underpin your programme. And then we will use a model called the Fully Engaged Curriculum as an extended example of how to apply a framework approach to facilitating generative discussions and creative thinking processes. If successful, the framework could be retained with whatever modifications the group wishes as a central reference as the design/change project progresses.

To shape the creative group process involved in course design, we will use 'diverge – take stock – converge' as a structure and, linked to this, will consider the leadership skills, behaviours and group processes that each stage entails. In many ways this model provides the format of the chapter as we move from enabling leadership (divergent) through to expressing objectives and organising the initial implementation plan (convergent).

It will also be important to acknowledge that when conflict arises – as it inevitably will as different backgrounds, perspectives and agendas brush together – enabling leadership involves listening powerfully with both the head and the heart, and having the poise to redirect your own disruptive emotions for the good of the group.

The final part of the chapter discusses how to keep engagement going: maintaining momentum through showing progress, quick wins and excellent communication. It will also briefly introduce implementation planning, project management and the importance of feedback loops to maintain creative flexibility.

LINKS TO THE PROGRAMME LEADERSHIP MODEL

Leading course design has two significant faces. It begins as fundamentally a piece of enabling leadership and then progresses through to organising. And both sets of skills are needed in equal measures: firstly, enabling the collaborative group processes that are not only essential to creativity and problem solving, but that also help to engender collective commitment and a sense of mutual accountability; secondly, the organising skills that support groups as their thoughts converge, as choices are made, as goals are expressed, as responsibilities are identified and as plans are moulded. These two sets of leadership skills should overlap and interplay as the course design/transformation process progresses, but the movement overall is from people-focused attributes to goal-focused attributes. The voice of the champion may also be heard within the leadership of course design as it may be necessary to make the case for change or to project energy into valuing a particular pedagogical approach or piece of educational framing.

In Table 6.1 below the key leadership skills and attributes associated with leading course design are highlighted (note: this is purely indicative – none of

TABLE 6.1 Programme Leadership Model – leading course design

Leadership skills			
CHAMPION	ORGANISER	ENABLER	MENTOR
Enthuse	Plan	Encourage	Listen
Promote	Organise	Shield	Invest
Model	Monitor	Support	Praise
Challenge	Control	Share/Convene	Review
Negotiate	Evaluate	Mediate	Relate

the leadership skills should be regarded as exclusive or restricted to just one area).

WHAT ARE YOU TRYING TO ACHIEVE?

In Chapter 5 we discussed in detail why having a clear brief matters. It is fundamentally about 'mandating yourself' and your team, and knowing that you are empowered to take forward the course design project. Those people you have identified as 'activists' should own the brief and either be champions for the project/initiative within the institution (and possibly beyond) or direct contributors willing to engage directly in the design, or both. But inevitably there will be others who have not so far been directly engaged, or who have had a relatively passive role, who will need to contribute in possibly quite significant ways. Presenting them with a firm set of objectives and a project plan at this stage might make it hard for them to discover a sense of commitment and ownership, and so a more emergent approach based around collaborative engagement could hold the key. In development processes of this kind, it is important for leaders to be aware that there is a clear relationship between engagement, commitment and accountability (see Figure 6.1 below).

There are three powerful starting points for collaborative engagement that can be brought to life in various ways:

- *What are the drivers for change?* This can focus on and include the institution, the discipline/subject/profession, the students, the higher education sector, and the national and international context.
- *What is currently good or great?* This question particularly applies when working on an existing module or programme and is intended to bring an appreciative spirit to the discussions. It will also help to identify your 'keepers' – those things you do not want to lose and, in fact, it would be great to potentially expand and develop elsewhere. A simple discussion exercise linked to this is 'stop – keep – start', which could be used at a later point in the process, focusing, perhaps, on particular areas. It simply asks the group:

Collaborative engagement

⬇

Collective commitment

⬇

Mutual accountability

FIGURE 6.1 Engagement, commitment and accountability

- What should we stop?
- What should we keep? And
- What should we start?

■ *What are the opportunities and challenges?* This is a nicely balanced question that brings to life an active and aware consideration of the things that may excite us and others about what we are doing (and why we are doing it), the opportunities, the possible difficulties we may encounter and the challenges we will have to transform or overcome. Exploring this may also help the group identify where their strengths lie and how they can best deploy their resources (personal, practical and professional).

The scale and nature of what you are trying to achieve is another important area to explore. Is it a focused initiative or is it far-ranging? Does it make incremental changes to a limited set of issues or is it a radical transformation affecting the programme overall? Are you in the realm of renovation, innovation or enhancement? And what is the balance of agreement and certainty?:

■ Agreement about outcomes – high or low?
■ Certainty about process – clear or unclear?

The responses to these questions and considerations should influence both your understanding of what you are trying to achieve and your approach. Picking out scope and complexity (Rowland and Higgs, 2008), an initiative that is simple, uniform and affects just one area may progress well with a relatively directive style of leadership (a voice saying 'this is what we're trying to achieve'), whereas an initiative that is complex and differentiated in its impact across a wide range of areas is likely to require an enabling approach to leadership where the change is more emergent (a voice asking 'what are we trying to achieve?'). This intersects with considering levels of agreement and certainty. Eddie Obeng (1996) developed a model around this which uses an attractive and memorable nomenclature:

■ *Painting by numbers*: high agreement on outcomes and strong clarity about process – 'know what' and 'know how' – a 'closed project' where

115

you are, perhaps, repeating a change of a kind you have done before (you have direct experience).

- *Going on a quest*: high agreement on outcomes, but low clarity about process – 'know what', but 'don't know how' – a 'semi-closed project' where all the stakeholders essentially agree what is needed ('wouldn't it be wonderful if . . .') but no one is really sure how to achieve it (you lack direct experience).
- *Making a movie*: low agreement on outcomes, but strong clarity about process – 'don't know what', but 'know how' – a 'semi-open project' where there has been investment in the methods or expertise you would like to use, and people may also have strong views about *how* they should be used, but what will come out of the project lacks clarity, detail and definition (you have related experience).
- *Walking in a fog*: low agreement on outcomes and low clarity about process – 'don't know what' and 'don't know how' – an 'open project' where you are, perhaps, having to react very rapidly to circumstances and are moving into, for you, uncharted territories – you have to move, but you are not sure how or where (you lack any kind of real and relevant experience).

Another aspect to consider in the framing of the challenge is how you position innovation. This is a term that is attractive to some, but possibly inhibiting to others. This could be an organisational inhibition: 'we like the idea of innovation, but can't accept your proposal because it's never been done before'. It could relate to team experience: people have becomes sceptical after waves of 'so-called' innovation have resulted in limited perceived improvement. Or it might relate to the psychological disposition of individuals: in the Myers-Briggs Type Indicator (Myers et al., 2003), one of the four personality preferences, or dichotomies, is concerned with the type of information people prefer to gather and trust, and this has on one side a preference for 'what is real' and practical applications (termed *sensing*), and on the other side a preference for 'what might be', imagination and insight (termed *intuition*). Someone with a sensing preference might be more inclined to trust experience and build on what has gone before (renovation); someone with an intuition preference might be more inclined to trust inspiration and be excited by future possibilities (innovation). These personality preferences, which have their origins in the work of the Swiss psychologist Carl Jung (1971), have been echoed in other models and frameworks, for example, the Change Style Indicator, which is an assessment designed to measure an individual's preferred style in approaching and addressing change. The Change Style Indicator places respondents on a 120-point continuum between Conserver and Originator, with Pragmatist in between:

- *Conservers* accept structure, look to retain existing systems, prefer change that is gradual/incremental and may appear cautious (but may ask the hard, detailed questions).

- *Pragmatists* explore structure, prefer change that best serves the function, and may appear reasonable and practical (but sometimes non-committal).
- *Originators* challenge the structure, prefer quicker, more expansive and radical change, and may appear disorganised and undisciplined (they enjoy risk, uncertainty and originality).

Most individuals are a blend of Conserver-Pragmatist or Pragmatist-Originator.

So be wary of assuming that everyone is excited by the idea of innovation in the same way or even that all of your colleagues share the same notion of what innovation is and of its merits. What you are trying to achieve might be better described as either renovation or enhancement. Renovating a great programme to ensure its currency, expand its reach or refresh the methods used is as significant a challenge as any other, and possibly of greater value to your institution than some misdirected attempts at innovation:

> For things to stay the same, things have to change.
>
> (Tomasi di Lampedusa, 1961)

This often quoted paradox inspires us to appreciate that not every change is about innovation, and that valuing the past and preserving existing narratives can be a vital part of change leadership. And the role of enhancement feeds into this as we look to continuously improve things that we already value. Norman Jackson (2002) put forward an interesting and provocative list of what enhancement might involve in the context of learning and teaching in higher education:

- Abandoning something that is not working
- Doing existing things better/more efficiently
- Making better use of something
- Expanding something that is considered to be desirable
- Adding new things to existing things
- Connecting things to make different things
- Doing entirely new things which replace or complement existing things
- Or it might be an improved capacity to do something different or new in the future.

Jackson goes on to observe that enhancement is understood by higher education teachers as change 'through the direct experience of doing it' and also through experiencing 'the results of doing it'.

Turning finally to innovation, it is easy to think of this as being something powerfully holistic and all-embracing, but the reality is that not all innovations are the same and often they are focused on specific areas. So, coming back to our headline question (what are you trying to achieve?), it is valuable to understand the six dimensions of innovation (based on Bessant, Hughes and Richards, 2010):

117

- Product innovation: changes in the things (products/services) which an organisation offers.
- Process innovation: changes in the ways in which they are created and delivered (creation, operation and delivery).
- Position innovation: changes in the context in which the products/services are introduced and branded.
- Performance innovation: how well we do what we do and how we can enhance skills, capabilities and capacity.
- Perspective innovation: how we see ourselves, 'our' world and our role in shaping the future.
- Paradigm innovation: changes in the underlying mental models which frame what the organisation does.

All of the above distinctions and consideration are important for you to consider as a leader of change, but may also be valuable as a stimulation for your group to consider as part of the early phases of collaborative engagement.

There is always another way of framing and portraying the kinds of distinctions we have been discussing above. The terms 'innovation', 'renovation' and 'enhancement' work well because they highlight, and perhaps even exaggerate, some important differences (and importantly the mindsets that tend to go with these differences). Another view is to conceptualise the distinctions as different levels of the same thing, from the basic to the transformational, as Middlehurst does below with reference to quality enhancement:

> At a basic level, enhancement of quality involves examining what one is doing, and as a consequence, making explicit aims, objectives and outcomes . . . At the next level, enhancement may involve making incremental changes so that teaching is more efficient or research more productive, while maintaining the current direction of each. At a third level, quality enhancement will involve doing things in new ways . . . The most radical forms of quality enhancement are those which involve transformational changes that call for a complete re-examination, re-conceptualization and re-direction of existing practice.
>
> (Middlehurst, 1997: 48–49)

WHO NEEDS TO BE INVOLVED?

> When I was a kid, there was no collaboration; it's you with a camera bossing your friends around. But as an adult, filmmaking is all about appreciating the talents of the people you surround yourself with and knowing you could never have made any of these films by yourself.
>
> (Spielberg, 2011)

It is easy for the answer to this question to be driven by concerns about what we will need to put into the course. The course is seen as a container of learning and the container needs to be filled with content! So, the imperative becomes to bring together all the people who can contribute content and then hope some harmonising force of nature will make things coherent. What a different proposition it would be instead to bring together the people who are great at collaborating. But there are two sides to this, of course: the qualities of people as collaborators, which can start to feel like an exclusive territory, and the characteristics of collaborative leaders. It has become quite popular in this age of talent management and competencies for organisations to try to express a set of collaborative attributes. The following nine attributes of highly effective collaborators is taken from the *Virgin Entrepreneur* website (Warawa, 2014):

1 Be transparent.
2 Say what you are going to do and follow through.
3 Allow for a little give and take.
4 Listen to understand, not to respond.
5 Stick to your guns.
6 Know which battles to fight.
7 Be authentic.
8 Be kind.
9 Step up.

But to keep things in balance, we also need to think of the characteristics of collaborative leaders, or 'the art of collaborative leadership' as Russell Linden (2010) describes it. Leaders model and seed the behaviours needed for success, and without this, leadership becomes disconnected and reduced to something like managerial oversight. 'Be the change you want to see', a quote often attributed to Mahatma Gandhi, teaches us that the qualities of behaviour and relationship we wish to see in others have to be congruently modelled in our own behaviour. The top five qualities of collaborative leaders identified by Linden are as follows:

1 Feel driven to achieve the goal through collaboration, with a measured ego.
2 Listen carefully to understand others' perspectives.
3 Look for win-win solutions to meet shared interests.
4 Use pull more than push.
5 Think strategically; connect the project to a larger purpose.

This is a fabulous 'list of five' that echoes the key leadership principles and practices relevant to leading learning and teaching in higher education: a quest to collaborate; leaders must never stop listening; the win-win philosophy of principled negotiation; the push/pull model of influencing styles; and leveraging the strategic goals of the organisation – creating a clear line of sight from the vision for the project to the vision of the organisation. This is the essence of

Boundary-Spanning leadership: 'the capability to establish direction, alignment and commitment across boundaries in service of a higher vision or goal' (Ernst and Chrobot-Mason, 2010).

A little more playfully perhaps, Archer and Cameron (2013) paint portraits, or caricatures, of four types of leaders who by their actions ruin a variety of different business collaborations:

- *The control freak*: character – the expert loaner.
- *The idealist*: character – a driving passion.
- *The incrementalist*: character – a safe pair of hands.
- *The selfish high achiever*: character – ambition without flexibility.

Archer and Cameron stress that these are not a random sample: 'these four portraits illustrate typical leadership styles, which in the right circumstances can take someone a long way in their career, but which prove disastrous in collaborative ventures'. Their narrative goes on to propose that collaborative leadership is 'one of the most sophisticated and mature styles of leadership' and that it involves three critical skills:

- Mediation – the ability to address conflict situations as they arise, building the confidence of others in the process.
- Influencing – that ability to match the most effective method of influence to the needs of the situation and the parties involved.
- Engaging others – building relationships, communicating with clarity and involving others in decision making.

(Archer and Cameron, 2013: 127)

It is as much, then, about creating a collaborative environment as it is about identifying and working with people who share collaborative qualities and values. And so much of the climate of any work environment is the tone set by the leader, initially at least. As engagement flourishes, collaborative leaders will become more and more inclusive in their approach, and will look to enable different forms of leadership within the group: leaders as enablers of leaders. This shared or distributed leadership allows complex ventures like course design to thrive. Ventures or challenges that have a 'wicked' (Rittel and Webber, 1973) edge to them because they are seen differently by different stakeholders, they are multi-dimensional in terms of what is needed for a successful outcome, there are deep values at work in determining the 'right' solutions and approaches, and the personal investment needed from individuals may be profound.

As well as an acknowledgement that subject specialists, disciplinary leads and relevant research colleagues will have strong contributions to make, you will also need to involve those with backgrounds/specialisms in educational design and development, and others known to have a flair for learning, teaching and student engagement in this area (some people may, of course, combine several of these qualities). And then there are other voices that could have important, if not essential, contributions to make. There are professional colleagues within the institution, employers or their representatives if they are willing to engage, and students.

Colleagues from professional services can contribute in a wide variety of ways to course design or learning transformation projects. The question to ask, though, is what should be the nature of that contribution: as equal partners in the process or as outsiders looking in (when invited)? The landscape of higher education is changing and part of that change is a remodelling of the status of relationships. For many years, a significant community within our universities had to tolerate being defined by what they are not – that is, 'non-academic staff'. This academic/non-academic binary stemmed from:

> a perceived split between collegial approaches, implying academic autonomy and freedom, underpinned by the contribution of higher education to the advancement of knowledge, and functional activity, such as planning and budgeting, that are geared to what are seen as management goals.
>
> (Whitchurch, 2013: 3–4)

It can be questioned whether terms like academic support or professional services take us much further than what Whitchurch terms the 'narratives of exclusion' in the previous negative labelling. The danger in this binary view is that it can polarise colleagues (almost suggesting master and servant, if one were to take it that far) and act as a barrier to collaboration. However, as Whitchurch goes on to observe, increasingly there has been a 'loosening of boundaries in the delivery of academic agendas'. As we contemplate what has been termed the 'third space' professional, we begin to see an increasing pro-portion of colleagues with a 'mix of academic and professional credentials, experience and roles'. So, drawing such colleagues into course design initia-tives as full partners in the process can only enrich the fully engaged approach that collaboration heralds. The student experience, learning technologies, information systems, library resources, quality assurance, validation require-ments, marketing, professional recognition, placement coordination, student support, international outreach – the list goes on – can all be fully integrated through an intentional convergence of participation, in line with the scale and needs of the project.

The best way to find out what students want is to ask them. This sounds simple enough, but it is amazing how often we neglect to do so. And whilst the picture may be improving in many areas of university life, when it comes to course design or re-design, a hesitancy creeps in. The premise for this hesitation usually takes the form of a question along the following lines: 'how can students know what they want (or need) until we've given it to them?' This is a good question. Surely students cannot be expected to know what they want to learn in advance of learning it. Well, to use a crude comparison, most diners have ideas about what a good meal is and the kind of restaurant experience they would enjoy before becoming acquainted with the menu. Likewise, in the commercial world, few people would contemplate developing a new product without engaging closely with the wants and needs of potential customers. So, notions of the novice/expert relationship in academic (particularly undergraduate) study, not unlike the apprenticeship model in many ways, can create a barrier to higher levels (quantity and quality) of student participation in course/learning design. A lot hinges here on how partnership is perceived or conceived within institutions and, indeed, the wider sector. There has been something of a proliferation of concepts around student engagement:

- Students as co-creators.
- Students as co-producers.
- Students as co-developers.
- Students as active participants.
- Students as agents for change.

Out of these has grown a broader and deeper sense of partnership, and this has started to gain significant currency. And a big part of putting student partnership into practice is engagement with curriculum design. Moving beyond more generalised ideas of student participation, which have been shown to improve student performance, persistence and satisfaction (Trowler , 2010), this level of engagement draws students in and welcomes them as part of the learning community involved in shaping courses. So, rather than having concerns regarding knowledge and expertise and whether students can be equal partners on this basis, a more positive reframing of partnership in this context is to express equality in terms of respecting each other's views.

Student engagement is an area where practice is moving into policy. Many good practices have been around for a while, although not consistently applied either within or across institutions, but as a policy priority, embedding the student voice into processes, structures and decision making is relatively recent. As part of the UK Quality Code, the Quality Assurance Agency for Higher Education published a chapter (B5) specifically on student engagement in June 2012. This states a very clear expectation that higher education providers are required to meet:

> Higher education providers take deliberate steps to engage all students, individually and collectively, as partners in the assurance and enhancement of their educational experience.
>
> (Quality Assurance Agency, 2012a)

Those few words are actually in my view momentous in the changing landscape of higher education and the relationship between students, university staff and institutions. Learning has moved from 'doing to you' to 'doing for you' to 'doing with you', and that is profound and potentially highly positive. The list offered in the chapter of the 'aspects of the educational journey into which students can offer insight' illustrates how wide-ranging student engagement is becoming as a policy priority:

- application and admission;
- induction and transition into higher education;
- programme and curriculum design, delivery and organisation;
- curriculum content;
- teaching delivery;
- learning opportunities;
- learning resources;
- student support and guidance;
- assessment.

There are not too many gaps there. And the mechanisms suggested for involving students are similarly broad, ranging from questionnaires through to involvement in new projects and dialogue with decision makers.

With regard to leading course design, or any related curriculum review or transformation process, the following are ten key principles to consider specifically with regard to student partnership:

1 Don't involve them as an afterthought.
2 Engage both experienced and less experienced students.
3 Involving a few students well is preferable to engaging a lot badly.
4 Discuss what partnering means – develop mutual expectations.
5 Support their development as part of the process.
6 No sitting on the side-lines – integrate them as equals into the group.
7 *Share the air* – facilitate in such a way that every voice is heard.
8 Make an asset of their fresh perspective and creativity.
9 Involve them in the whole process and share fully the outcomes.
10 Seek to recognise their involvement appropriately.

This is not put forward as a perfect, comprehensive or exhaustive list, but may act as a springboard for developing a set of principles of your own (or even for your department or institution).

WHAT IS YOUR EDUCATIONAL PHILOSOPHY?

Leading change often involves changing how you lead. As we have discussed before in Chapter 3, it involves moving beyond or letting go of the managerial, but, more than that, it creates a narrative within which people individually and collectively can find the inspiration to achieve something great. Something great!? Well, going beyond the ordinary, exceeding expectations, excelling at some aspect(s), creating something original, overcoming significant obstacles, re-defining success, transforming relationships or simply turning around a failing situation. What makes it great is that reflective moment that dispels doubt when individuals turn to each other and with a nod, and probably a relieved smile, acknowledge that 'this is going to be good'. That is the spark of inspiration that begins to ignite a transformation process.

Leadership counts! Research carried out by Deborah Rowland and Malcolm Higgs has further confirmed that when it comes to change there is a statistically significant relationship between leadership and success:

> Our research identified . . . that what leaders do makes the biggest differ-
> ence between success and failure in implementing high magnitude change,
> in fact it accounted for 50% of the variance. Put another way, if leaders do
> not reflect on and pay attention to their own leadership behaviour they could
> reduce their chances of successfully implementing high magnitude change
> by a half.
>
> (Rowland and Higgs, 2008: 61–2)

The term 'high magnitude' refers to a combination of the scope (the extent of the impact) and the complexity of the change, and usually suggests something with external drivers, a relatively short timescale and the need for emergent approaches. And whilst programme design or transformation projects are unlikely to have an organisation-wide impact (unless, perhaps, a suite of very large, core programmes are involved, or the transformation concerns significant aspects of the overall learning and teaching strategy), the complexity, the external dimensions and the active interests of multiple stakeholders make this very relevant for our consideration.

So what shifts perceptions, engages energy and focuses intent? An aspirational narrative that is authentic because it respects the past, is grounded because it acknowledges the present and is inspiring because it starts to shape an attractive future. Only 'starts to'? Yes, because if the leader imposes a vision that is rounded, fully formed and complete, it can never (or rarely) be fully owned by others. But it may be possible to present a framework that the group can develop as its own – a framework it can inhabit both conceptually and emotionally as the design/ change project progresses. This could, for example, set out the frame and edges for the project, or propose a particular pedagogical approach for the discussions to operate within:

> Being forward-looking – envisioning exciting possibilities and enlisting others
> in a shared view of the future – is the attribute that most distinguishes leaders
> from nonleaders. We know this because we asked followers.
>
> (Kouzes and Posner, 2009)

Despite what the words may suggest, the leadership attributes around vision and narrative do not necessarily have to involve *performance skills*. The key to collaborative engagement, as always, is to bring people together and ask good questions. Good question are usually simple questions in a well-crafted sequence. This is what creates transformative spaces (or 'space for change':

Summerfield and Smith, 2011), in which colleagues can challenge and develop ideas, discover fresh insights, build relationships, find commitment and start to focus and plan.

Rather than taking a deep dive into content, begin by exploring wider principles that will frame the design/transformation initiative overall. A question sometimes used to challenge and stimulate participants on educational development workshops is: 'What is your educational philosophy?' This is not intended to put them on the spot as individuals, but rather to encourage them to reflect on the discourse in or around their programme team. And it is a big question – a question that invites some big thinking around the character of learning and teaching on a course, and that can form the basis of a vision if the thinking is pursued far enough and deep enough. It is also a question that belongs very much to the divergent phase of the change dialogue (more on this below).

If the response to the question 'what is your educational philosophy?' were to be 'that learning on our teaching programme is fundamentally student-centred', then begin by asking why. And continue asking why (in a variety of supportive facilitative ways, of course) until the answer starts to come into really sharp focus:

- Why?
  - So that students take responsibility for their own learning.
- Great – why?
  - So that they start to develop independent learning skills.
- Great – why?
  - To encourage deeper learning that's more integrated with the specific needs and interests of individual students.
- Great – why?
  - To ensure that they develop personal and professional skills that will support them as effective practitioners in their field.
- And, once more, why?
  - To develop students as future professionals who have learnt how to learn in novel and complex situations, equipped and ready for the challenges and opportunities of a rapidly changing world.
- Sounds good . . .

The '5 Whys' technique was originally developed by Sakichi Toyoda in the 1930s and was used within the Toyota Motor Corporation in the 1970s during the evolution of its manufacturing methodologies. Toyota still uses it to solve problems today.

Questions could then turn to 'what?' What does that look, sound and feel like? Can we build up a rich picture of what student-centred learning is like? What is the reality of it?:

- What would we see students doing?
- What would we hear students saying?
- How would we see students interacting?
- What sort of questions would they be asking each other?
- How would students be interacting with us?
- What sort of questions would they be asking us?
- What would they produce?
- How would they produce it?
- What would this feel like for them?
- What would this feel like for us?

There clearly might be nuances to all of these questions based on the subject discipline, the level of study and other factors, but the intention is to be generative in the area of learning and student engagement, and to craft a vision around this prior to thinking about structures, methods, curriculum components and content.

Another approach mentioned above for this initial phase of engagement in course design would be to present a model or framework for the group to develop as its own. The leader might need to project energy into this and champion the value of it as either a particular pedagogical approach or a piece of educational framing. This would operate as a framework for the group's discussions to operate within initially, and could possibly be retained with whatever modifications the group wishes as a central reference as the design/change project progresses. It could even become a structural device within the curriculum itself. Such an approach could, of course, be used by leaders alongside the 'educational philosophy' questions above or other tools/techniques for collaborative engagement.

THE FULLY ENGAGED CURRICULUM

The Fully Engaged Curriculum shown in Figures 6.2 and 6.4 below is a model I have developed which could be used as an example of this framework approach. It is generic in its nature and can be applied to any higher education programme. The model incorporates a range of contemporary ideas on curriculum, student engagement, the nature of adult learning and the purpose of higher education.

The model begins by setting out four equal learning domains (knowing – doing – creating – being) and the flow is from 'knowing' in the north of the model around both sides to 'being' at the south. 'Knowing' is about information and 'being' is about identity. The flow around the model is through performance on the 'doing' side and production on the 'creating' side, and it is

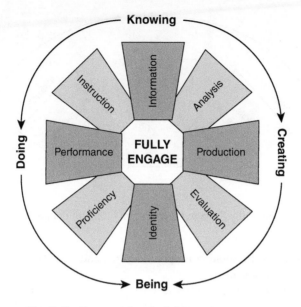

Knowing

Doing

Creating

Being

Instruction

Information

Analysis

Performance

FULLY ENGAGE

Production

Proficiency

Identity

Evaluation

the combination of 'doing' and 'creating' and the behavioural proficiency and self-reflection that goes with each respectively that develops personal meaning and identity. This is the central proposition in the model and it is called the Fully Engaged Curriculum because firstly it aims to fully engage students (that is, engagement of the whole learner) and secondly it asserts that each domain needs to be fully engaged with the other three.

Within each domain, there are three areas of learning engagement: the domain itself, the primary area (re-labelled as an area of learning engagement – shown in brackets in the list below) and two further areas to either side and immediately adjacent (termed crossover areas):

■ Knowing – instruction and analysis (and information – primary area).
■ Doing – instruction and proficiency (and performance – primary area).
■ Creating – analysis and evaluation (and production – primary area).
■ Being – proficiency and evaluation (and identity – primary area).

The intervening areas of learning engagement are shared with two domains, which is crucial to the fully integrated nature of the model. For example, analysis belongs to both the 'knowing' domain and the 'creating' domain. So, the representation of each domain includes three areas of learning engagement. Figure 6.3 below shows how the 'doing' domain is represented.

The purpose here is not to give a full exposition of this model and all of the educational and theoretical links and associations, but to consider the use of a framework such as this in the leadership of course design. However, broadly we can note links with:

127 ■

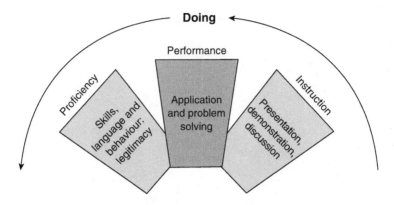

FIGURE 6.3 The Fully Engaged Curriculum – 'doing' domain

- The idea of threshold concepts (Meyer, Land and Baillie, 2010) in the 'knowing' domain;
- The progression through the cognitive levels in Bloom's Taxonomy (1956) as the model moves from knowledge through analysis to evaluation;
- Echoes of the three-circle schema in the dynamic curriculum model put forward by Barnett and Coate (2005);
- The importance of creativity and discovery within the curriculum and students undertaking research and inquiry (Jenkins, Healey and Zetter, 2007);
- Notions of legitimacy and being 'on an inbound trajectory' (Wenger, 1998) that relate to 'professional' performance;
- Constructivist ideas to do with students creating personal meaning out of the experiences available to them and growing as a result: 'constructing meaning is learning; there is no other kind' (Hein, 1991);
- The critical transformational impact of self-reflection in student work or 'upgrading the significance of reflection' (Reid, Dahlgren and Dahlgren, 2011);
- Recognition that identity formation, the process of becoming, is about both personal discovery (based on things like competence, emotional maturity, autonomy, positive relationships, sense of purpose and integrity: Chickering and Reisser, 1993) and the consolidated expression of expert attributes (Johns, 2004).

Figure 6.4 below puts a little bit of flesh on the bones of the model. It provides a brief description of the types of learning and teaching activities, resources and learner attributes that fall under each of the eight headings in the model. In presenting this to a group, the leader should find examples that are relevant to both the context of the institution and the subject discipline to bring it to life, but without implying that this is purely re-framing 'what we do already': the process should be a balance of validation and discovery. By contrast, some playful examples could be used to stimulate a more immediate and impactful recognition of the core proposition behind the model. These could be simplifications of what goes on in other disciplines (becoming a medical doctor, perhaps) or looser examples that are more metaphorical:

- Knowing – types of architecture.
- Doing – building a house.
- Creating – designing a house.
- Being – enjoying the location (the property you built starts to transform you).

In a more generalised way, you may want to emphasise the key importance of shifting the curriculum out of the 'knowing' domain: the curriculum as disjointed parcels of knowledge. The following is an 'invented' quote from a successful business studies graduate (good degree) who has been unable to find work:

It was as though I left knowing everything there is to know about what a flower is, but with no idea how to grow one.

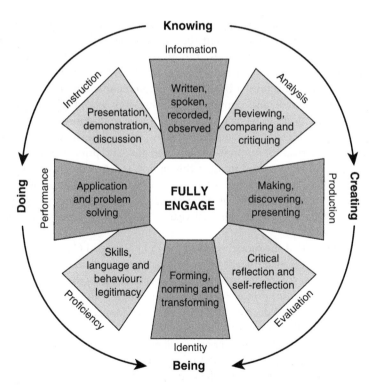

FIGURE 6.4 The Fully Engaged Curriculum, with details

Having presented the model to the group, the main intention is to encourage some collaborative engagement. This is likely to involve workshop-style activities and discussions. The model lends itself to being split into the four domains, using the format shown above in Figure 6.3, and small groups can be formed to discuss, explore and experiment with each one. The following is a simple set of four questions that each sub-group could consider (initials have been used to label the four domains):

1   How will your domain be achieved?
2   How will it be 'fully engaged' with the other three domains?
    -   separate activities;
    -   linked activities (e.g. K before D);
    -   integrated activities (D generates K and involves C);
    -   holistic activities (the ultimate focus is on B).
3   What will you stop/keep/start:
    -   in your curriculum design?;
    -   in your approach to assessment?;
    -   in your interaction/relationship with students?;
    -   in your work . . . As a team? As an individual?
4   And what excites you? What will this transformation achieve?

To share and capture the learning outputs from this activity, and to start building an action plan, groups could present their main ideas, insights and recommendations to each other. Alternatively, the groups could rotate World Café style (originators of this method, Juanita Brown and David Isaacs, 1995) and build upon each other's ideas until a broad set of recommendations arise with a sense of shared commitment and consensus. Another way would be to follow the exploration of the four domains with a further phase of discussion taking each of the eight areas of learning engagement, drilling down into the detail of each as related to the curriculum in question. Keeping alive the principle of integrating the domains will be very important if this option is selected. You do not want to end up with a curriculum that is 'knowing' in year one and most of year two, with the odd bit of 'doing' that is not assessed, and only a cursory engagement with 'being' halfway through the final year, if at all, and virtually no 'creating' (sound familiar?).

Remembering that the model is called the Fully Engaged Curriculum because it asserts that each domain needs to be fully engaged with the other three, it is important to fully explore the crossovers in the model. All of the areas of learning engagement that are not prime areas are crossover areas. So, for example, analysis is part of the 'knowing' domain and the 'creating' domain, and is the crossover between the two. Fully exploring and articulating the variety of ways in which within the curriculum the crossover areas will enable the domains to engage with each other is an absolutely critical part of the discussion and the eventual design.

Now, we need to keep in mind the maxim that 'the model is not reality'. It is a conceptual framework, a representational scheme, a deliberate and intentional simplification put forward, in this case, as a stimulus for co-creation and co-design. Whilst, as broadly outlined above, it has links and associations with a wide range of established educational ideas and theories, it does not pretend to be entirely definitive. Looking at it, there could be a mass of arrows linking each of the areas of learning engagement with all of the others, and the arrows could be thick or thin to denote significance depending on the subject, the level of study and the character of learning and study in the institution. So, allow the model to facilitate and support your thinking and discussions, but do not be restrained by it. If you start to see links and overlaps that run across the model, for example, points of engagement between analysis and performance or between production and proficiency, then capture and celebrate them. To achieve full engagement, each domain needs to become fully integrated with the other three.

Returning to the four domains, the following provides a quote and six prompt questions for each that leaders could use to seed reflection and stimulate discussion ('them' and 'they' in the text below refers to students as learners, and is used for no other reason than to make the questions dynamic):

- Knowing: 'Information is not instruction' (David Merrill, quoted in Zemke, 1998).

  - What knowledge – where, when and how?
  - How will you know what they know?
  - What will make it stick – go deeper?
  - How will the knowledge be used (knowledge in action)?
  - How will they develop their knowledge to reason and critique?
  - How will the knowledge transform them?

- Doing: 'Knowing is not enough, we must apply' (Goethe, 1749–1832).

  - What must/should they be able to do?
  - How will you know they can do it?
  - Which comes first: the knowledge or the problem?
  - How will they develop flair and proficiency?
  - Can they perform both independently and as part of a team?
  - How do these skills transfer to the 'real word'/other contexts?

- Creating: 'Learning will be grounded in research and research-like activities, so that much of what students are learning will be through their own discoveries' (University of Lincoln, 2013).

  - What would we like them to be able to produce?
  - What opportunities must there be for originality, discovery and expression (independently or collaboratively)?
  - How will they take responsibility for developing their own learning and possibly the learning of others?
  - What critical skills or faculties must they be able to demonstrate?

- How will they reflect critically on their own performance and the things they produce?
- How will their creative/research activities transform them?

■ Being (learning is transformational as well as transmissional): 'In contrast with novices, experts intuit and respond appropriately to a situation as a whole without any obvious linear or reductionist thinking' (Johns, 2004).

- What would we like them to aspire to?
- What models of professional identity will be significant within and around the programme?
- How will they be encouraged to reflect upon the transformational aspects of both their personal and professional development?
- How will we create opportunities for quality discussions?
- Are there frameworks which capture and express professional competencies in this area? If so, how will they be integrated?
- What marks, measures or milestones would be appropriate for recognising/celebrating progression and development?

These questions are, of course, only suggestions. Leaders can use and adapt them, and find others that better fit the needs of their group and the specifics of their design/transformation challenge. And do not be inhibited or feel that specialist or professional skills are needed to facilitate a process of this kind; this is an opportunity to express and assert your leadership and model core values around collaborative engagement. Remember, *amateurs made the Ark, professionals made the* Titanic. The more connected you are as an enabling leader, combining passion and compassion, the more connected others will become.

I have used my model of the Fully Engaged Curriculum as an extended example of how the framework approach can be used to lead course design. Whilst I commend it to you as a model, many others could, of course, be employed in a similar way. Another approach would be to use two or three models in combination and as part of this invite the design/transformation team to identify and combine elements to propose, as it were, a model of their own.

COLLABORATIVE ENGAGEMENT: DIVERGE – TAKE STOCK – CONVERGE

Most of the focus in this chapter has deliberately been on the divergent phase of the design/change dialogue. At this stage, the leadership dimension should be high because the challenge is fundamentally energy-based, as it primarily relates to engagement, collaboration, creativity and vision. Getting the environment right is crucial as we look to create transformative spaces in which design/change teams can perform and use divergent processes of the kind described above.

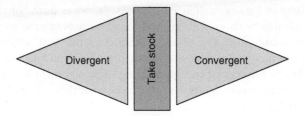

FIGURE 6.5 Divergent and convergent

Figure 6.5 above shows how creative group processes typically progress from a divergent phase to a phase of taking stock and, finally, to a third convergent stage.

The three phases can be broadly categorised as follows:

■ *Divergent* – this phase is generative, expansive and creative. It has a free-wheeling feel to it and looks to rule everything in and nothing out. The goal is a storm of ideas that can seed the new approaches you will need. The climate of the group is crucial and it is good practice to establish ground rules around inclusivity, mutual respect, full participation, being appreciative, welcoming 'silly' ideas, and powerful listening. Group processes, questions, models and frameworks should be selected to promote, encourage and structure the generative/creative engagement that is involved.

■ *Taking stock* – this phase is a pause for breath that looks to gather up and in some way order everything that the divergent phase has generated. It is at once both a celebration and a mini-audit. One aspect of taking stock is making sure that everything is captured. There is the spoken word, and having someone dedicated to making comprehensive notes is a very good idea, and then there are artefacts such as posters, table sheets and idea walls (usually involving repositionable notes of various kinds). Digital cameras and smartphones are extremely useful for capturing the visual artefacts, and there are very easy-to-use applications that can turn a set of photographs into a single document that can be readily shared. The second aspect of taking stock – and this is really the art of it – is successfully identifying groupings, common themes and repeated messages that can feed into the final convergent phase. A word of caution when it comes to taking stock is to watch for discarding ideas inadvertently, possibly by combining ideas inappropriately, for example, or, worse, allowing ideas to be prejudged, whether consciously or not.

■ *Convergent* – the convergent phase begins to ask: 'So what?' If the divergent phase is about creating choices, then the convergent phase is about making choices. If divergent thinking is about creating a lot of ideas, then convergent thinking is about excluding some and selecting others. The convergent phase sorts ideas, categorises, summarises, begins to evaluate and starts to draw conclusions. It moves from 'what we could do' towards 'what we will do', and with a more pragmatic mindset starts to formulate a plan. Out of many alternatives, the 'best' solutions should start to emerge. To achieve convergence, some guiding principles may need to be formulated and applied, and these may include organisational imperatives or constraints (but you know what they say, question before complying . . .).

These three phases look distinct as they are presented here, but inevitably each one bleeds through into the other. There is therefore a choice for leaders regarding whether to run them into each other or intentionally make them separate. There are virtues to both approaches. A full day devoted to course design could need the shape of all three phases to make it feel complete, and if the group gets energised, it may well have the momentum to do so. Another approach that is often used is for the divergent phase to be followed by a relatively short phase of taking stock which the leader then undertakes to take forward and complete, sending a summary to all of the participants for their comments. The convergent phase could then, perhaps, be delegated to individuals or sub-groups with responsibility for specific aspects or areas of the curriculum. The role of the leader is then to maintain an overview, ensure coherence and, above all, to go on sharing.

No phase is absolute, of course, and rocking back and forth between the phases may well be necessary for a larger project. For example, if the convergent phase at the end of the first cycle of engagement produces a broad curriculum structure and a set of core learning principles that people are committed to, then a further divergent set of activities could be initiated to explore creative ideas for approaches to learning within each of the main curriculum components.

There are a variety of processes and techniques that leaders can use to facilitate each of the three phases. Some are well known, such as structured brainstorming, SWOT Analysis (strengths, weaknesses, opportunities and threats), Force Field Analysis, Stakeholder Analysis, Fishbone Analysis, ranking options and many more. There are books, websites, workshops and other resources that provide details and guidance on how to facilitate these processes. Others are more specialised and may need additional support. Alternatively, you can design processes of your own based on developing a sequence of questions, progressing from very liberating questions (for example, 'if you could change anything, what would it be?' or 'what would be the most active ways to engage students in "x"?') through to more focused and specific questions, perhaps inviting participants to rank items or make a selection. Having identified your question sequence, the challenge is then to identify a variety of active and interesting ways for participants to both engage with the questions and with each other (mixing and re-mixing sub-groups can enhance the depth and breadth of outcomes generated). It may also be that you wish to use some reflections on the changing external context, or data around student participation, or student feedback, or student destinations or employability as a springboard for discussions, and your question sequence could be designed to incorporate this in a positive way. The Fully Engaged Curriculum was used above to illustrate a framework approach particularly focused on the divergent phase, but if such a model was well received, it could also be used to structure the convergent phase and could even go on to become a structural and philosophical underpinning of the course overall.

It is not the purpose of this book to provide a long list of group processes with a detailed description of each. Our focus is on leadership. And it is interesting to note the movement in leadership style that occurs through the three phases described above and to relate this back to the Programme Leadership Model. Essentially the movement is from enabler to organiser – from people-focused to goal-focused attributes. The divergent phase as a team-based function calls for a high level of enabling leadership, possibly with flavours of the champion if there is a particular model, framework or pedagogical approach that you need to put energy into introducing or promoting as a piece of educational framing. But the main leadership skills involved in the divergent phase are to convene, encourage, support and mediate.

'Mediate' appears in this list of four leadership skills because any generative group process is likely to include conflict: hopefully healthy, constructive conflict in an atmosphere in which discussions are open with disagreements not leading to a fear of loss or rejection, but some level of mediation may nevertheless be necessary. And conflict of this kind is very important as it can produce the synthesis of ideas that leads to new insights and realisations, or third-way thinking as a *kind of* active dialectic unfolds. However, the reality is that sometimes this can be a bumpy ride, which is why this chapter began with the quote from David Caruso on emotional intelligence. Enabling leadership involves listening powerfully with both the head and the heart, and having the poise to redirect your own disruptive emotions for the good of the group. That is the essence of emotionally intelligent leadership:

> The ability to monitor one's own and others feelings and emotions, to discriminate among them, and to use this information to guide one's thinking and action.
>
> (Salovey and Mayer, 1990: 189)

The four factors of emotional intelligence proposed by Mayer and Salovey in their Four-Branch Model (1997) are as follows:

- Emotional perception – the perception and expression of emotions.
- Emotional integration – the ability to reason using emotions.
- Emotional understanding – the ability to understand emotions (feelings and their meaning).
- Emotional management – the ability to manage emotions (openness and personal growth).

135

It is important to realise that the leadership challenge is at least as much about monitoring and managing your own emotions as it is resolving other people's conflicts. Indeed, emotions are likely to take over in some situations if leaders are unable to redirect their own responses in positive ways. 'Disagree with the idea not the person' is a great ground rule to have in place to help enable you to do so. It gives healthy conflict permission whilst hopefully ruling out personal attacks. And if the leader can go on listening with their head to the ideas and insights arising, whilst their heart listens to and manages the emotions, then there is a good chance that the group can be productive in terms of both content and climate.

The taking stock phase in a sense bridges from enabling to organising. It can still be a facilitated group process, and in most cases probably should be, but the intention is not to generate anything new. However, originality can still arise in the ways in which links, connections, groupings and associations are identified. Discussions can be rich and challenging as colleagues ask, for example: 'Are these two things saying the same thing or should they be in different groups?' And depending on how the divergent phase was structured, colleagues may already be thinking about grouping ideas under headings such as employability, assessment, team-based activities and so on.

In essence, the convergent phase should be the start of a planning process. From the rich picture of possibilities rendered by the divergent phase and taking stock, a set of priorities and objectives should start to emerge. The decision making that is part of the convergent phase is also an opportunity to build consensus and commitment, but to do this, it may help to have some processes and structures designed to support convergent thinking. These can be simple: 'yes – no – maybe' is probably the simplest tool for sorting options, but there are others:

- Must – should – could (the imperative nature of the ideas – 'which must we do?').
- Now – soon – later – never (to sort priorities in relation to time or urgency).
- New – nearly new – similar – mostly the same – old (considers ideas in relation to what we do already).

Another approach is to categorise ideas/options using a four-box grid. The two axes for the grid can be formulated in various ways:

- The x-axis (the horizontal axis) is impact (low to high). The y-axis (the vertical axis) is ease of implementation (hard to easy). This identifies in the top-right or 'positive' quadrant options that are high impact and easy to implement.
- The x-axis is how innovative (low to high). The y-axis is how feasible (low to high). This identifies in the top-right or 'positive' quadrant options that are both highly innovative and very feasible.

■ The x-axis is potential for student engagement (low to high). The y-axis is amount of resources required (high to low). This identifies in the top-right or 'positive' quadrant options that have a high potential for student engagement and require a relatively low level of resources.

You can, of course, formulate your four-box grid in whatever way best serves your course design or transformation challenge. This technique tends to involve combining an aspirational dimension (for example, impact) with a restraining dimension (for example, ease of implementation).

A third approach for structuring convergent thinking is to create as a diagram a six-pointed star. This provides three sets of opposing points that can be labelled in various ways, depending on the main drivers of your design/change initiative (you are restricted to identifying three key dimensions, which is probably enough in most cases). In the example below, the team has, let us say, a vision that involves making the programme more professionally focused and therefore more student-led with a higher proportion of assessments based on applied skills/knowledge and proficiency:

■ First dimension: academic – professional.
■ Second dimension: tutor-led – student-led.
■ Third dimension: knowledge assessed – application/proficiency assessed.

The ideas and options that came out of the taking stock phase are then each given a number so that they can be plotted on the points of the star in response to the three key dimensions. So, if idea number one supports a professional focus, is able to be student-led and can be assessed through a piece of group problem solving (application), then a '1' should appear on each of those three points of the star. Relative levels can then be shown by placing the number

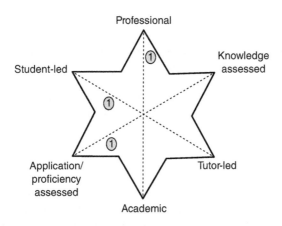

FIGURE 6.6 Example of a six-pointed star

either at the apex point (high level) or close to the centre of the star (low level). This process should create a strong visual representation of those ideas and options that will move the design project most powerfully in the direction desired. As an alternative to the six-pointed star, a diagram of six intersecting circles can be used in the same way – the advantage of this is that it allows more crossovers to be identified, but the downside is the visual complexity of the image overall.

To whatever extent you can, it is important to pull out of the convergent phase a set of objectives that encapsulate the core ideas that have arisen. Some may be quite sharp and focused (for example, 'no more than 30 per cent of the summative assessments will take the form of written and timed examinations'), while others may be overarching and require interpretation (for example, 'opportunities for creative exploration and expression will run throughout the curriculum'), but both will have their place. What is critical is that you and the group have something concrete to reflect upon and take forward. It is even valuable if some of the objectives say no more than certain aspects/issues will be given further consideration, perhaps with an indication of by whom and within what timeframe.

So, within this process of moving from divergent to convergent processes and discussions, the enabling leader starts to become the organiser, and Fayol's core functions of management will start to emerge (see Chapter 3). However, engagement is not a one-stop shop and commitment can never be taken for granted: 'There you go, you are now engaged!' The leadership dimension may reduce, but it never goes away – leadership and management are dimensions that always exist in unison to some degree, as we discussed in Chapter 3. Leading engagement is a continuous process; *the road to success is always under construction*. Going back to 'business as usual' should not be an option, and to avoid this, some tangible piece of change needs to be seen and celebrated very quickly after the design/change initiative is initiated. John Kotter, the eminent author on change leadership, refers to this as generating short-term wins:

> Running a transformation effort without serious attention to short-term wins is extremely risky. Sometimes you get lucky; visible results just happen. But sometimes your luck runs out . . . short-term wins help build necessary momentum. Fence sitters are transformed into supporters, reluctant supporters into active participants, and so on. This momentum is critical . . . because the energy needed to complete (the change) is often enormous.
>
> (Kotter, 1996: 119)

In terms of engagement, you may, in fact, experience a net loss if as a leader you facilitate a process of collaborative engagement and then return to 'business as usual' without anything happening. My rule of the three Ms is that *maintaining momentum motivates*, and two words that cannot be underestimated when it comes to change leadership are 'progress' and 'achievement'. So, even if the focus is moving towards planning and organising, it is important to continue to:

- keep people interested;
- keep people informed; and
- keep people involved.

And rather than slipping back into the procedural, keep people active. You cannot do everything yourself, and it would be foolish and counterproductive to try, so a very empowering outcome of the convergent phase is a broad plan (a masterplan, perhaps) that delegates to individuals or sub-groups responsibilities for ideas/action points relating to specific aspects of the curriculum.

And finally, again on the subject of change leadership and keeping people interested, informed and involved, there is communication. Within Kotter's eight-stage process for leading change, generating short-term wins is one of the stages, while another is communicating the change vision. In Kotter's model, each of the eight stages corresponds to a common 'error' identified through research and the one for communication is 'undercommunicating the vision by a factor of 10 (or 100 or even 1,000)', which is quite startling until you start to think about it. Coming up with a communication strategy that involves sending everybody involved an update email about the design/change initiative every two weeks initially sounds like quite a concrete and satisfactory thing to do, but when you set it against the incredibly high amount of communication that people receive in an organisation, it becomes almost laughably insignificant:

> A great vision can serve a useful purpose even if it is understood by just a few people. But the real power of a vision is unleashed only when most of those involved in an enterprise or activity have a common understanding of its goals and direction. That shared sense of a desirable future can help motivate and coordinate the kinds of actions that create transformations.
>
> Without credible communication, and a lot of it, employees' hearts and minds are never captured.
>
> (Kotter, 1996: 9)

PLANNING AND KEEPING IT ALL ON TRACK

The planning and organising that should emerge from the principles of and approaches to leading course design/transformation described above will start to take you towards the models, methods and good practices of curriculum design and review. Your institution will have policies and guidelines on this, and there are other good books and resources available that will take you into the detail, including another in this series (Butcher, Davies and Highton, 2006).

Aspects of this may inform how you structure and lead the collaborative engagement with colleagues, students and other stakeholders, but it may be wise particularly in the divergent phase not to include too many restraints or limiting factors (for example, set module structures or assessment weightings) and, indeed, you may deliberately encourage people to think beyond them so as to liberate creativity. But with a clear set of objectives and priorities coming out of the convergent phase, it is now time to start translating these across into the formal landscape of curriculum design. Important areas for consideration will include the following:

- The principles of outcomes-based learning and teaching.*
- Level descriptors and benchmark statements.*
- Frameworks for professional accreditation.*
- Constructive alignment and the relationship between aims, intended learning outcomes, teaching and learning activities, and assessment tasks.*
- Educational taxonomies or hierarchies that mainly classify levels of cognitive or intellectual demand (particularly Bloom's taxonomy and subsequent variations thereof).*
- Intended learning outcomes and identifying verbs as the markers of alignment.*
- Dimensions of learning: deep vs. surface; active vs. passive; rote vs. applied; exposition vs. exploration; declarative vs. functioning knowledge.
- The positioning of students in relation to their learning: student-centred, self-directed, student-led, student autonomy, independent learning, peer-supported learning or team-based learning.
- Student motivation: intrinsic, extrinsic, social and competitive, and ideas relating to self-efficacy (Bandura, 1977) and building learner confidence.
- Curriculum shapes: linear, spiral, building blocks, jigsaw, etc.
- Modes and methods of delivery: placement-driven, field-based, face-to-face, distance-based, online, blended, etc.
- Assessment and feedback: what, when, where, who and how.*
- Assessment: validity, reliability, transparency and authenticity.*
- The structure of the academic year – opportunities and constraints.
- Credit frameworks and module configurations and combinations.
- Formats for programme/module specifications and descriptions.
- Teaching methods and skills tables or matrices.
- Curriculum maps: programme or module mapping (sometimes linked to teaching allocation models).
- Policies and requirements for course validation or revalidation.
- Learning spaces and resources.
- Roles and responsibilities (departmental and institutional).
- Course handbook formats and structures.
- Learning plans for individual components or sessions (lesson plans).

- Student regulations and discipline (expectations, conduct, plagiarism and cheating).
- Equality and diversity: access, inclusion, assistance, support, culture and community.

(* Further details on these items are included in Chapter 7.)

This is quite a list already and it could be much longer. Some of the items apply to the wider higher education system and frameworks governing the quality, standard and consistency of educational provision. Some are to do with established theories of student learning, educational design and learner engagement. And others are items that, whilst perhaps common in the sector, will be tailored by your institution based on factors to do with context, mission and culture.

If your course design/transformation process has produced a strong vision and a powerful set of ideas expressed as curriculum design objectives, and if your team has become inspired with a real sense of collective commitment and a drive to make them happen, then you may be in a position to broker with the institution, senior figures and administrative gatekeepers to challenge, bend or even break some of the conventions and received wisdom. Sometimes the perverse logic of rules is that it is easier to enforce them than it is to change them, even when the said rule has become the root of poor decisions or injustice. This is seen from the world stage right through to petty office politics. As regards brokering, it could, indeed, be said that by some definitions, the process of leading course design described so far has been one of brokerage:

> Brokerage is an intentional act in which the broker seeks to work in collaborative and creative ways with people, ideas, knowledge and resources to develop or change something. The professional actions typically include:
>
> - Envisioning the change(s) to be made;
> - Creating the conditions to enable change to be made;
> - Engaging people/organizations in debate/consultation/negotiation to help shape the nature of the change and facilitate the process of change;
> - Creating the infrastructures and processes to facilitate development and support change;
> - Facilitating the development, diffusion and use of knowledge for change;
> - Behaving honestly and ethically.
>
> (Jackson, 2003: 5)

The above list includes formats for programme/module specifications and descriptions. Institutions will have a format that they require programme leaders and design teams to use based on good practice in the sector, national guide-lines and frameworks, and this requirement will be a point of review through validation/revalidation processes. The programme/module description can be regarded as a piece of leadership in itself, as it gives definition to the course, the curriculum and the educational experience. It frames not only goals and objectives but also expectations in terms of the character of learning and the purpose of study. It should therefore be far more than a list of content. It should from the outset capture a sense of purposeful alignment in terms of the learning to be achieved and how that learning will be represented in terms of what the student will be able to do, say and think at the end of the programme of study (what they will be able to do and say, the cognitive, practical and professional levels they will be able to demonstrate, and how they will be able to interpret, understand and interact with the world). 'Work from both ends in' is the single best piece of advice for anyone involved in the challenge of course definition and design. The two ends are firstly the intended learning outcomes for the course or module, and secondly the opportunities students will be provided with, or able to negotiate, to demonstrate how and to what degree they have achieved both the intended outcomes and other 'unintended but desirable' (Biggs and Tang, 2007) outcomes. These opportunities we generally refer to as assessment or assessment tasks. Only once having given considerable thought to the two ends, intended outcomes and how the outcomes will be assessed, should you then start to consider what learning and teaching activities will help the students individually and collectively to engage with the subject material and achieve the required outcomes. It is this process of active engagement and purposeful achievement that lies at the heart of course definition and design. Whilst such documents need to be clear, accurate and precise in their overall nature, and follow the format prescribed, it is worth considering how to bring some life and spirit into the language to give it energy and make it appealing for a wide readership, including students. As an example, consider the following two lecture titles and see which most appeals to you:

- Bentham and Kant: the key differences between consequentialist moral reasoning and categorical moral reasoning.
- What's the right thing to do? The moral side of murder.

The second is the actual title of one of Michael Sandel's lectures on the Justice course at Harvard University (Sandel, 2005). The lecture is inspirational in all sorts of ways, and so is its title!

Another aspect of planning relates to project management and developing and articulating an implementation plan. However good the vision, it is worthless if we do not have the practical management skills to turn the vision into reality. One way of looking at this is that creating the vision and communicating it in an inspiring way is about leadership, but the execution of tasks and activities to bring the change about involves the core functions of management (to plan, organise, monitor, control and evaluate: P-O-M-C-E). This is a good example of the modern manager having to be both a leader and a manager. Your implementation plan, or transition plan, should take you from the present situation to the one you want to achieve in the future.

Depending on the scale of your change initiative, producing a simple logic diagram and overlaying it with some estimated timings may be sufficient to give you a workable plan. However, it is often useful to take your planning a stage further by scheduling the activities on a bar chart (or Gantt chart after Henry Gantt) to show clearly timings and the relationships between activities. Computer-based packages of varying levels of complexity and cost are available to facilitate this, and some of them possess a much wider range of project management functionality. Even using these, it often works well to go through the more fluid process of drawing up a rough logic diagram before attempting a more detailed plan. It is also useful to put together a grid linking activities with time and resources (an ART (activity, resource, time) grid – see Table 6.2 below) and then looking to see where activities can be combined, at least to some degree, to create efficiencies.

The fundamental planning skills of goal setting, activity grids, timelines, sequencing, scheduling, milestones, resource allocation, assigning roles, forwards and backwards planning, critical paths and so on, appropriately applied, will help you and others to organise and manage the implementation of the new course design. They can also be a powerful tool for communication. I well remember an occasion on which the support for a project I was leading was, let us say, lukewarm, but when I circulated a well written-up and reasonably detailed plan, it seemed to have the effect of crystallising the idea in people's minds. It also provided a more solid basis for engaging key decision makers.

'Life is what happens while you are busy making other plans' is a wonderful quote (and wonderfully true) attributed to John Lennon. And precisely for this reason, the skill of management is as much about keeping a plan on track as it

TABLE 6.2 ART grid

Activity (or group of activities)	Resources	Time
A single activity or a series of linked activities	People	Expected duration
	Numbers and capacity Who exactly?	Informed estimate of how long this activity is likely to take
	Information, policies and processes	Risks and contingency
	Equipment and materials	Note any particular risks that could influence the time
	Financial	Must start by
		Must end by

is coming up with the plan in the first place. If we go right back to the model of management functions we looked at in the framework for management in Chapter 3, we have so far mainly covered the planning and organising functions ('P' and 'O'). It is now time to turn our attention to monitoring and control ('M' and 'C'). A point well worth making here is the importance of feedback within the systematic approach to programme management. Static, inflexible plans are usually hopelessly constraining, and it is actually the process of feeding back revisions, enhancements, and even the impact of apparent setbacks and enforced changes that leads to an enriched plan as it is transformed into action. That being so, we need to ensure our management is conscious and considered rather than a mishmash of haphazard changes.

This is where the idea of feedback loops can take on significance (see Figure 6.7 below). For example, a particular professor may be firmly written into your module plan as making a key contribution – maybe she has done so for the past several years and as a result that contribution has grown in size and apparent importance. A quite unexpected, quite unforeseen ten-minute phone call delivers the bad news – let's say the professor concerned is taking on a major new commitment at another institution and is no longer available. Rather than a knee-jerk response to patch things up and keep things on track, typically twisting the arms of one or more hard-pressed and perhaps less well-qualified colleagues to take on the commitments, a feedback loop would encourage you to review and re-appraise this element of the plan, going right back to the underpinning objectives. The result of this might be as follows:

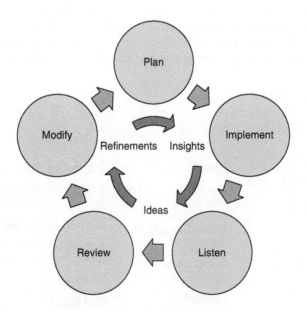

FIGURE 6.7 Example of a continuous feedback loop

- A fundamental shift in the emphasis given to this element of the module, reflecting perhaps a new realisation that the high emphasis given to it hitherto was not fully in line with the modules learning outcomes.
- A review and updating of the material covered.
- A critical revision in the approach to learning, possibly providing greater student choice and self-direction – who knows . . .

The point is that there should be feedback loops running all the way through the planning and implementation process, as a vibrant and fully engaged approach works to keep the programme alive for all concerned with a combined sense of continuous improvement and conscientious delivery.

Beware of underestimating planning or regarding it as something pedestrian or mundane. 'A well-planned and executed module' may sound like something of a stale compliment, but it is actually the greatest compliment of all in this regard. It is also a rare compliment, partly because not all modules are well planned, but more importantly because great planning nearly always enables other fantastic qualities to emerge that quite rightly steal the limelight. For example, a module review may highlight the tremendous levels of student engagement that were achieved or the self-directed nature of the learning that took place, but will overlook commenting upon the excellent planning and organisation, and the key decision making that fundamentally enabled this. So, a department or institution that does not make efforts to recognise and reward good teaching planning and management is neglecting the foundations of its achievements.

QUESTIONS FOR ACTION AND REFLECTION

1 What do you see as your strongest collaborative qualities?

2 What are currently the most significant drivers for change impacting on your module/course/suite of programmes and what challenges and opportunities do they present?

3 How would you describe or characterise the educational philosophy of your course or module?

4 Who are the people most routinely involved in considering questions of course design or change in your area? Who is not generally involved that could/should have a significant contribution to make (include students in your considerations)?

5 How would you describe or define 'innovation' in relation to the ambitions you and others have for your module/course/suite of programmes?

6 What is the nature of the relationship with students on your course (for example, how is their voice heard?) and how would you like this to be transformed?

1

7   Identify three open questions that you feel would stimulate members of your programme team to think differently about issues like the purpose of your course, the impact of your course, the engagement of students and the quality of the learning experience.

8   With regard to your module/course/suite of programmes, if you could change anything in terms of course design, what would it be?

Chapter 7

Leading assessment and feedback

THE CHALLENGE IN THIS CHAPTER

Beginning with thoughts about the balance between 'giving' and 'receiving' as regards assessment and feedback, and the inequalities that may exist between 'giver' and 'receiver', this chapter will explore the leadership challenge of influencing colleagues to make feedback in particular more valuable and transformative.

It is all too easy for assessment to become reduced to a game of templates and targets in which the focus is on the assessment of learning rather than *assessment for learning*. Too much of an emphasis can result on the skills of the organiser: who does what, where and most crucially when, as we strive to cross the administrative finishing line. These aspects matter, of course, as timeliness, quality and consistency are important, but the danger is that we lose sight of purpose.

Developing a shared understanding of the purpose of feedback and creating space for colleagues to collaboratively engage with this question can help transform assessment from being an isolated and 'isolating' activity to a collective undertaking with real energy and direction. This is a great example of enabling leadership.

The spotlight on feedback is strong in higher education and this is an area where student expectations are high and voices can be critical. It is important, therefore, to establish a conversation with students about assessment and feedback, to understand their needs and to reposition feedback as a dialogue that has the intention to influence, if not inspire, the future direction of their learning. In this way feedback can start to be seen as something transformational rather than transactional. The intention is to 'feedforward'. Within this, the role of self-assessment and peer assessment can be equally significant.

At the heart of this chapter, a list of the types of questions, challenges and provocations that could be used to engage a group in a deeper consideration of the purpose and nature of feedback (and its impact) is provided. This suggested question sequence is put forward as an example to provide a flavour of the approach rather than a script to follow. The culture and mindset which surrounds such a conversation is as critical as the precision of the questions explored: the co-creation of ideas requires an appreciative spirit of enquiry.

The chapter goes on to look at types and modes of assessment, and detail is provided on four core aspects of assessment that it is imperative that programme directors and others involved in the leadership of learning and teaching are able to consider, review and act upon. These are:

■ load;
■ level;
■ alignment; and
■ authenticity.

LINKS TO THE PROGRAMME LEADERSHIP MODEL

From the perspective of leadership, it is important to re-balance the perceived emphasis as regards assessment and feedback. Seeing it as primarily an organisational challenge, interacting with a variety of willing, less willing and some reluctant colleagues diminishes what could and should be a significant enabler of student engagement. And if shifting and focusing mindsets through collaborative engagement, appealing to the head and the heart, is the essence of the challenge, then this points more towards the leader as champion and enabler than it does the leader as organiser.

One of the pitfalls, it seems, of leading assessment and feedback is that in the face of difficulties, we are inclined to focus on systems rather than people. It is seen as chiefly a goal-focused undertaking and we look to improve quality and consistency mainly by enhancing the systems designed to support the process. As a result, our institutions are replete with templates, proformas and schedules which many people are reluctant to use or follow. This is not to diminish good management and sound management practices, but the roots of real enhancement, as we look to transform assessment and feedback into something that will inform, stimulate and energise student learning, lie in the inspired commitment of a well-engaged team with a real sense of shared purpose.

In Table 7.1 below, the key leadership skills and attributes associated with leading assessment and feedback are highlighted (note: this is purely indicative – none of the leadership skills should be regarded as exclusive or restricted to just one area).

TABLE 7.1 Programme Leadership Model – leading assessment and feedback

Leadership skills

CHAMPION	ORGANISER	ENABLER	MENTOR
Enthuse	Plan	Encourage	Listen
Promote	Organise	Shield	Invest
Model	Monitor	Support	Praise
Challenge	Control	Share/Convene	Review
Negotiate	Evaluate	Mediate	Relate

GIVING AND RECEIVING – WHAT IS THE BALANCE?

Assessment takes up so much time and the students never appreciate it.

The above is not a direct quote, although it easily could be. Rather, it is a distillation of the sentiments of frustration expressed by many academics in many contexts. But where does the flaw lie – in the giving or in the receiving? The appreciation of human effort implies something mutual between the spirit of the craft and the spirit of the enjoyment of the craft. Something created with great care and then experienced by another with equal care is likely to lead to a relationship of appreciation that will be satisfying to both those involved. Are we in danger sometimes, then, of expecting students to invest more in the spirit of appreciation than we perhaps invest in creating our feedback?

The Russian psychologist Lev Vygotsky (1978) challenges us to consider what really defines human activity and suggests that it is 'for the other' before it is for the self. Relating this to the long-running debate about the relationship between learning and teaching, this suggests that teaching is defined by learning; 'unless learning has taken place, there has been no teaching' would be one way of expressing this, which is not to say that learning cannot exist independently. This aspect of social development theory reinforces the notion that it is the appreciation, use and application of something by another that gives it true definition. So feedback and learning only emerge fully in relation to each other.

Now this may all feel a bit rich, fruity and philosophical, but the expectations placed around assessment and feedback generally are in certain respects unrealistic, unequal and, worst of all, in some cases almost unachievable. Let's look at some of the practicalities:

- There is a status difference of at least an administrative kind between the marker and the marked.
- The student to assessor ratio is often many-to-some or even many-to-one.
- Time invested in the student performance is nearly always considerably more than time invested in the assessor performance.

- We generally assume a novice to expert relationship, and there is an unwritten assumption that this will somehow mitigate the two points above.
- The over-riding assumption is that students have been prepared for the assessment (or given every reasonable opportunity to prepare themselves); assessors may be expected to be prepared to assess simply by virtue of who they are and, to varying degrees, their credentials.
- Supportive, nurturing structures (human and otherwise) should surround the student performance; sometimes (I hesitate to say 'often') only administrative structures surround assessor performance.
- The student performance should be embedded within or flow out of a rich learning experience with which they have been personally engaged; assessors may have been engaged with the learning process, but in some cases may have had no direct connection (although in some respects this objectivity can be seen as a strength).
- Students should be clear about what they are trying to demonstrate and achieve (if not, has the system let them down?); assessors may have very inconsistent notions of what they are trying to achieve.
- Student workload is normally a carefully considered factor in course design, course management and quality assurance; assessor workload is often managed in a haphazard way based in some cases on no more than proximity to the subject and availability.
- The consequences of outcomes may be seen as potentially life-changing by students; assessors may or may not relate to the importance of the outcomes to students, but within their own frame of reference, the assessment activity may rank some way below other priorities.

It is interesting and provocative to compare what a student invests in producing a piece of work with what an assessor may or may not invest in assessing that piece of work, and there are wide variations which make it a little controversial to generalise – for example, direct observation and immediate oral feedback (say a student doctor taking a patient history) suggests a more equal level of investment by student and assessor and a more authentic experience. But a marker with a pile of scripts or assignment reports and a relatively short amount of time surrounded by other academic and administrative priorities is a reality to which many can relate.

There is also sometimes the issue of students valuing and using the feedback they receive. The inequality here, perhaps, can switch the other way. The assessor invests conscientiously in detailed feedback intended as a constructive basis for ongoing learning and future performance, but the student only looks for and sees those points that justify the mark, or that appear to diverge from it more problematically. Whilst this is by no means just a recent phenomenon, some would point to this as evidence of a more consumerist relationship between students and institutions.

THE LEADERSHIP CHALLENGE IN RELATION TO ASSESSMENT AND FEEDBACK

If we begin from the premise that leadership is influence, then leading assessment is a considerable challenge. At the institutional level, influencing the organisation to create frameworks for assessment to maintain quality, ensure consistency and encourage good practice, whilst adhering to external standards and codes of practice, is a major strategic undertaking. However, as a strategic endeavour and a badge of institutional credibility, this sort of process may be strongly championed by senior figures. By contrast, at the course or module level, influencing colleagues to contribute to assessment as a shared endeavour with a common sense of purpose and a commitment to standards will require a leader with energy and tenacity, whilst quite possibly receiving very little structural support.

Relating assessment to the Programme Leadership Model, it is easy to see leading assessment and feedback as primarily a goal-focused undertaking. The functional skills of the organiser are paramount from an administrative perspective as considering workloads, scheduling activities and fretting over deadlines are probably a daily reality for most module and programme leaders. But where assessment is enhanced, the roots of transformation are often found in a range of enabling behaviours. Bringing people together, creating space for collaborative engagement and moving assessment from being an isolated 'I did it at the weekend' activity to a collective undertaking with shared energy and purpose is a great example of enabling leadership. I distinctly remember a workshop participant frustrated at the standard and consistency of assessment feedback on her programme saying 'I put together a feedback template carefully linked to the criteria but hardly anyone will use it'. This was probably an example of where instead of enabling, the programme leader decided to do even more organising, and institutions are replete with templates and proformas devised in well-intended isolation and then either neglected or completed in a perfunctory way by colleagues.

Assessment is an area where sometimes the distinction between management and leadership can come across quite profoundly. Targets can take over from purpose as we push to cross the administrative finishing line. There is the big question of who does what, when and where when it comes to assessment, and those who are tempted to retreat to the safe ground of management will quickly find themselves putting together spreadsheets or, if they have the clout, workload allocation models. The different tribes and territories of academic disciplines (Becher and Trowler, 2001) can sometimes reveal their predispositions here, and I remember a significant variation between two faculties in one institution where for one, the allocation of assessment had been reduced (or elevated) to virtually a statistical model, whilst in the other, it seemed to be a 'black art' combining tradition and patronage. Was one more successful than the other? Hard to say, looking back, but whilst the objectivity of a system can seem appealing, it does not necessarily render a higher degree of efficiency,

151

productivity, or certainly quality than the more arbitrary use of relationships, customs (for want of a better word) and, crucially, willing engagement.

When discussing this area with groups, there is one question that throws the spotlight firmly back on to leadership:

- Does your team have a shared understanding of the purpose of feedback?

Two other questions that accompany this are as follows:

- Do individuals see themselves as part of an assessment team?
- Have they received training in assessment and feedback?

The initial response to the first question is often interest and curiosity; the other two questions tend to elicit discomfort.

Perhaps this is moving us towards the essence of leadership in relation to assessment. On the one hand, the 'organiser' role, leading the task, may focus on getting people to contribute, and who does what, when and where; on the other hand, the enabler will look to bring people together to develop collaboratively a shared sense of purpose. And if assessment is truly going to be 'for learning' (or for future learning: Black, 2006) rather than 'of learning' (justifying the mark and so forth), then this shared purpose is crucial. The feedback becomes intentional rather than procedural.

As we have discussed before, leadership is about interest and energy – energy that flows from the connection of people with task or purpose in a way that brings it to life, and that is often where assessment can falter. It can be lifeless and stale (both in the giving and the receiving), not just as a piece of work, but as something that 'brings to life' and engenders further student learning and discovery. A brilliant distinction that has entered the educational vocabulary regarding assessment is the difference between 'feedback' and 'feedforward' because it is precisely about this issue of energy. Feedback in isolation is an invariably bland and therefore fairly lifeless commentary that 'hopefully' linked to some form of pre-defined criteria attempts to highlight what was good and less good about a piece of work. The focus is on the past and it is left to the student to extrapolate for the future . . . or not. Feedforward includes feedback, the process of review and comment, but projects the emphasis towards the future. So, whilst feedback focuses on past or possibly present performance, depending on the proximity of the assessment to the learning, feedforward looks to the next assignment (Smith, 2010), the next phase of learning or the wider development of the individual (the 'being' aspect of learning). And this brings with it a sense of life and energy, an excitement about learning and potential. It also brings with it a genuine curiosity from the assessor about where the student could take their learning next. It is like two different voices:

- Voice one: a good exploration of the key issues, but lacking critical engagement.

■ Voice two: so far, you are identifying effectively the key issues in the situation. The next stage is to start really questioning what lies behind the outbreak and to propose alternative approaches.

Voice two starts to feedforward (much more could be said, of course, in a full scenario) and is underpinned by the intention to influence, if not inspire, the future direction of the student's learning. There is also a sense of relationship in the way in which the assessment is framed, and relationship is central to student engagement (lecturer, role or relationship? – more on this in Chapter 8). Ideally there should be a dialogue around feedback, whether face-to-face or virtual, that closes the gap between reflection and future action and creates a sense of there being a feedback loop that is sustained or continuous. Taking this idea a step further, the feedback process could itself be regarded as a piece of leadership, inspiring in the student the commitment and energy for future learning.

Voice one, on the other hand, is written in a sort of educational code which some students might decipher usefully, perhaps with the help of a tutor or a more experienced fellow student, but which many others would probably disregard or worse find discouraging: the 'good exploration' is overshadowed by the rather deflating 'lacking critical engagement' (whatever that means). It is also likely that the terminology in the first voice has been chosen to reflect the language in a slimly rendered set of marking criteria, and whilst this 'proportionate language' does reflect one aspect of perceived good practice, it is an example of 'feedback on learning' rather than 'feedback for learning'. This distinction is vital to understanding the role of leadership in assessment.

A voice we have not mentioned yet is the student voice, and in relation to feedback it would be inexcusable not to do so. The National Student Survey (NSS) in the UK in 2008 showed that the majority of students (57 per cent) were not satisfied with the standard of feedback they were receiving. Issues of lateness, ambiguity and negativity were highlighted as commonplace in the sector and, in response, an initiative by the National Union of Students (NUS) called 'The Great NUS Feedback Amnesty' put forward ten compelling principles of good feedback practice:

1 Feedback should be for learning, not just of learning.
2 Feedback should be a continuous process.
3 Feedback should be timely.
4 Feedback should relate to clear criteria.
5 Feedback should be constructive.
6 Feedback should be legible and clear.
7 Feedback should be provided on exams.
8 Feedback should include self-assessment and peer-to-peer feedback.
9 Feedback should be accessible to all students.
10 Feedback should be flexible and suited to students' needs.

On its own, this would be a brilliant list for stimulating engagement with a group of colleagues on what to assess and how to assess, and when combined with other questions about the purpose of assessment, the specific disciplinary and professional considerations arising on a programme and the vision for students in terms of their wider development and employability, the discussion could potentially become very rich indeed. This would be a good example of using the student voice to generate energy and engagement in a staff group, and in addition to this, various forms of student survey data specific to either the programme or the institution could also be discussed. The energy we get from considering, including or even being led by the student voice is something that institutions in the UK are now realising in powerful ways, with initiatives flourishing on students as partners (Birmingham City University), students as producers (University of Lincoln) and students as change agents (University of Exeter), to cite just three examples.

Over the decade since the UK NSS was launched in 2004, there was an overall improvement in levels of student satisfaction with assessment and feedback (reaching 72 per cent in both 2013 and 2014), but it nevertheless remains the lowest scoring of the six survey categories. Compared with an overall satisfaction rating of 86 per cent for UK undergraduate courses and 87 per cent for the 'teaching on my course' category, the 72 per cent for assessment and feedback still lags some way behind. The six survey categories are as follows, with the 2014 satisfaction results shown (combining 'strongly agree' and 'mostly agree' responses):

- The teaching on my course   87 per cent
- Assessment and feedback   72 per cent
- Academic support   81 per cent
- Organisation and management   78 per cent
- Learning resources   85 per cent
- Personal development   82 per cent

It should be mentioned that there are some who question whether the NSS is fit for purpose, from various perspectives, and in relation to assessment and feedback, there has been concern that drives to improve turnaround times in particular may have compromised quality and also increased pressure on staff in some instances.

Looking back at the list of ten compelling principles of good feedback practice put forward by the NUS in 2008, it is notable that point eight says that feedback should include self-assessment and peer-to-peer feedback. To enable this, courses need to be open regarding intended learning outcomes, marking criteria and grade descriptors. And this is not just open in terms of written information – that's the easy part – but open in terms of the active and aware dialogue that takes place in and around the learning itself: 'students need to understand assessment criteria in order to spot weaknesses in their own work' (Carless, 2015). A powerful part of 'learning how to learn' (Bateson, 1972), which is a key graduate quality, is being provided with opportunities, structures and support for self-evaluation. As professional and vocational expectations increase on university programmes of all kinds, particularly undergraduate studies, it is of key importance that leaders of learning and teaching strengthen the appreciation in their teams that self-evaluation or self-reflection unlocks new kinds of potential in students:

> Independence, creativity and self-reliance are all facilitated when self-criticism and self-evaluation are basic and evaluation by others is of secondary importance.
>
> (Rogers, 1969: 114)

True enough, our immediate associations with the above may be more linked to postgraduate study and the qualities of independent research, but increasingly we need to think of the whole person and the 'journey of becoming' that is central to developing the graduates of tomorrow. In some rapidly evolving subject areas, knowledge learnt in year one has been overtaken by new knowledge before the end of year three, and this leaves us as educators facing perhaps more starkly than ever before the fact that 'knowing is not enough'. What graduates know (or knew) as a result of their studies is starting to matter less than what they can do, what they can create, the questions they can ask, and the qualities of person and character they possess.

THE PURPOSE OF ASSESSMENT AND FEEDBACK

To build commitment, a phase of collaborative engagement is critical. This is well known from the broader field of change leadership:

> Since change is the primary function of leadership, being able to generate highly energized behaviour is as centrally important here as are direction setting and alignment.
>
> (Kotter, 1990: 61)

> Participatory decision-making is a key facet of effective leadership in higher education . . . together with 'fostering a supportive and collaborative environment'.
>
> (Gentle and Forman, 2014: 3)

There are a variety of levels at which colleagues can engage and these can be captured with the following words:

- Why?
- What?
- How?
- Who?

The pity is that generally we are far more inclined to engage people in 'how and who' than we are 'why and what'. And yet starting with 'why' holds the key to

155

true colleague engagement. As Simon Sinek tells us, it is altogether more inspiring, purposeful and collaborative to give everyone a stake in considering 'why':

> Imagine if every organization started with WHY. Decisions would be simpler. Loyalties would be greater. Trust would be a common currency. If our leaders were diligent about starting with WHY, optimism would reign and innovation would thrive . . . No matter the size of the organization, no matter the industry, no matter the product or the service, if we all take some responsibility to start with WHY and inspire others to do the same, then, together, we can change the world. And that's pretty inspiring.
>
> (Sinek, 2009: 225)

These concluding words from Sinek's bestselling book *Start with Why* could be applied at an institutional level as universities seek to better understand, define, shape and articulate their distinctiveness in a sector facing ever-increasing competitive pressures (from both within the sector and beyond). And likewise individual teaching programmes need to express their 'why' more cogently to attract and retain students, and thrive in a market where, through funding changes and other measures, student choice is being placed 'at the heart of the system'. But it is in relation to staff engagement that in many ways Sinek's 'why' holds the most powerful key, particularly when it comes to rejuvenating something like marking and assessment, an activity which can all too easily be seen as a labour, an imposition or even an unwanted distraction.

For all sorts of reasons, good and bad, it can be difficult to transform an established teaching programme, at whatever level, but the approach to assessment and the ethos surrounding feedback can shift the learning culture in significant ways and transform student engagement. So if you are looking for an entry point for transforming learning and teaching, then focusing on assessment can provide a good return on your leadership investment.

Getting under the skin of the purpose of assessment and feedback (the why) and asking 'what are we trying to achieve?' can be a great way of bringing a programme team together. The transformational aspect is creating attractive goals that can engage both the head and the heart of those involved. We see this in all sorts of contexts: running round a park for several hours on a wet and windy day may make sense to a small number of people because of the rational health benefits of exercise (it appeals to the head), but add a red plastic nose and a cause like childhood leukaemia, and people are inspired to turn out in their thousands (it appeals to the heart). The fundamental difference here is vision – and not a pedestrian vision linked to organisational targets of parochial interests, but a vision that is about making a meaningful difference in the world or reshaping the future. This is central to understanding what really inspires people:

> People change what they do less because they are given *analysis* that shifts their *thinking* than because they are *shown* a truth that influences their *feelings*.
>
> (Kotter and Cohen, 2002: 1)

To facilitate this involves bringing people together in a collaborative space. 'Meeting helps', they say, as a starting point for discussion. Virtual spaces could be used, and if online interactions are an authentic part of the learning experience for students, then it can be good for staff to explore leadership and collaborative behaviours using similar learning technologies, dialogues and exchanges. Whatever the nature of the collaborative space, the process is then about agreeing objectives for the interaction and identifying the questions with which the group will engage. The following is a short list of the types of questions, challenges and provocations you could consider (provided as an example question sequence to give a flavour of the approach rather than a script to follow):

- *What is our vision of students today?* Starting with the widest lens, this question encourages the group to think about outputs and impact as expressed in the student. It is a question clearly with wider significance than just assessment, but that needn't inhibit the group's engagement.
- *What would we like students to do with our assessment feedback?* This is key to debating purpose. If we don't think about how something will be used, we will lack both clarity and conviction regarding its purpose. And although intention can never entirely define use (nor should it), it can breathe life into what might otherwise be left as a fairly abstract activity. A question like this may invite a bit of gap analysis, with colleagues considering, on the one hand, how they see students currently using feedback and, on the other hand, ways in which they feel it could be used more fruitfully. At this point you may wish to include a sample of student comments, for example, from survey feedback or other data, to help frame the discussion around the student voice (more radically, perhaps, you may consider including some student representatives in the discussion).
- *Blockers and enablers?* As a follow-up to the question above, a further discussion could be facilitated around, firstly, what may 'block' students from using the feedback in the ways identified and, secondly, what would 'enable' them to be more likely to make full use of it. Sub-headings could, perhaps, be used to encourage colleagues to think about things like timing, format, language, relationship, environment, motivation, resources, etc.
- *Which aspects of students are we developing well (or supporting them to develop)?* Beginning with an appreciative phase in the discussion is both productive in itself and also helpful in terms of liberating people's thinking for phases that will invite them to reflect critically.
- *Which aspects of students are we developing less well (or not supporting them to develop)?* With reference back to the vision, there may be acknowledgement that as an assessment team, we tend to focus on and emphasise certain aspects of student performance and development much more than others, and exploring the reasons for this could either provide

157

useful affirmation of the practice or insights into ways of re-balance it. Feedback sends messages to students at many levels, and what you give attention to (whether related to pre-defined criteria or not) will have a significant influence on where they direct their learning.

- *What needs to be clear in our feedback? What's currently not as clear as it could be?* Firstly, this should link the group to the assessment criteria and a critical consideration of how well assessment tasks trigger the active verbs which are the markers for alignment in the course design (see Figure 7.1 below). Secondly, the group should discuss how well they are reflecting student achievement in the feedback provided and the degree to which relative levels of performance are expressed and celebrated. Thirdly, and perhaps most importantly, what is the discourse around gaps, improvements, next steps and potential? What will feed forward into their next assignment, what will inspire them to pursue their reading/enquiry in particular directions, and what will help them reflect on themselves and their personal development (or even professional identity)?

- *What flavour of language do we use in our feedback? How could this be developed?* I remember in one assessment team there being quite a debate about whether or not assessors should directly address the student: the difference between 'you have captured well' and 'this piece captures well', for example. Now, some would say that it is the substance of the feedback that matters, and it does. But style and tone matter too, and if your vision is for there to be a dialogue around feedback, then establishing a relationship in the way feedback is shared is a vital starting point.

- *How could we make our feedback even more inspiring/impactful/accessible/developmental/consistent/other?* (Select and insert whichever adjective(s) apply in your situation, of course, but inspiring can be a challenging lens to look through as colleagues may not have considered feedback in this way.) The question sequence should flow through quite logically to this point, and the discussion will hopefully come full circle back to 'vision' and what really matters: the students and their needs. As well as appreciating the strengths and limitations in a piece of work, the feedback should be at least equally about what the student learns next. Some students (we could call them 'deep learners') may be very attuned to discovering this for themselves and have an instinct for identifying their own questions for development, but in a diverse student group, part of the meta-learning may be developing precisely this capability (learning how to learn). Well-composed feedback can be a great way of modelling these skills and, crucially, this developmental mindset. This cannot be done without some life and energy, and a focus on the future within the feedback itself.

- *Are there any efficiencies or improved ways of working we should be considering?* Now this is, perhaps, more in the nature of a managerial question, but that shouldn't preclude it. Assessment generates a high workload for programme teams, and discussing, sharing and comparing effective ways of working can be very valuable. Creating structures may help with efficiency, such as articulating levels within assessment criteria that more readily enable markers to differentiate 'good' from 'very good' or 'outstanding' performance. Precedents and model answers can also be useful to help colleagues align the unique voice they bring to assessment with the assessment narrative in the wider programme team, and this can also assist with issues of consistency. And then there is the wisdom of experience which shares, in ways that can all too easily be regarded as superficial, approaches for remaining fresh, reducing distractions, staying on task and remembering that student 39 is just as important as the student who wrote the first script you read.

The culture which surrounds a meeting like this is in many ways as important as the structure and content. If it can be approached with an appreciative spirit, an openness to co-creation and a growth mindset, then productive and energising outcomes are almost assured. Being appreciative boils down to how we talk about the world, whether we revel in what's bad, oppressive and dysfunctional from our own limited perspective, or whether we choose to celebrate and build upon what's good:

> From a conversation-based perspective, how we talk about the world affects how we see, experience, make sense of and understand the world, and hence the way we act in the world. From this perspective both continuity and change are inherently contained and expressed in patterns of conversation. It's not so much that we talk about the world as we see it, it's more that we see the world as we talk about it. When we change the patterns of talk or conversation, we change the world.
>
> (Lewis, Passmore and Cantore, 2011: 24–5)

The fundamental idea behind a growth mindset (Dweck, 2008) is the notion that who you are is just the starting point for who you can become. Carol Dweck

1. **Embed** the verb – in the intended learning outcome
2. **Activate** the verb – in the teaching and learning activities
3. **Trigger** the verb – in the assessment task(s)

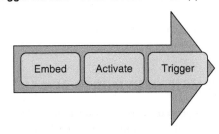

FIGURE 7.1 Verbs are the markers for alignment

highlights key differences between the outcomes generated by a 'fixed mindset' and those of what she terms a 'growth mindset'. It has been shown that when it comes to development, the power of our beliefs can strongly affect both what we desire for ourselves and others, and also whether we/they succeed in achieving those desires. The 'growth mindset' sees things as fluid, not fixed, full of potential rather than full of limitations, and capable of enhancement instead of fashioned by circumstances. Such a mindset is powerful for fully buying into a philosophy like 'feedback for learning' and its impact on students, and it is also liberating for co-creation in discussions of the kind described above about purpose, vision and re-invention.

It is easy to be apprehensive and anticipate that there will be resistance to collaboration, co-creation and shared discussions about purpose and enhancement – and with good reason in an environment that has, perhaps, historically favoured individual autonomy over collaborative working:

> It's really hard to get people to understand why collaboration is so important and that these are higher-order skills they need to acquire. They can acknowledge this intellectually, but every fibre in their body (and their experience, and history) is pointing diametrically in the other direction.
>
> (Garrett and Davies, 2010: 14–15)

But there are signs that this tension is diminishing as the environment around higher education evolves. Technology is transforming the world in terms of both communication and knowledge. A far wider spectrum of society is engaged in adult education and professional development. Globalisation is creating transnational educational programmes and notions of borderless education. Research is becoming increasingly multi-institutional, multi-national and multi-disciplinary. 'Real-world' impact and application has become a prominent feature of academic achievement and recognition. And professional expectations are starting to achieve parity with academic attainment in an ever wider range of disciplines. All of these factors, and others, are rendering collaboration and collaborative skills the higher-order attributes of tomorrow, and so it is well worth encouraging your team in this direction and creating opportunities for co-creation and collaborative engagement. Investing in building a high level of trust and appreciation, and a learning community in which challenge is welcomed rather than feared will produce greater long-term benefits than introducing or revising yet another policy.

In educational environments, policies are sometimes seen as things which *stand between us and our freedom to perform.*

TYPES OF ASSESSMENT AND MODES OF ASSESSMENT

There is a relationship between the type of assessment and the type and quality of feedback. Considering this takes us more into the realm of leading course design, but we should acknowledge here that the more fit for purpose the assessment task, the more we can expect in terms of how feedback is given, received and used – and how great the transformational impact of the feedback will be.

This is a book focused on leadership. There are other books that will admirably explore types of assessment (diagnostic, formative, summative, ipsative, norm-referenced, criterion referenced, etc.), modes of assessment (exams, essays, multiple-choice questions (MCQs), reviews, journals, portfolios, projects, oral presentations, problem-based and team-based challenges, etc.) and methods of assessment (tutor, peer, group, automated online and self-assessment). For our discussion here, however, it is useful to consider the role of leadership in challenging things like the constructive alignment of courses with assessment and the degree to which assessment tasks are tailored to provide opportunities for a diverse range of students to demonstrate their ability, engagement and attainment.

A more humorous classification of assessment that I have used in workshops is to identify that there are essentially two types of student work: those you can put in a pile and those you cannot. It seems in higher education that our preference or predisposition is towards assessments you can put in a pile. This links, of course, to a much wider discussion about what knowledge is and how it can be demonstrated. It also links, perhaps, to what you can put in a briefcase and take home on a Friday evening – although that is undoubtedly far too cynical a portrayal of academic life . . .

So, without getting into the detail of assessment design and practice, there are four aspects that it is imperative that programme directors and others involved in the leadership of learning and teaching are able to consider, review and act upon. These are:

- load;
- level;
- alignment; and
- authenticity.

Load

Put simply, assessment should be a test not a burden. And yet we get very tied up in preoccupations about the amount of assessment on a course. Is it assessment-heavy or is it assessment-light? Are we over-assessing or are we under-assessing? It is sometimes as though our primary consideration is hitting a kind of Goldilocks zone for assessment – the point where it is 'just right'. External examiners are often asked to comment on this by making comparisons with courses elsewhere, and this becomes even more problematic when word counts become the main (or only) comparator. And there can, dare I say, even be an element of institutional benchmarking involved as more 'prestigious' institutions look to have more demanding assessment loads:

The idea that a single external examiner could make a comparative judgment on the national, and indeed international, standard of a programme has always been flawed.

(Higher Education Academy, 2012: 29)

A way for leaders to turn this on its head is to stop thinking about 'the demands of the course' and to think instead about opportunities for students. What are the opportunities for students to demonstrate that they have achieved or exceeded the intended learning outcomes and built for themselves a framework of personal learning to take forward? Do the opportunities enable them to show consistency, proficiency and, if appropriate, originality in a dynamic range of situations (i.e. that they can take their learning and apply it in a variety of unique contexts)? These questions, and others like them, bring a more qualitative dimension to considering the assessment load and help us escape merely quantifying the number of essays, the cumulative word count total and the hours spent in examination halls.

Level

Pitching and differentiating the academic level of assessments is challenging for even the most closely engaged subject specialists. Initial and ongoing programme validation processes will give particular attention to this and will often come up with recommendations to fine-tune programme specifications and approaches to assessment.

For leaders, this is a question of fluency (either your own or that of other people) in the range of frameworks, standards and benchmarks that operate in your higher education system and relate to your institution and your discipline. There are a range of valuable reference points that help course leaders, and those working closely with them, to determine the appropriate level and standard:

■ National or regional qualification frameworks – for example, the Quality Assurance Agency (QAA) in the UK has published a Framework for Higher Education Qualifications (FHEQ) in England Wales and Northern Ireland (2008) that applies to degrees, diplomas, certificates and other academic awards granted by higher education providers in the exercise of their degree-awarding powers. Within the framework, detailed descriptors are given for five generic levels (qualification level descriptors), or academic standards, and these are linked to 'typical' higher education qualifications (the mapping of awards also takes in the three cycles used in the European Higher Education Area (EHEA)).

■ Subject specific standards – for example, Subject Benchmark Statements are used as part of the UK Quality Code for Higher Education to set out expectations about standards of degrees in a range of subject areas. They seek to define what can be expected of a graduate in the subject in terms of what they might know, do and understand at the end of their studies. In the UK this is a key part of setting and maintaining academic standards, and ensuring reasonable levels of consistency and parity across the sector.

- Professional standards linked to accreditation – there are a range of subjects where academic programmes operate on a dual basis. As well as being academic awards, they are also professionally accredited or recognised as 'qualifying' degrees for particular professions. Examples in the UK would include medicine, law, nursing and midwifery, engineering, surveying, journalism, accountancy . . . and the list is growing. In some cases, such as law, regulatory bodies provide recognition that links with an essential requirement to practice; in others, the association is looser and is more about professional standing and competence. It can sometimes be challenging when programme teams are looking to refresh a course and innovate that within their thinking, one eye at least has to remain focused on the professional accreditation or qualifying requirements.

- International standards – a feature and challenge of transnational education is the issue of course validation and the operation of potentially several sets of national standards, and this is in addition to the other challenges of culture, learning traditions and stakeholder expectations. A word that is seen a lot in the literature relating to this is 'harmonising'. Even within Europe, or the EHEA, efforts towards the harmonisation of academic degree standards and quality assurance standards have been slow. And so whilst there are calls for more to be done on international quality standards, and organisations like the QAA in the UK are looking to take a leading role in such developments, the onus remains on institutions and even programme teams to ensure that 'the standards of any of their awards involving learning opportunities delivered by others are equivalent to the standards set for other awards that they confer at the same level' (Quality Assurance Agency, 2012b). This can, of course, present a major challenge to international partnering, particularly getting the balance right between maintaining the spirit of partnership whilst also attending closely to issues of monitoring and control around standards.

- Institutional standards – all of the above will (or should) feed into the institution's own quality assurance policies and codes of practice of various kinds. These tend to come in hard and soft versions, with some having the weight of regulations and others in expanded form being more in the nature of user guides with examples, precedents and guidelines to follow. These have great value, particularly if they have visibility (in other words, people know they exist and where to find them) and there is staff development in place to support and encourage their application in practice. Additionally, there is the institutional knowledge that resides in people. This institutional memory, or programme heritage, is often carried by key individuals, without necessarily much formal recognition. They know, for example, what went before, why certain decisions were made, what worked well with different groups of students, the contributions made by colleagues no longer at the institution and how one programme relates to another in important ways. They instinctively know that 'at this level' in this subject, certain things seem to work well, and that the key difference between a certain module at Stage 1 and another at Stage 3 is 'X', and that this relates to how a specific set of outcomes are achieved. These individuals should be cherished by leaders, for without this institutional memory, our thinking and decision making will often lack true context. Linked to this, two further considerations for leaders are firstly knowing when to challenge the 'received wisdom' and secondly, where it is valuable, how to capture and preserve it for the future.

Alignment

Curriculum alignment or constructive alignment is a significant concept fundamental to both course design and management, and for programme leaders it is an absolutely key principle to hold in mind for many aspects of their role, but particularly, perhaps, leading assessment. Linked to the wider idea of outcomes-based education, coherence, integrity and structural consistency are qualities that flow from constructive alignment, and the model also draws strongly on constructivist theory and notions of student-centredness:

> It is 'constructive' because it is based on the constructivist theory that learners use their own activity to construct their knowledge or other outcome. It extends in a practical way Shuell's statement that 'what the student does is actually more important in determining what is learned than what the teacher does' (1986: 429). The intended outcomes specify the activity that students should engage if they are to achieve the intended outcome as well as the content the activity refers to, the teacher's task being to set up a learning environment that encourages the student to perform those learning activities, and then assess the outcomes to see that they match those intended.
>
> (Biggs and Tang, 2007: 52)

Referring back to Figure 7.1 above, the alignment flows from an intended learning outcome (ILO) into a teaching and learning activity (TLA) and finally into an assessment task (AT). And verbs which express the learning activity are the markers for alignment that run throughout. The verb is embedded in the ILO, activated in the TLA and triggered in the AT. John Biggs, who put forward the model of constructive alignment in 1999, uses learning to drive a car (car driving is the verb) as his example. Figure 7.2 below takes this up, but adds an aim to the start of the alignment process.

As verbs are so critical to constructive alignment (they express the learning activity), it is critical that the right ones are selected, and to help achieve

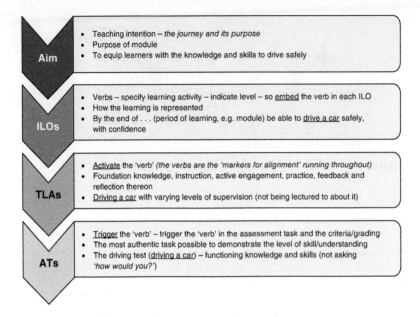

FIGURE 7.2 Constructive alignment

precision in this, various educational taxonomies are used. This links to the section above on academic levels, and in a generic way qualification level descriptors set out to use verbs and language to express what students should be able to do and demonstrate at different academic levels. At the much more specific level of individual programmes and modules, the art is finding the right verb to fit the intended learning outcome. Bloom's Taxonomy of the Cognitive Domain (Bloom, 1956), and other more recent variations thereof (Anderson and Krathwohl, 2001), are used to help achieve the kind of precision needed (see Figure 9.3 below).

To give an even finer grain and closer guidance, various verb lists have been put together that articulate across to the levels of Bloom's Taxonomy, and these should help us as educators escape from lazy verbs like 'understand':

- What do you mean by . . . understand?
- How do you know I . . . understand?
- What should I be able to do with what I . . . understand?
- How has it changed me . . . ?
- And do I really . . . understand?

Other lazy verbs include 'appreciate' and 'demonstrate': what do they mean, what would the student need to do and how would you measure it?

Here are a few examples of more precise verbs that should trigger appropriate learning activities at the various levels of Bloom's Taxonomy:

165

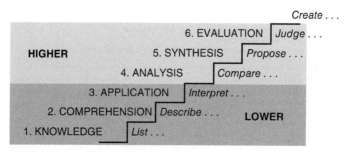

FIGURE 7.3 Bloom's Taxonomy – Cognitive Domain

- Knowledge – name, list, define . . .
- Comprehension – discuss, describe, explain . . .
- Application – interpret, apply, illustrate . . .
- Analysis – compare, debate, contrast . . .
- Synthesis – propose, construct, design . . .
- Evaluation – judge, critique, assess . . .

Looking at constructive alignment overall, assessment is, perhaps, in practice the most critical of the three stages. Why? Because whilst everything flows from the quality and precision of the intended learning outcome (so getting that right is undoubtedly crucial), it is actually at the assessment stage that the alignment can most easily come adrift. How? By simply asking the wrong question. And that creates not just a fault with the curriculum, but also a potential injustice for students. If the intended learning outcome is that by the end of the period of study, students 'should be able to compare the impact of . . . using a range of established methodologies', then the assessment task needs to provide students with an opportunity to demonstrate that they can do so (and also how well they can do so). Getting the question right involves asking them to 'compare' – triggering the verb at the level of analysis. If we ask them to 'list' a range of appropriate methodologies, then the assessment task is too low. If we ask them to 'judge' the most favourable impact and articulate why, then the assessment task is of a higher order than the intended learning outcome. Both would be out of alignment in significant ways.

Programme leaders should resist being cast as the guardians of alignment. Not only would that be unrealistic in terms of personal capacity in most cases, but it would also go against the spirit of collective commitment and mutual accountability. However, in a similar way to exploring the purpose of assessment outlined above through collaborative engagement and discussion, awareness-raising can be done around the theme of alignment. And to bring this to life, it will be important to put across and emphasise that this is not a dull administrative alignment, but rather a dynamic alignment that looks to inspire significant learning across the breadth of the curriculum and beyond. The interplay between intended learning outcomes, the relationship between modules/study years (stages), the integration of contemporary themes, the inquiry-based nature of study, the scope for originality and the 'elbow room' for 'unintended but deliberate outcomes' (Biggs and Tang, 2007: 7) are all factors to sit alongside the virtues of constructive alignment to ensure that it frames good practice, but does not stifle innovation.

Authenticity

The last of the four aspects of assessment design and practice to cover here is authenticity. It is perhaps the simplest and most profound of the four, and concerns how we invite students to demonstrate their learning. The level and alignment of the question may be impeccable, but the method of assessment can fail to give the student an opportunity to show their knowledge in action. The example I used earlier in this chapter concerned a student doctor taking a patient history. What is the assessment and feedback challenge here? Is it to find out if they know the steps involved in taking a patient history? Or is it to find out if they can do it and to feedback on the qualities and attributes they bring to this vital task?:

- On page two of the examination paper, we find a question along the following lines: *Describe the seven steps involved in taking a systematic medical history.*
- A look of relief and contentment spreads across the student's face because they committed this to memory the night before, and the words begin to flow:
  - Step 1 – introduce yourself in a friendly manner if you do not know the person . . .
  - Step 2 – get the chief complaint . . .
  - Step 3 – explore the main problem in more detail . . .
  - Step 4 – gather the past medical history . . .
  - Step 5 – gather a family history . . .
  - And so on . . .

In reality, the health sciences are likely to use what is termed in the UK an objective structured clinical examination (OSCE) for a test of this kind, bringing together clinical skills performance with communication and knowledge of medical procedures. Without going into full detail, this would involve direct observation in a clinical setting (real or simulated).

And that is the principle of authentic assessment. How closely can we move the assessment towards actual performance (functioning knowledge) and away from 'knowing about things' (declarative knowledge)?

There is a link here back to the first aspect we discussed, load, because authentic assessment invites us to create assessment tasks that are multi-faceted. A problem-based assessment, for example, working in a group could bring together knowledge, application, analysis and evaluation as well as professional skills vital to future employability and a range of broader graduate attributes (and be a piece of learning in itself). And would this not be preferable to a piecemeal set of smaller assignments that do not invite students to integrate their learning and construct personal meaning out of the experience? Are we, perhaps, sometimes in danger of allowing custom and perceived administrative convenience (student work you can put in a pile) to inhibit us from designing assessments that provide the best and most authentic experiences for students?

Large-scale curriculum reviews can be impressive and result in all sorts of changes to where teaching happens, when teaching happens, levels of student involvement and empowerment, the use of technology, the integration of research and so forth. But sometimes when you then turn the page and look at the assessment strategy, it is once again all timed exams and essay assignments. Because of the leading influence of assessment on both the character and nature of student learning (an extremely well-documented relationship), the truth is that if you haven't innovated assessment, then you haven't innovated your programme.

QUESTIONS FOR ACTION AND REFLECTION

1   What is currently the strongest aspect of assessment and feedback on your module/course/suite of programmes? And how do you know it is strong?
2   Which aspect of assessment and feedback on your module/course/suite of programmes is most in need of improvement? And how do you know it needs improvement?
3   What do you regard as the purpose of feedback on your module/course/suite of programmes?
4   How could you strengthen the sense of shared purpose regarding assessment and feedback in your team? What open questions would help to stimulate your team to consider this?
5   How could you engage students in improving or refining the approach to assessment on your module/course/suite of programmes?
6   What do students value most in terms of feedback?
7   How well aligned are your assessment tasks with your intended learning outcomes? And how could this be improved?
8   How satisfying and satisfactory are the opportunities for formative assessment on your module/course/suite of programmes?
9   What is the most 'authentic' example of assessment on your module/course/suite of programmes? What changes could be made to make other assessment activities more authentic?
10 With regard to assessment and feedback on your module/course/suite of programmes, if you could change anything, what would it be?

Chapter 8

Leading course delivery

The real role of leadership in education – and I think it's true at the national level, the state level, at the school level – is not and should not be command and control. The real role of leadership is climate control, creating a climate of possibility. And if you do that, people will rise to it and achieve things that you completely did not anticipate and couldn't have expected.

(Robinson, 2013)

THE CHALLENGE IN THIS CHAPTER

What do we mean by delivery? This is the question that begins the first section of this chapter enabling a discussion that leads to the clear acknowledgement that teaching is not a delivery system. Teaching does not deliver learning; at its best, it facilitates learning. At an institutional level, the term 'delivery' may be an apt way of describing broadly what the institution offers, but it is far less appropriate as regards modern conceptions of learning and teaching. A significant element of the leadership challenge is therefore to shift colleagues' notion of 'delivery' away from the transmission of content and towards facilitating learning. And this brings forward an important recognition of the shared ground that learning and leadership inhabit – they are both unmistakably about liberating potential.

The central challenge in this chapter concerns the difference between compliance and participation. *Shall I tell them what to do, show them what to do or leave them to it?* Leadership in this sense, just like the facilitation of learning, is a balancing act, a combination of styles involving more or less direction from the leader/facilitator and higher and lower levels of active engagement from followers/ learners. A range of leadership theories are discussed that focus on the issue of follower participation, balancing freedom and control, autonomy with hierarchy and direction with empowerment. Another way of considering participation is to

explore what leadership qualities/attributes inspire and encourage willing participation: what are the practices of exemplary leadership?

We will discuss liberating leadership as an approach (really a set of
approaches) to facilitating empowerment and, in the context of leading course
delivery, what this means for both supporting a change team and empowering
teachers to make their own decisions in response to student needs. A disconnect
between the two (leading the team and leading individuals) can cause change initiatives to unravel, which is why leading course delivery should involve a strong
commitment to supporting and mentoring individuals.

The second half of this chapter is focused on leadership modelling – how
leaders model values and behaviour. This is the basis of true influence, or deep
influence, and is ultimately the main reason why followers follow. The leader of
teaching delivery has the opportunity to model critical values and behaviours at
three levels:

- *Level one – leadership and learning* (the enabler).
- *Level two – explicit learning values* (the champion).
- *Level three – modelling the pedagogy* (the teacher).

Based on this, we go on to explore some broad examples of what leadership
modelling might involve (areas concerned, and what it might look, sound and feel
like), firstly at the team level and secondly in greater detail when working with or
alongside individuals: ten points on each.

As is the case throughout this book, the emphasis is on leadership, not management. This chapter will not itemise or explore the specific management
actions and responsibilities involved in leading course delivery. It will not go
into the mechanics of things like teaching allocation, timetabling, securing
resources, room availability and reading lists. These things are important, and
teaching programme leaders have a responsibility to know what needs to be
done, when, where and who to work with. Within individual institutional contexts, there should be training and guidance available on these responsibilities
and when roles are transferred between course/module leaders, there should,
ideally, be handover periods to ensure that knowledge and insights are shared
and that there is continuity. Relying on policies and guidelines alone, particularly a proliferation of poorly structured and linked webpages or manuals with
sometimes devastating levels of complexity, is not enough. Training, mentoring
and support should be seen as a critical part of inducting and developing new
course and module leaders.

A great piece of advice for curriculum review or development is to *work
from both ends in*. In Chapter 6 we looked at leading course design and then
in Chapter 7 we explored leading assessment and feedback. Now, we will work

from both ends in and will discuss leading course delivery. The idea of 'working from both ends in' is linked to constructive alignment (Biggs and Tang, 2007) – *if these are the intended learning outcomes (ILOs) and those are the assessment tasks, then what learning and teaching activities will we need to put in the middle to activate the ILOs and provide students with the best possible opportunities for discovering and demonstrating their learning?*

LINKS TO THE PROGRAMME LEADERSHIP MODEL

The challenge of leading course delivery is to align task, team and individual. This therefore calls for a wide spectrum of the skills in the Programme Leadership Model. From a managerial perspective, it picks up from the implementation planning that was part of course design/redesign and brings in the skills of the organiser, particularly the ability to organise, monitor and control. But the main themes in terms of leadership are participation and empowerment. The 'delivery' of the course is done through the programme team and the individuals within that team, and so the role of the course leader is to influence participation and facilitate empowerment. Creating a 'climate of possibility' (Robinson, 2013) where people move away from delivering the content of the course and start seeing teaching as a creative process that supports students to construct their own learning, that is the line of development for leading course delivery. It is a courageous line and will rarely, if ever, be the path of least resistance. For both leaders and teachers, the line of least resistance invariably involves *retreating to the safe ground of instruction.*

The enabling skills of encouraging, supporting and sharing are central, particularly to leading the team, but it is the leadership of individuals that is particularly important to course delivery as it develops competence, increases confidence and inspires commitment. The leadership attribute of the mentor is therefore particularly significant here, as are the skills of listening, investing, praising, reviewing and relating. We will devote a significant portion of this chapter to the challenge of leading and supporting individuals, and the skills of the mentor. And by investing as a leader in the development of a range of key individuals, you can reach a tipping point in terms of the strength of performance, and collective commitment, of the team overall.

And finally there is also a role for the champion attribute in leading course delivery linked to explicitly modelling learning values. This may be done in a quiet way, modelling the pedagogical approach to which the group is committed in their own teaching practice, but on other occasions they may need to expressly state and directly model values and behaviours that they believe with conviction encapsulate the way the programme needs to be or become.

In Table 8.1 below the key leadership skills and attributes associated with leading course delivery are highlighted (note: this is purely indicative – none of the leadership skills should be regarded as exclusive or restricted to just one area).

TABLE 8.1 Programme Leadership Model – leading course delivery

Leadership skills

CHAMPION	ORGANISER	ENABLER	MENTOR
Enthuse	Plan	Encourage	Listen
Promote	Organise	Shield	Invest
Model	Monitor	Support	Praise
Challenge	Control	Share/Convene	Review
Negotiate	Evaluate	Mediate	Relate

WHAT DO WE MEAN BY DELIVERY?

In typical academic fashion, the first thing we are going to do here is have a problem with the terminology. And that's not a bad thing because, firstly, terms matter and precision is helpful and, secondly, it provides an opportunity to question and clarify the notion of 'delivery'. It is not unusual to talk about course delivery or delivering a course in the world of education and training. Other similar terms might include running, convening, giving or providing. The word 'convene' stands out in this list because whilst it feels a little old fashioned, it literally means to come together or to bring together. This feels rather more inclusive in its nature than the directive qualities of giving, providing or delivering. So, the distinction we need to make is between the contractual sense of delivery, as in delivering a service, and our understanding of where learning resides. A university runs, provides and delivers courses, and it has ways of specifying them, expressing them, offering them and explaining them to hopefully attract students appropriately. There is then a sense in which the university delivers and the student receives an educational experience, although ideas of student partnership are beginning to reshape the hierarchical relationship that this implies. However, to be on the receiving end of a good education, to use that colloquialism, is still the expectation of many students, their families and supporters, no matter what we may try to say about being equal partners in the learning process.

It remains useful then to be able to talk about delivering a course because that in a very real sense is the undertaking. However, it is less useful to talk about delivering learning. This is where the distinction matters:

> As I began to trust students . . . I changed from being a teacher . . . to being a facilitator of learning.
>
> (Rogers, 1983: 26)

There is an important, long-running debate about the relationship between teaching and learning. It is one of those debates which is as valuable for the discussion it generates as for the answers it provides – and long may that continue. What it most crucially points towards is that teaching does not deliver learning; at its best, it facilitates learning. And so to move away from the didactic associations with teaching, it is, perhaps, better to think of being a facilitator of learning. This learning-oriented conception of teaching shifts us usefully from the transmitter mode, where the focus is on 'delivering' the content of the curriculum: once delivered, like a postman moving on to the next property, it is up to the recipient to make something of it. A student-centred approach moves the focus strongly away from delivering content and towards knowledge as something constructed by the student. The focus of the facilitator is on supporting and improving learning, and crucial to this is firstly making the learning active (learning through doing) and secondly closing the gap in the relationship between teacher and student:

> Content and knowledge occur as a result of student learning, of the student constructing it for him or herself. In this situation, the teacher is a facilitator of this learning, having a responsibility to help students in their 'constructions of knowledge'.
>
> (Light and Cox, 2001: 33)

And with regard to dialogue, engagement and relationship:

> Knowing and communicating are virtually the same and are grounded here within a situation in which the overlap between the premises of the student's 'world' and the teacher's 'world' are extended and as fully shared as possible.
>
> (Light and Cox, 2001: 34)

Why spend time discussing this in a book that's about leadership? Well, here's why. Learning and leadership have something incredibly important in common: they are both about facilitation. As Ken Robinson said in the quote that opened this chapter, the role of the leader is to create 'a climate of possibility' – brilliant words that capture the essence of facilitation. The same could equally be said of teaching. In their book on small group teaching in higher education, Exley and Dennick (2004: 35) also emphasise the importance of climate:

> Facilitators should engender a climate of trust in which curiosity and the intrinsic desire to learn can be nourished and enhanced.

There is a shared ground that learning and leadership inhabit and that is unmistakably about liberating potential: the potential of the programme team to facilitate a rich, challenging and exciting learning experience for students, and the potential of students to discover, flourish and grow.

So, questioning the term 'delivery' has taken us in some important directions. Firstly, it is useful to acknowledge the term at an institutional level as an apt way of describing what the university offers, but it is far less appropriate as regards modern conceptions of learning and teaching. Secondly, a significant element of the leadership challenge will be to shift colleagues' notion of 'delivery' away from the transmission of content and towards facilitating learning. Thirdly, the approach to leadership is also about climate and self-discovery, and the same spectrum of directive to non-directive behaviours exists for leaders as it does for teachers in the classroom. We can choose to tell or we can choose to ask – one may get people to comply, while the other will support them to learn.

Another factor in this is the orientation of the individual student or colleague. The one-way, didactic approach to 'delivering' teaching content will at best work for a small proportion of students who because of their educational background or disposition are able to naturally bring 'an active engagement even to more passive forms of learning' (take a deep approach; Biggs and Tang, 2007). For the wider, more diverse spectrum of students, it is through a well-facilitated, active and aware engagement with 'questions that matter', problems, discussions and challenges that deeper levels of learning and personal discovery will be achieved. The problem is that teaching in higher education has not progressed and adapted at the same rate as the widening levels of participation in our university systems:

> Higher Education provision is moving so quickly, but when it comes to what education looks like and how we assess things, it hasn't changed for centuries . . . We still do the same things that universities did in the Middle Ages.
>
> (Vieru, 2015)

The orientation of colleagues follows a similar pattern. Driven by their own sense of what brings learning to life, a natural curiosity for what inspires students from all backgrounds to engage and develop, and a desire to make learning a collaborative process based on relationship, some colleagues will enthusiastically experiment with learning styles, teaching formats, resources and processes, and will look to innovate. They naturally, as it were, take a deep approach to teaching. These activists in your group will inspire you and inspire each other, and an encouraging but hands-off approach to leadership will probably suit them well. But for others, the safe ground of instruction may feel like an easier and more familiar place to be, not through fault but disposition, and they may consider that other priorities have first call on their energies. The role then for the leader will be to build a climate in which teaching becomes accepted as a creative process of facilitation and not a delivery system:

> Teaching is a creative profession. Teaching, properly conceived, is not a delivery system . . . You're not there just to pass on received information. Great teachers do that, but what great teachers also do is mentor, stimulate, provoke, engage.
>
> (Robinson, 2013)

SHALL I TELL THEM WHAT TO DO, SHOW THEM WHAT TO DO OR LEAVE THEM TO IT?

If a vice-chancellor or a college principal told the faculty at their institution that from now on, lectures must be 'much more inspiring' and seminars must 'fizz with interaction', the chances are that the improvements would be minimal. In fact, there is a high likelihood that it would be counterproductive, because it more than implies a criticism and very few of us like to be told how to do our jobs. Some people would also, no doubt, challenge the assumption, as they might see it, that 'inspiration' and 'interaction' improve learning – they did very well at university *without the need for any of that.*

When it comes to engagement and individual motivation, there is a huge difference between compliance and participation, and in organisations that traditionally value autonomy and independence of thought, participation needs to both touch individuals and create a sense of collective commitment across the community. It is also problematic, to say the least, to command or coerce higher-order attributes like creativity and innovation. A far more fruitful way to approach the same challenge would be for the leader(s) to firstly dedicate attention to developing the best possible environment for these qualities to flourish and be recognised, and secondly to seed the behaviours needed for success through modelling and example.

The same sort of thing can occur at an institutional level when under the banner of strategy, the university starts to use value-based statements to promote its distinctiveness. 'Students are at the heart of everything we do' could be an example of this, and whilst there is absolutely nothing wrong with the philosophy that underpins such a statement, there could be issues in terms of participation. To close the gap between values stated and values seen, it is crucial to have the participation of staff and other stakeholders in crafting such a vision. The danger otherwise is that by imposing a vision of this kind hierarchically, the leadership risks creating a sense of alienation amongst those who will be called upon to fulfil it: alienation from the institution that needs their loyalty and commitment.

Going right back to the work of Kurt Lewin and colleagues in 1939, leadership theories have focused in various ways on the issue of follower participation in decision making. Lewin's original work identified three styles of leadership decision making:

- Autocratic – the leader(s) makes the decisions themselves without consulting or involving followers. In Lewin's experiments, he found that this caused the highest level of discontent.
- Democratic – the leader(s) takes an active role in the decision-making process, but involves and consults others. This can be problematic when there are a wide range of opinions and there is no clear way of reaching an equitable final decision.
- Laissez-faire – the leader(s) has very little involvement in decision making and allows others to make their own decisions. This approach can be

175

empowering when followers are capable and motivated, but may need to be introduced gradually if this has not been the norm in the work environment. It is also a more challenging approach when a high level of central coordination is needed.

With a focus more specifically on facilitation, John Heron reframed these three styles as hierarchical, cooperative and autonomous. These three modes as they are termed operate quite distinctly (1999):

- The hierarchical mode – leading from the front the facilitator directs the learning process, exercising power over it. The facilitator decides on objectives, provides structures, takes charge of decisions, interprets and gives meaning to things that matter, and thinks and acts on behalf of the group.
- The cooperative mode – by sharing power over the learning process, the facilitator looks to enable and guide the group to become more self-directing. The facilitator works with and alongside the group to identity objectives, give meaning to experiences, confront resistance and negotiate outcomes.
- The autonomous mode – leading from behind, the facilitator respects the autonomy of the group and the freedom they have to explore meaning and find their own way, exercising judgements and making decisions. The facilitator delegates responsibility to the group and creates transformative spaces for their interactions. This is not about abdicating accountability, but is rather 'the subtle art of creating conditions within which people can exercise full self-determination in their learning' (Heron, 1999).

Whilst Heron talks about facilitation in relation to learning, it is easy to see the crossover into the leadership of teams and initiatives. The leader is equally a facilitator and the learning engagement involved in transforming processes, approaches and, most crucially, behaviours is powerfully the same:

> What I mean by a facilitator . . . is a person who has the role of empowering participants to learn in an experiential group . . . By an experiential group I mean one in which learning takes place through an active and aware involvement of the whole person.
>
> (Heron, 1999: 1)

Heron's work goes into many layers of elaboration and sophistication. For example, the three modes are linked across with six dimensions of facilitation to create a grid that stimulates facilitators/leaders to consider 18 options. The grid in Table 8.2 below shows this, with some labelling of the planning dimension included.

No behavioural framework such as this can ever pretend to deal in absolutes, but it is nevertheless an excellent construct for both considering and developing

TABLE 8.2 Facilitation – dimensions and modes

	Planning	Meaning	Confronting	Feeling	Structuring	Valuing
Hierarchy	direction					
Cooperation	negotiation					
Autonomy	delegation					

facilitation/leadership styles and behaviours. The dimensions can, of course, interweave and overlap, and the modes can include each other: for example, an approach that is hierarchical overall could include elements of cooperation and autonomy. Facilitation is above all else a balancing act, and so in many ways is leadership.

A model more expressly focused on leadership that echoes again the theme of control and participation is called the Continuum of Leadership Behaviour (Tannenbaum and Schmidt, 1958). This puts forward seven degrees of management authority and team-member freedom that can be nicely captured with seven short words: *tells – sells – tests – consults – involves – joins – empowers* (these were not the words used on the original model, with the exception of 'sells'). To the left of the model (*tells*) is what was originally called boss-centred leadership where essentially 'the manager makes the decision and announces it'; to the right of the model (empowers) is what was originally called subordinate-centred leadership where 'the manager permits the group to make decisions within prescribed limits'. Whilst the language used in this paper may come across as dated, it is interesting to reflect on the similarities and associations with the terms 'teacher-centred' (or 'content-centred') and 'student-centred'. The authors, Robert Tannenbaum and Warren Schmidt, in a retrospective commentary in 1973 acknowledged that 'today's' employees are likely to 'resent being treated as subordinates' and 'expect to be consulted and to exert influence'. They also reflected on the importance of open-system theory and the interdependencies not only within the model, but also within the wider organisation, and the forces at work in the external environment.

Taking the two endpoints and the mid-point from Tannenbaum and Schmidt's model (*tells – consults – empowers*), it is striking to see how this contingency theory of leadership, as it is sometimes classified, mirrors the models of both Lewin and Heron, and reinforces the important relationship between leadership and participation. In Figure 8.1 below the three models are presented together.

The balancing act of facilitation is matched by the flexibility of style for leaders. It is not about one right style, or even about a single right style for how things are today; the truth is that it is actually about versatility, responsiveness, using the styles in a dynamic combination and having the emotional intelligence to navigate both your intrapersonal and interpersonal surroundings. However, just as the safe ground of instruction is a tempting place for teachers to head when the going gets tough, so it is for leaders. So challenge yourself to push towards the non-directive in most situations:

177

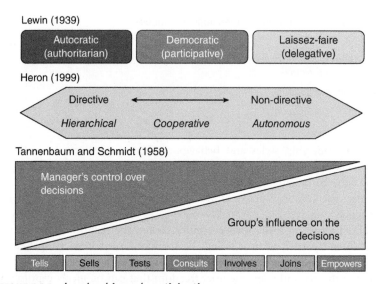

Lewin (1939)

| Autocratic (authoritarian) | Democratic (participative) | Laissez-faire (delegative) |

Heron (1999)

Directive ←——————→ Non-directive

Hierarchical   *Cooperative*   *Autonomous*

Tannenbaum and Schmidt (1958)

Manager's control over decisions

Group's influence on the decisions

| Tells | Sells | Tests | Consults | Involves | Joins | Empowers |

FIGURE 8.1 Leadership and participation

Successful managers of people can be primarily characterised neither as strong leaders nor as permissive ones. Rather, they are people who maintain a high batting average in accurately assessing the forces that determine what their most appropriate behaviour at any given time should be and in actually being able to behave accordingly. Being both insightful and flexible, they are less likely to see the problems of leadership as a dilemma.

(Tannenbaum and Schmidt, 1958: 101)

Kouzes and Posner took a very different approach to exploring participation by basing their extensive research on the idea of *willing participation*. At the heart of their investigations (from 1982 onwards) is the question: 'What do you most look for and admire in a leader, someone whose direction you would willingly follow?' Respondents select from a list of 20 personal traits and characteristics derived from earlier research, and with well over 75,000 contributors from across six continents over more than 20 years, there is a remarkable consistency in the top four:

- honest;
- forward-looking;
- competent;
- inspiring.

Building upon this and a very extensive collection of stories from 'ordinary people' recalling their peak leadership experiences (what leaders do when they are at their personal best), Kouzes and Posner (2002) have gone on to propose five practices of exemplary leadership:

1   *Model the way* – they 'know that if they want to gain commitment and achieve the highest standards, they must be models of the behaviour they expect from others . . . People first follow the person, then the plan'.

2   *Inspire a shared vision* – they 'breathe life into the hopes and dreams of others and enable them to see the exciting possibilities that the future holds . . . Leaders cannot command commitment, only inspire it'.

3   *Challenge the process* – they 'search for opportunities to innovate, grow and improve' and change the status quo, and they 'know well that innovation and change all involve experimentation, risk and failure' (and see these risks as learning opportunities).

4   *Enable others to act* – 'they foster collaboration and build trust . . . They engage all those who must make the project work – and in some way, all who must live with the results'. They 'enable others to act not by hoarding the power they have but by giving it away'. They 'turn their constituents into leaders themselves'.

5   *Encourage the heart* – they 'show appreciation for people's contributions and . . . create a culture of celebration'. They 'know that celebration and rituals, when done with authenticity and from the heart, build a strong sense of collective identity and community spirit that can carry a group through extraordinarily tough times'.

These exemplary practices come to the fore when the 'leadership challenge' (which is also the name of Kouzes and Posner's bestselling book) concerns 'how to make extraordinary things happen in organisations'.

Let us return, then, to the question that headed this section: shall I tell them what to do, show them what to do or leave them to it? Well, yes to all three is no doubt the answer, but try to avoid too much telling, particularly when it concerns higher-order attributes like creativity and innovation, and if you want to create a community with both a shared vision and commitment. Telling is also best avoided in situations where there are hazy power relationships and you may not have the authority to tell: people are likely to be quick to point this out. As we discussed in Chapter 4, in these situations influence based on relationship, vision and behaviour is likely to be more effective and enduring. Part of the problem with the question is that it has succumbed to the poetry of the tricolon and has presented us with a list of three. There could be a fourth option capturing the collaborative qualities that occupy the centre ground in the three models described above (democratic, cooperative and consultative). This might be something like 'work with them to explore and discover what to do', capturing the spirit of collaborative engagement that was the key theme of Chapter 6.

FACILITATING EMPOWERMENT AND LIBERATING LEADERSHIP

Collaborative engagement takes participation in a direction that links the three models described above (Lewin, Heron, and Tannenbaum and Schmidt) with the practices of exemplary leadership put forward by Kouzes and Posner. It starts to provide ideas on facilitating empowerment. This combines high levels of participation, including looking to enable leaders within the group, with modelling, inspiring, encouraging the heart and challenging processes. And it is about both an empowered group and empowered individuals, because facilitating learning transformation in an educational context involves a combination of 'building and supporting a "change team"' and the 'empowerment of teachers to make their own decisions' (Gibbs, Knapper and Piccinin, 2009). A disconnect between the two can cause the change initiative to unravel, which is why leading course delivery will involve a strong commitment to supporting and mentoring individuals. This may often be in large part the role of the programme leader, but through something like a 'team charter' (a statement of values in action – more on this below) and the distribution of leadership, colleagues can find roles in mentoring and supporting each other. The formation of small teaching teams can also help to foster and maintain the sense of empowerment, and avoid the lonely road of the solo lecturer *doing their bit* whilst blinkered to the rest of the curriculum and the overall ethos of the programme.

Facilitating empowerment is linked to ideas of liberating leadership – a form of leadership that focuses on firstly creating the best possible environment, secondly removing the interference (institutional, interpersonal and psychological) that blocks performance and thirdly raising awareness of potential (group and individual). Empowerment itself can be defined as:

> A process in which people achieve the capacity to control decisions affecting their lives. Empowerment enables people to define themselves and to construct their own identities.
>
> (Hamelink, 1994: 132–3)

Liberating leadership is an approach based on various aspects of positive psychology and supporting groups and individuals to start to win what Timothy Gallwey (1975) refers to as the 'inner game'. The inner game looks to remove interference so that potential and performance can flow together, and interference is seen as something that sits as a barrier between the two. The inner game 'is played to overcome all habits of mind which inhibit excellence in performance' (Gallwey, 1975). In a blog piece I wrote for the Leadership Foundation for Higher Education (UK) in July 2013 called 'Winning the Inner Game: Imagine Being the Best You Could Possibly Be!', I identified four fundamental types of interference that block performance and corresponding leadership approaches:

- *Low inspiration* – the opposite of being actively inspired. Active inspiration gives us life, fresh energy, enthusiasm, vigour and positivity. It inspires us in a way that enables us to inspire others! *A liberating leader will look to tune into the things which inspire individuals, teams and even organisations. They will also openly share the things which inspire them.*

In their approach to business planning and achieving change, they will focus heavily on the inspiration that lies behind the initiative. They know that we are inspired by a dream, not a plan and will look to make the 'dream' or vision a clear part of their dialogue around goals and performance.

- *Self-limiting beliefs* – the things we tell ourselves about ourselves, our inner dialogue about what we can and cannot do and, crucially, what we are *good at* and what we are *bad at. Stemming from a steadfast faith in human potential, a liberating leader will work with individuals to raise awareness of self-limiting beliefs and release potential through coaching, great feedback, developing relationships and demonstrating personal commitment.*

- *Deficit relationships* – relationships that are cynical, deflating and uncaring. There is no winner, just a sharing of interference that makes doing challenging work/study more onerous than ever. *A liberating leader will look to set the tone in terms of creating relationships based on empathy, compassion and passion. These relationships are energising, inspiring and fulfilling, and go beyond the difficulties of today. They are based on trust, respect, warmth and a desire to understand the emotional needs of others.*

- *Pain language* – our outer dialogue has a very strong influence over our inner dialogue and can become a source of interference. Pain language like 'I can't . . .', 'I have to . . .' and 'it's never going to happen . . .' feeds through into our thoughts, beliefs and even values. They can create or reinforce self-limiting beliefs. *A liberating leader will aim to lead with a narrative and a way of interacting that is all about power language* (in place of the pain of 'I have to . . .' we have the power of 'I want to . . .', for example). *They will set out to model power language for colleagues in all directions, not just the immediate team, and will develop relationships on this basis.*

Liberating leadership is an approach (and in some senses a belief system) which aims to set potential free by focusing on interference and which uses empathy, compassion and passion to move towards a more fully engaged workplace and learning environment. Whether working with staff, students or both, a liberating leader knows:

- that we are inspired by a dream not a plan;
- the importance of removing interference so that people can thrive; and
- the value of creating organisations that people enjoy.

Releasing potential through liberating leadership applies equally to leading the student experience. It can impact on student motivation, strengthen learning relationships, transform the environment, and give students the confidence to access and use the resources they need. If we want students to be (or become) *the best they can possibly be*, on their own terms, then leadership that empowers is the key to engagement.

181

More recently I have expanded the Liberating Leadership Model to bring in four further keys to sit alongside the interpersonal aspects described above. These four are more strategically focused – they focus on interference as strategic and structural deficiencies – and relate to leading the organisation and connecting people with mission and purpose. Unlike the four above, these do not express the interference, but rather focus on the approach to leadership:

- *Roving line of sight* – a liberating leader develops and reinforces a direct line of sight from the work contribution of the individual and team to the strategic direction of the organisation. As a result, a positive and tangible connection is seen and felt between the team/individual's work and the aspirations and achievements of the organisation as a whole. This leads to individual adoption – *your goals are my goals* – and personal leadership. A 'roving' line of sight is strong and does not become easily obscured as circumstances change, teams evolve and priorities shift. For leading teaching delivery, this is a crucial aspect of engagement because if you can bring together the mission-driven factors (the needs of the organisation) with the student-driven factors (the needs of students), then you will create a powerful sense of coherence and connectedness that will give the programme a mission of its own.

- *Collective commitment* – a liberating leader will use collaborative engagement to build a strong sense of collective commitment around both the process and the outcome(s) of what needs to be achieved and delivered. This ownership and personal investment creates a condition of mutual accountability around not just the mechanics of delivery, but also enhancement themes such as quality, values and innovation. Referring back to Figure 6.1, collective commitment sits between collaborative engagement and mutual accountability, and is the energy that links the two. As Paul Gentle (Gentle and Forman, 2014) powerfully encourages us to realise, the qualities of leadership that inspire collective commitment include participatory decision making, collective learning, enabling others to lead, personal authenticity and high-quality discussions.

- *Self-direction* – the liberating leader knows that fundamentally we are all self-empowered individuals and that the key to rediscovering that power lies in self-direction. As Hamelink teaches us in the quotation at the start of this section, we construct our own identities as we achieve the capacity to control decisions affecting our lives. This is highlighted nowhere more clearly than in the recent work of Daniel Pink (2011) on the *puzzle of motivation* for people working in complex and creative roles. Rejecting 'if/then' reward systems as ineffective and even sometimes counterproductive as regards motivation and performance (such rewards can cause the kind of functional fixedness and blinkered thinking that inhibits creativity), Pink proposes three elements of motivation:

- autonomy – the urge to direct our own lives;
- mastery – the desire to get better and better at something that matters;
- purpose – the yearning to do what we do in the service of something larger than ourselves (this links with the 'roving line of sight' described above).

Ryde and Sofianos (2014) in their discourse on creating authentic organisations focus in further on the central importance of autonomy and freedom and explore three freedoms in the context of bringing meaning and engagement back to work: freedom to operate, freedom to speak and freedom to actualise. And as regards leading teaching delivery and specifically teacher involvement, teachers have been found to be much more likely to adopt a student-focused approach where they 'have scope to make their own decisions about their own teaching practice and also contribute to departmental decisions about the curriculum and about how teaching is undertaken' (Gibbs, Knapper and Piccinin, 2009).

■ *Building trust* – the liberating leader knows that without trust, teams and organisations unravel and come apart: 'trust is the emotional glue that binds followers and leaders together' (Bennis and Nanus, 1985). And this foundation of team development must never be taken as a given. In Patrick Lencioni's model (2002), the absence of trust is the first of five dysfunctions that cumulatively build towards an inattention to collective results. So, leaders need to know that 'trust walks in but rides away' and give it their constant and consistent attention. Because consistency is a big part of it, if leaders continually break or try to rewrite the narratives they create with their teams, they will not only lose commitment, but they will start to alienate people. Consistency is one of the key behaviours for leaders to model if they want to build and maintain a foundation of trust in their teams. And for leaders, consistency involves conviction: showing conviction is easy, maintaining conviction is hard, and holding on to conviction in the face of discouragement, adversity and pain requires courage – sometimes great courage (that is why it sits at the centre of the Programme Leadership Model).

All of the eight keys to liberating leadership apply to the challenge of leading course delivery, both those focused on the interpersonal and those focused on the strategic. If the team can share their inspiration, overcome self-limiting beliefs and support each other's potential through relationships based on listening, empathy and positive reinforcing language, then they will become empowered 'to make extraordinary things happen' (Kouzes and Posner, 2002) as they work together to facilitate student learning. And if you can help facilitate this empowerment by developing with them a clear line of sight from the contribution of the programme to the goals of the organisation, and a mutual foundation of trust reinforced by both personal conviction and collective commitment, then they will become self-directing in their approach to both delivering and enhancing the programme.

183

1. SHARING INSPIRATION Sharing and tuning in	**2. ROVING LINE OF SIGHT** Staying connected – personal leadership	**3. EMPOWERING BELIEFS** Inner game: removing interference
8. BUILDING TRUST Sharing personal stories and listening	**Liberating Leadership**	**4. COLLECTIVE COMMITMENT** Be the change you want to see
7. LIBERATING RELATIONSHIPS Empathy, compassion and passion	**6. SELF-DIRECTION** Autonomy, mastery and purpose	**5. POWER LANGUAGE** A power narrative and the multiplier effect

FIGURE 8.2 Eight keys to liberating leadership

LEADERSHIP MODELLING – VALUES AND BEHAVIOUR

> You must be the change you want to see in the world. [Sometimes shortened to just 'be the change you want to see'.]
>
> (Attributed to Mahatma Gandhi, 1869–1948)

People are far more likely to do what they see than do what they're told. This is evidenced from families to workplaces to international affairs – people are influenced more deeply by the behaviours they see and experience than the fine words leaders say. The upside and downside of leadership is that everything you do sends a message. So, simply put, if you don't do it, why should anyone else? And if your actions aren't congruent with your words, then why should anyone follow what you say? A combination of command and coercion may, perhaps, bring about compliance with the letter of your words, but the spirit will be absent or lacking (and the *shadow* side of the organisation may think and say quite different things).

Modelling key values and behaviours is not about being a role model. It is not an imitation game, and never should be, and amongst the limitations linked to the idea of having role models is the observation that they can quickly become distant, rather passive aspirations. Leadership modelling, by contrast, should be dynamic, in the moment and authentic. Going back to the work of Kouzes and Posner described above, exemplary leaders 'know that if they want to gain commitment and achieve the highest standards, they must be models of the behaviour they expect from others . . . People first follow the person, then the plan' (Kouzes and Posner, 2002). So, leaders *model the way* not in an abstract or distant manner, but in a way that is visible and makes sense to people in the here and now. This is the main part of why followers follow.

Modelling values and behaviours is not the exclusive domain of the leader. In fact, sometimes those labelled 'leader' fail to do so and it is others in the group who naturally take on this role. More proactive leaders may model themselves and also encourage and recognise this in others – an example of leaders being enablers of leaders. And modelling is never mimicry. Followers always mediate behaviours through their own personality based on their background, perspective and prior experience. In turn, what leaders see in followers will influence them back (positively or not) and the process becomes to some extent cyclical: a constant evolutionary process.

Sometimes the challenge of leadership modelling is to break cycles of negative behaviour in teams. On occasions, for example, teaching teams can develop the mindset that students are the problem and have a narrative that in effect blames students for being disengaged, weak, lazy, uncommitted to their studies or even 'a poor batch'. A word of encouragement, though – negativity nearly always looks bigger than it is. There is a magnifier effect that interprets the outwards signs, the behaviours, as being the manifestation of some almost terminal internal issue or dilemma. It looks like a giant, it looks insurmountable, but a 5 per cent change in behaviour can often be transformational. The problem is that in our anxiety to correct things, we often go for 50 per cent instead of 5 per cent. Discussing with a team how we can make a 5 per cent improvement in the way we communicate, for example, feels achievable, brings the issue to attention and is likely to raise awareness and a wide range of ideas people can commit to. Once an approach is decided, the rest is about modelling, reinforcing and recognising. What never works, though, is being negative about the negativity – that amounts to entering the negative cycle yourself and in a sense giving it your endorsement. So, borrowing rather simplistically ideas from cognitive behavioural therapy, the approach is problem-focused and action-oriented. How can we come up with a specific strategy for remodelling behaviour and, through this, challenge thoughts and feelings that may have become ingrained? The same approach to breaking cycles of negative behaviour and thereby influencing both thinking and feeling can be applied at a personal level. If this interests you, try the following: *go 24 hours without complaining (not even once), then watch how your life starts changing!*

The leader of teaching delivery has the opportunity to model critical values and behaviours at three levels:

- *Level one – leadership and learning* (the enabler): by adopting a facilitative style of leadership, they show that they value collaborative engagement, collective learning, participant-centred discussion and activity, and self-direction. They create 'a climate of possibility' (Robinson, 2013) in which the team's potential can flourish. These values and behaviours mirror the qualities that are central to facilitating student-centred learning (see Figure 4.1 – 'Learning-focused teaching and leadership').
- *Level two – explicit learning values* (the champion): they expressly state and directly model values and behaviours they believe with conviction encapsulate the way the programme needs to be or become (and they will also have evidence that informs this conviction, such as student feedback).

185

At the start of a transformation initiative, whether large or small, they may, for example, need to make the case for change and project energy into valuing a particular pedagogical approach or piece of educational framing.

■ *Level three – modelling the pedagogy* (the teacher): they establish trust, credibility and respect by modelling, if not exemplifying, the pedagogical approach to which the group is committed. They 'walk the talk' and bring an infectious energy to so doing. They may also initiate scholarly activity around this, such as pedagogical research and/or disseminating practice to a wider community.

Under the heading of establishing credibility and trust, Gibbs, Knapper and Piccinin (2009) identified the following activities for the departmental leadership of excellent teaching:

■ maintaining credibility as a scholar;
■ establishing credibility as an outstanding teacher;
■ modelling the proposed pedagogy – 'walking the talk';
■ fostering open communication with all stakeholders;
■ listening carefully to all viewpoints;
■ planning and preparing carefully before taking decisions;
■ being available to staff and soliciting their ideas.

These activities span the three levels of leadership modelling described above, but with less emphasis on level two (explicit learning values).

So, where do values come into this? Are they expressed through behaviour or are they different, deeper or distinct? Well, if behaviours are consistent, congruent with each other and across situations, and if they flow from the individual without apparent force or interference, then there is a good chance they are the expression of something more deeply held. Values, explicitly or unconsciously, are things we live by, and if we have free will and confidence, they will flow through us into the things that we do. 'Doing' and 'being' will flow together, to return to the Fully Engaged Curriculum explored in Chapter 6:

> When you do things from the soul, you feel a river moving in you, a joy.
> (Rumi – Jalāl ad-Dīn Muḥammad Rūmī,
> 1207–73)

When teaching becomes a flow of expression and joy not just about the content or the love of the subject, although that is important and infectious, but about the process of supporting learning and discovery, the environment itself becomes energised and empowered. Going back again to Chapter 6, this is where an educational philosophy takes off as it is embodied by the leader and the teaching team and becomes part of the relationship with students:

The power and purpose of a personal philosophy statement lies not in its eloquence or its fit with some current discourse of teaching, but in its ability to reveal what is hidden, yet essential, to understanding someone's teaching.

(Pratt, 2005: 35)

If a leader can model at this level, showing consistent behaviours that are powered by values that are central to the vision to which we are collectively committed, then this should provide a strong inspiration to followers:

If you embody the ideals of your vision, not for show but because those ideals are a real part of you, collaborators perceive you as trustworthy . . . They know that you believe, practice, and live the ideals you are asking them to champion.

If you don't stand for what you want others to seek, they will not stand for you.

(Burchard, 2009: 108)

TEAM-LEVEL LEADERSHIP MODELLING AND LEADING INDIVIDUALS

Within the context of leading course delivery, the following are some broad examples of what leadership modelling might involve (the areas concerned and what it might look, sound and feel like), firstly at the team level and secondly in greater detail when working with or alongside individuals: ten points on each.

Team-level leadership modelling

1   *Meeting* – bringing the team together (physically or virtually). The most powerful way to connect people is to meet; the most effective way to isolate people is to prevent them from meeting or to exclude them from meetings. A learning community grows, makes choices, evolves and develops based on the transformative spaces it inhabits. *People should grow together, not apart!*

2   *Forming and developing* – investing time in processes that enable the group to bond, form relationships, develop the confidence to challenge each other in constructive ways and establish effective ways of working together. There is a very well-known model that puts forward the idea that groups progress through predictable stages, all of which are necessary and inevitable, on their way to becoming effective teams. This is Tuckman's Group Development Model (1965) that articulates four phases of development with the headings 'forming, storming, norming and performing'. This model can be applied to both work groups and learning teams (see Figure 8.3 below).

3   *Listening* – allowing others to speak first and speak longest:

187

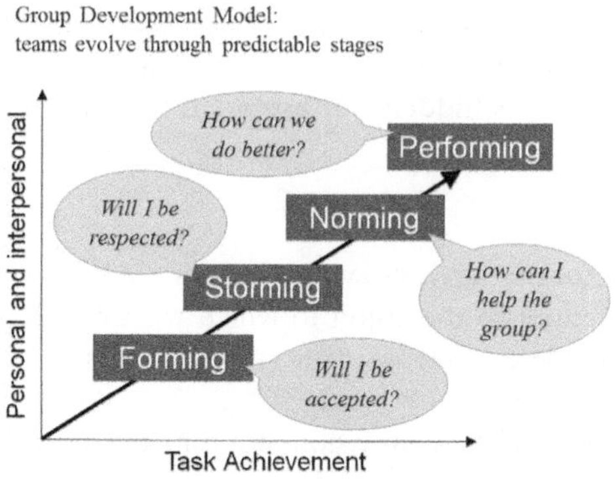

Group Development Model:
teams evolve through predictable stages

FIGURE 8.3 The Group Development Model

Forming	Storming	Norming	Performing
• Coming together • Polite and formal • Uncertainty . . . • Concerns about belonging and acceptance • Need for task definition • **Leader directs**	• Turbulence and conflict • Power struggles • Looking for position and respect • Competition • Factions and cliques may emerge • **Leader contains**	• Group settles down • Trust starts to emerge • Mutual respect • Groundrules are established • Sense of purpose • Want to contribute • **Leader facilitates**	• Enthusiasm and energy (now '*we*') • Feelings and thoughts expressed • Team roles emerge • Constructive criticisms shared • Creative flow (*fun*) • **Leader empowers**

The quality of your attention determines the quality of other people's thinking . . . When you are listening to someone, much of the quality of what you are hearing is your effect on them. Giving good attention to people makes them more intelligent.

(Kline, 1999: 36–7)

Consider both who you are listening to and what you are listening to. The student voice, as it is popularly referred to, needs an attentive listener just as much as the staff or colleague voice: it needs Kline's 'quality of . . . attention' in just the same way. So think broadly about your team and ensure your listening takes in all of the contributors and stakeholders, all of the voices. And use listening as an opportunity to encourage people to think freely and expansively: listen to both the 'high dreams' and the 'low dreams'. And don't stop. In order for our teams and organisations to survive, *leaders must never stop listening.*

4   *Eliciting views* – achieving a balanced set of contributions and facilitating diversity (for example, supporting both introverted and extroverted personality types). This will involve some of the classic skills of facilitation like bringing people in, redirecting discussion, allowing silence, closing

down people who are over-contributing, using summaries and facilitating rounds in which everyone gets a turn to speak.

5   *Showing confidence* – demonstrating a firmly based belief in the group's ability to succeed: *no one wants to be led by a pessimist*. Leaders do not hesitate to affirm what the team can do and they look to ignite potential by tuning ideas into outcomes and moving the conversation from 'what' to 'how'. They also support the group to reframe self-limiting beliefs, as described in the section on liberating leadership above.

6   *Enabling leadership* – identifying quickly your 'first followers' and encouraging them through praise, support and delegation to step forward as leaders within the team and 'model the way'. There is a theory called the diffusion of innovations (Rogers, 1962), which suggests that it is the early adopters (also known as first followers, lighthouse customers, transformers and even trendsetters) in a change situation who actually provide a high proportion of the leadership energy (see Figure 8.4 below).

7   *Identifying and using strengths* – finding roles for team members that will allow their strengths to flourish and their contribution to the group to be welcomed and appreciated. Within the dynamic of the team, this will also be about identifying complementary roles that will help enable high performance overall. The best-known model of team roles was developed by Dr Meredith Belbin (1981) and this identifies nine team role behavioural styles that in combination, and in reasonable balance, help enable teams to be successful and high performing. Within the model, based on a combination of personality and learned behaviour, individuals will have a primary team role, one or more secondary team roles and allowable weaknesses (roles where they are less strong). There is an inventory that

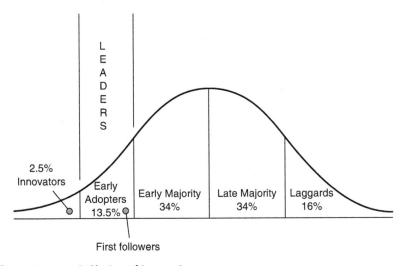

FIGURE 8.4 Diffusion of innovations curve

goes with the model (the Belbin Team Inventory) designed to identify the role we typically adopt in terms of our contribution and relationships with the rest of the team. Overall, the model is about balance and valuing diversity. The nine roles fall into three groups of three: thought-oriented, action-oriented and people-oriented.

8 *Fostering debate* – encouraging different views to emerge and be challenged to inspire new ways of doing things. This will be a process both informed by evidence and inspired by values. The data generated by programme monitoring and review will be fed into the discussions, and the first phase of debate will be grounded in understanding and exploring the current reality: *how are we doing?* The leader as facilitator will keep the group focused on the first phase, without straying, before progressing. The second phase will look to generate a diverse and expansive range of options, and different or opposing ideas will be welcomed: *what could we do?* Again, the role of the facilitator is to keep the group focused on this phase until ideas for options have been exhausted. The third and final phase (*what will we do?*) encourages the group to make a decision by considering a range of convergent questions like:

- what interests us most?;
- what would have the most impact?;
- what would best address the issue?;
- what would be most efficient and effective?;
- what would give us a premium return (extra added value)?

9 *Representing the group to other groups* – the leader mediates between the team and other groups, giving them a voice and enabling them to hear and be heard. Sometimes this can be about spanning boundaries within the organisation to enable collaboration to flourish or to share ideas or resources. On other occasions it could be almost the opposite – shielding the group and creating a holding space in which the team can focus and perform, and also grow as an entity (becoming an 'us'). The enabler attribute within the Programme Leadership Model includes both 'mediate' and 'shield' as leadership skills. Social identity theory as it relates to leadership emphasises the importance of crafting a sense of 'us', and that involves both relationships within the group and relationships beyond the group. The leader's role in this sense is about:

> Shaping social identities so that the leader and his or her proposals are seen as the concrete manifestations of group beliefs and values.
>
> (Haslam, Reicher and Platow, 2011: 143)

Representing the group can also just be about spreading the word, celebrating achievements, sharing good practice and even promoting your 'brand'. Even the most collaborative environments include competitive dimensions and leaders have a responsibility not to undersell their teams. And it will be for the good of the institution overall to hear about successes so that they can be promoted (internally and externally), built upon and reviewed for future development.

Another aspect of this could involve creating a team charter. This is something that can be done with high levels of structure and formality, but a more informal approach is probably appropriate for most teaching teams. A charter provides a point of reference about who we are, our purpose, what we value and how we intend to work together. The purpose aspect can be re-stated from the work done previously around course and assessment design. This reinforces the idea of 'working from both ends in' linked to constructive alignment (Biggs and Tang, 2007) – *if these are the intended learning outcomes (ILOs) and those are the assessment tasks, then what leaning and teaching activities will we need to put in the middle to activate the ILOs and provide students with the best possible opportunities for discovering and demonstrating their learning?* To develop the 'ways of working together' aspect of the charter, a simple process to facilitate begins with the following question:

In terms of communication and support, what do we need from each other:

- To perform?
- To collaborate?
- For inclusion?
- For motivation?

Team members can work together in pairs or groups of three or four (depending on the overall size of the team) and can then be asked to contribute their top three ideas. Pulling these together into a short list of six or eight core principles will then work in a similar way to establishing ground rules for a student project team. There are then many choices for how you keep these active and present, and how you revisit them when necessary, but the sense of ownership a team can develop around such a charter can be surprising (by the way, don't use the word 'charter' if people find it off-putting, just use the principle).

10 *Seek feedback* – great leaders seek feedback on their leadership – not once or twice, not here or there, but constantly. Emotional intelligence tells us that all of our actions and interactions as leaders spring from self-awareness. But aside from our own perceptions, what data do we have to inform our thoughts, feelings and emotions? How do we sculpt our self-awareness without feedback? Part of the art of seeking feedback is to create a climate in which people can be fair and honest: few people want to speak from the heart if it is going to make someone angry. In many ways the best way to elicit feedback is to be explicit (Gallo, 2012) by acknowledging as part of the team culture that everybody makes mistakes, including you, and explaining why you need feedback, how you will receive and welcome it and, most importantly, how you will use it. A culture of healthy, constructive criticism is a sign of a high-performing

191

team, and this involves feedback flowing in all directions. Another important aspect of seeking feedback is that it again enables you to 'model the way' as people will see that that in your leadership you 'personify the shared values' (Kouzes and Posner, 2007).

All of the above ten points could very readily be translated to apply to leading and facilitating student learning. This is level one leadership modelling – *leadership and learning*. As a leader of the team, your leadership models how to lead and facilitate student learning. The culture both within the team and across the course delivery is about collaborative engagement, collective learning and facilitating both individual and group potential (see Figure 4.1 – 'Learning-focused teaching and leadership'.

Now to turn to leading individuals and a further ten points, but with increased detail. Leading individuals is one of the most powerful aspects of leading course delivery. It develops competence, increases confidence and inspires commitment. Competence, confidence and commitment are the three legs that support a platform of high individual performance, as shown in Figure 8.5 below. And by investing as a leader in the development of a range of key individuals, you can reach a tipping point in terms of the strength of performance, and collective commitment, of the team overall. Linking this back to the Programme Leadership Model, the leadership attribute of the mentor is particularly significant here, as are the skills of listening, investing, praising, reviewing and relating.

Leading individuals

1   *Walk the talk, and talk the walk* – at a wonderful institution where I worked, there was a powerful premise that underpinned the teaching allocation model: everybody teaches. So, from research fellows through to faculty heads and even the director of the institution, all academic staff contributed to teaching. Those in appropriate professional service roles also participated in teaching and student support, and their contributions were valued

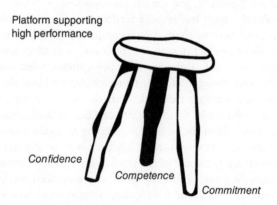

FIGURE 8.5 Confidence, competence and commitment

and recognised. And the impact of this was that the learning environment was energised through its leadership. At closer range, it is important not only that programme leaders teach, but also that they facilitate learning in the way they have espoused and agreed: 'often the most powerful way to communicate a new direction is through behaviour' (Kotter, 1996). This doesn't mean they have to be the best (whatever that means) – in fact, leaders being the best can be quite off-putting or even intimidating – but they do have to demonstrate both their own engagement and credibility. It also forms a bond with individuals in the team because it shows that you are both an active part of a shared endeavour: you are *in it together*. A track record of high achievement can also put you in a position to 'talk the walk' – that is, to be a voice of authority or even a thought leader regarding teaching in your area. Having a reputation, formal recognition, strong and consistent student ratings, and even relevant publications all work as outward signs of credibility that can help you to influence individuals:

> The more time I spend with game-changing innovators and high-performing companies, the more I appreciate the need for leaders to 'talk the walk' — that is, to be able to explain, in language that is unique to their field and compelling to their colleagues and customers, why what they do matters.
>
> (Taylor, 2014)

2   *Friend and mentor* – the leader acts as a companion on the individual's journey of development: a fellow or friend. In learning and teaching in higher education, the role of mentor could be part of the support given to someone new to teaching, it could be linked to peer observation, it could be a broader educational supervision arrangement, it could be a component in a staff development initiative or it could be a looser arrangement between colleagues/friends. What matters in whatever scenario is that mentors develop the 'ask don't tell' habit. It is so easy when someone says 'I've got a problem with X' to say 'OK, do Y'. And even if your solution is a good one, the thing you have deprived them of, whether they realise it or not, is learning: the journey from X to Y. If X is the experience, then the fundamental learning journey is:

■   *What happened?* (reflection)
■   *So what?* (conclusions – ideas and theories)
■   *What next?* (planning – a commitment to action)
■   *And when?* (the next experience)

The questions balance looking back and reflecting with looking forward and planning, and the process follows David Kolb's experiential learning cycle (1984) and other models linked to one-to-one coaching and supervision such as the GROW model, which was developed in the 1980s with significant contributions from Sir John Whitmore, Graham Alexander and Alan Fine. GROW stands for:

- *goal* (stemming from the problem/issue/experience, the outcome the person would like to achieve);
- *reality* (reflecting on what happened in sharp detail);
- *options and obstacles* (considering freely a wide selection of options regarding what they could do differently and at the same time noting potential obstacles);
- *wrap up with commitment* (selecting and committing to the option that they favour most in the circumstances).

Clearly the notion of a learning cycle suggests something that is continuous with a series of iterative stages. So, one cycle leads to a new experience, which feeds into the next reflective cycle and so on. And out of this a learning practice spiral develops (see Figure 8.6 below).

The 'ask don't tell' habit is driven by the belief that we are all born with an innate capacity to learn from experience, and the role of the mentor (coach or supervisor) is simply to support that potential by using the process described above and asking great questions:

- What happened? What's the current situation?
- What have you done so far?

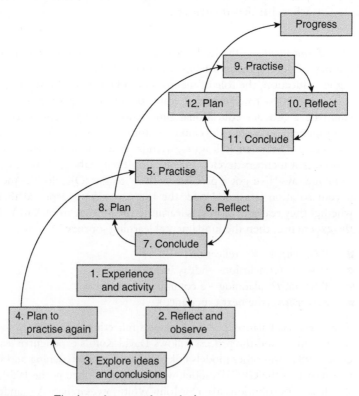

FIGURE 8.6 The learning practice spiral

- What else could you do? What are the options?
- Of those what interests you most?
- How would that work?
- What else do you need to consider?
- OK, so what *are* you going to do, and by when?
- What support are you going to need?
- Who else do you need to speak to?
- Great. Well, let me know how it goes.

3   *Listening* – people love to talk about their teaching experiences. Even people who claim not to like teaching love to talk about it, although not necessarily in a way that is positive. And linked to the previous point on mentoring and the 'ask don't tell' habit, the only way to ask great questions is to listen powerfully. A strange thing happens when you listen, really listen, with an attentive mind and an open heart – people start thinking for themselves. And you may be surprised how few questions you have to ask, particularly after they get used to your listening and the simple power of it. Stephen Covey refers to this as empathic listening:

> Empathic (from empathy) listening gets inside another person's frame of reference. You look out through it, you see the world the way they see the world, you understand their paradigm, you understand how they feel . . . It's deeply therapeutic and healing because it gives a person 'psychological air'.
>
> (Covey, 1992: 240–1)

When leading teaching delivery, you work with individuals who are not just trying to understand their teaching experiences intellectually – they are also trying to understand them emotionally. *Why didn't the students want to participate? Why were they confused? Why didn't they understand me? Why did only some of them enjoy the exercise? Why couldn't they think for themselves?* The learning is a relationship with students, a to-and-fro of discussion and engagement made up of both rewarding and turbulent encounters, and relationships trigger emotions at every level. So, listening isn't just to plan and problem-solve, it is also to make sense of the emotional dimensions of experience. It is about raising awareness both in the head and in the heart.

But listening is not easy. In a busy world that looks to fill every silence and communicate every thought, the stillness of listening can be hard to achieve. We can be all too ready to give people 'a good talking to', but a 'good listening to' is a much rarer thing to find. So to develop your listening skills, try to remember LISTEN:

- *L – look interested* – if you look interested, you probably will be;
- *I – involve yourself by responding* – but you don't necessarily need to respond out loud and with words or vigorous active gestures;

195

sometimes just by genuinely feeling and acknowledging what they are saying inside yourself will show through your body language (in gentle affirming nods, for example, and eye contact);

- *S – stay on target* – if you feel they are straying onto something new or different, simply bring them back on track with a simple 'tell me more about . . . ?' question;
- *T – test your understanding* – use short platform summaries to simply replay and check what you have heard;
- *E – evaluate the message* – express and name the essence of what has come across to you, if possible using their language;
- *N – neutralise your feelings* – don't judge, just listen. Don't impose what you would do (or have done in the past in similar situations), just listen. Don't look for right or wrong, just listen. *It's their learning, hands off!*

When you listen in the way described above, you may sometimes feel that you have not contributed very much – that is part of how we value things in our society. But rest assured, you have given them a great gift. And they will know it, even if you don't. And you may also be left wondering sometimes what they are thanking you for.

4 *Sharing your stories* – good leaders are not afraid to relate authentic stories that reveal who they are. When people are frustrated with a leader, you may hear them say: 'Who is this guy anyway?' This is an expression of doubt around credibility, integrity, status and, most importantly, authenticity. A gap has emerged in the relationship and people are struggling to connect. The power of stories is that they help people to relate to each other in powerful ways, particularly if hitherto they have not shared a common history. Ryde and Sofianos (2014) talk about the 'schism of the self' where who we are at work is partitioned off, as it were, from who we are overall: we lead behind a mask.

Sharing your stories is a way of dropping the mask and relating with both teams and individuals, and also showing empathy for people and situations. The leadership of teaching delivery is an undertaking full of stories: stories of triumphs and tragedies, stories of heroes and villains, and stories of creation and catastrophe. This is because there is a drama about learning and teaching that involves new people meeting, going on a journey, forming relationships, making discoveries, overcoming problems/challenges, being tested, making breakthroughs, having conflicts and hopefully emerging into a brighter future. And as we said in the section on listening above, people love to talk about their teaching. Telling and sharing stories is a very human thing to do, and leaders need to be aware of how communities are shaped by the stories they collectively craft and develop over time: the evolutions of the team's stories.

The stories you tell may be about your own teaching experiences, to close the gap and move towards the individual. And there may or may not be a message in the story – whatever our intent, that ultimately will be for the listener to decide. It is usually advisable not to use stories as a way of telling the individual what to do: *I had a similar situation and you should do the same as I did*. But if your story captures a value that amplifies something central to the issue, then sharing it may help the individual reframe their experience in a useful way. You may also relate stories from other aspects of your life as a way of sharing perspectives, enriching communication, triggering motivation, helping to create meaning and as a natural part of building the relationship:

> Stories touch us in ways that other forms of communication do not. A good story, well told, can slip past the defences of the rational mind, pluck at our hearts, and stir our souls.
>
> (Mead, 2014: 17)

5   *Hope* – 'A leader is a dealer in hope' (Napoleon Bonaparte, 1769–1821). Hope is about the future, usually a better future, and in leadership terms that means vision. In a blog piece I wrote for the Leadership Foundation for Higher Education (UK) in May 2015 entitled 'No More Heroes . . .? Leading Engagement', I introduced the idea of 'the land of the possible':

> What these heroic qualities enable leaders to achieve is moving people from the 'land of the not possible' to the 'land of the possible'. This is not just important for organisational success and resilience in the face of change, but also because the 'land of the possible' is simply a happier place to be.

Working with individuals to facilitate student learning is very often a transformative undertaking; people moving from things they, perhaps, consider conventional and safe to approaches that are less familiar. Typically this is a movement from instruction to interaction, participation and, further along the scale, self-direction. This movement requires energy and encouragement, as well as a leader who projects both hope and optimism. One of my stories is of a lecturer on a postgraduate certificate in learning and teaching who was preparing for a lecture that I was going to observe: I call this story *a game of two halves*. In our briefing discussion ahead of the lecture, she memorably told me 'I've put in a piece of interaction but only because you're observing'. Her honesty was refreshing and based on a genuine scepticism regarding whether interactive activities in lectures did anything to enhance learning. The day came and the lecture began. The first half progressed at a terrific speed with slide after complex slide flicking by at a rate matched only by the pace of her delivery. Some students made frantic notes, others attempted a few scribbles, most quickly gave up and either disengaged or relaxed to enjoy the spectacle. And then midway through came the interaction. In

197

groups of three or four, as they were sitting in the lecture hall, the students had to consider a table of data in four columns, representing four countries, and decide together for which country a certain health policy intervention would be most beneficial. The students engaged, suddenly there was a lovely buzz of chatter in the room, and the lecturer, who had looked very serious and a little nervous up to that point, smiled. She then took their responses through a show of hands and instinctively led a productive discussion with contributions from students exploring why and a few related issues. Then came the second half of the lecture. It was slower, there was more expression, there was more eye contact with the students, and the lecturer picked out certain slides to talk about and emphasise, and passed over others. So, when we came to our feedback discussion after the lecture, you will not be surprised to learn that this bright and intelligent lecturer had already formed her own conclusions. And whilst she acknowledged that the interaction seemed to enhance the learning, her main motivation for becoming a convert to interaction in lectures was that she had enjoyed the second half far more than the first. She had enjoyed the quality of the learning relationship. This experience, and her reflections on it, had moved her to 'the land of the possible' and opened up a whole spectrum of new potential in terms of facilitating student learning (not just in lecture halls). And my role as a leader of course delivery, whilst a fairly passive one in the portion of the story told here, had inspired enough 'hope' to encourage her to *reluctantly* try something different.

6   *Feedback and review* – the leader is courageous in sharing feedback and knows that it must always be approached constructively. The tragedy of the workplace is the absence of feedback. Individuals only have their own reference points for deciding where they are performing well and where they could improve, and unless their disposition propels them to do otherwise, the tendency will be to *plod on*. This results in teaching delivery, or any other activity for that matter, becoming a fairly lifeless activity, a routine, conforming to an administrative structure. According to Roland and Frances Bee (1996), constructive feedback 'is the characteristic that differentiates between managers who successfully motivate and develop their staff and those who struggle in their people-management role'.

Feedback, whether critical or not, should be informed by data, clear examples or direct observation. The person giving the feedback should be clear about their intent and should share this openly with the individual concerned. Any emotional charge associated with the feedback should be carefully considered by the person giving the feedback beforehand so that they can reflect on how this may come across. Data, intent and emotional charge (Downey, 1999) are the three ingredients that combine to determine whether or not individual feedback comes across as constructive (see Figure 8.7 below).

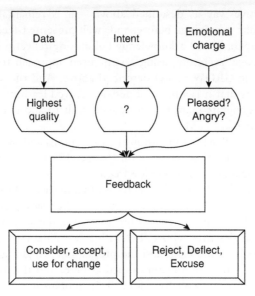

FIGURE 8.7 The ingredients of effective feedback

If the individual does not regard the feedback as constructive, if it seems unfair, unfounded, badly intended or driven by anger, for example, it is likely not to be accepted. The three behaviours that tend to flow from this are reject, deflect or excuse, none of which is a useful or positive basis for learning and improvement. However, if the feedback is seen as constructive, the individual is likely to consider it and, through a process of review and reflection, use it for change. Here is a quick exercise based on the above:

EXERCISE

Think of a piece of feedback you recently shared with a member of your team:

- What was the *data* (the information itself) – did you ensure it was accurate and of the highest quality?
- What was your *intent* in sharing the feedback? What did you say you were looking to achieve? What were you actually trying to achieve?
- What was the *emotional charge*? If you were angry, upset or disappointed, how did this come across?
- How did the person respond to the feedback? Was it constructive for them (a basis for positive change)?

If it is possible, the best approach for reviewing feedback is self-appraisal. The skill for leaders here is twofold: firstly, sharing the feedback in a constructive way as described above – it is remarkable how often, despite our misgivings beforehand, well-presented feedback is recognised by people and acknowledged alongside reflections on their own performance; secondly, using a structured approach to the discussion such as the GROW model described above. And the strength of self-appraisal is that it is a piece of person-centred learning and, as such, is likely to generate plans that people commit to and that become transformational.

Whilst feedback should ideally be continuous and organic, part of the culture of a learning organisation (Senge, 1990), the process of review tends to be more formal and less frequent. It is nonetheless valuable as an opportunity for individuals to agree for themselves performance goals and objectives linked to a specific timeframe. The leader's role is essentially to support and encourage this process, using the same principle of self-appraisal as described above, but with a coordinating perspective linked to the goals of the team and the programme. Aligning task, team and individual is the coordinating function here, and this process of alignment also provides a platform for broader monitoring and evaluation. But ownership of the development objectives still rests with the individual and, once again, participation rather than compliance should be the mindset. And the most significant part of the process, whatever system your organisation has in place, is the interaction that occurs at the review stage and the learning conversations that spring from this. Above all else, review is an opportunity for engagement.

7 *Opening the gate* – the leader can make connections for individuals and help enable people to be a resource for each other. Leaders are often gatekeepers within networks and at the intersection of networks, and part of the boundary-spanning role of leadership is to take a far-sighted approach, connecting people for both immediate goals and future possibilities. Jealously guarding contacts and networks is a curious thing to do, probably betraying either insecurity or an obsession with status, and it can seldom if ever be a recipe for growth. And when leading course delivery, an endeavour that may well involve people working across divisions, departments and disciplines, the skill of generously connecting people is of high importance:

> A tribe is a group of people connected to one another, connected to a leader, and connected to an idea. For millions of years, human beings have been part of one tribe or another. A group needs only two things to be a tribe: a shared interest and a way to communicate.
> (Godin, 2008: 1)

One aspect of leadership influence is to do with controlling access to resources, and this extends to social capital. People's interest, motivation, sense of community and performance can be affected either positively or adversely by the links and human connections they are able to make around the challenges they face. If those connections are free-flowing and people are available to each other, that effect is likely to be positive. In this sense, solutions and decisions are not necessarily driven by the leader in a bureaucratic or administrative way, but instead through enabling connections, collaborations and quality conversations. This links well with the notion of collegiality, in some people's view the cornerstone of a university and the antidote to managerialism, which is not a forced-fit relationship for the purpose of achieving target-driven goals, but rather a multi-layered set of relationships based on interest, mutuality and synergy.

8   *Praise and recognition* – a leader who instinctively knows when and what to praise is a leader who really understands the individuals they work with. Praise needs to be personal, prompt and precise. Recognition is the celebration of praise – singular of accumulated – to the wider community. Praise is for the spirit of the individual; recognition is for the spirit of the collective. Some people suggest that praise should be used sparingly, otherwise it becomes devalued: the thinking is along the lines that if everything is excellent, then nothing is excellent. In an environment that values critical evaluation and the assessment of performance against carefully graded criteria, this perspective is understandable. And the purpose of praise is certainly not to create a positive illusion where the facts speak otherwise. However, praise is one of the simplest and most human ways to energise a work environment, and it should be used liberally and generously by leaders. Despite what some might say, I think that most of us are suckers for it. Put simply (and this avoids elaborate debates about self-esteem and efficacy), it makes us happy. Even those, I think, with a cultivatedly serious visage enjoy a lift in energy when well-deserved praise comes their way. The following is a playful, made-up dialogue intended to suggest a paradox:

> PERSON A: I don't respond well to praise.
> PERSON B: Well done. That must keep you critically alert and aware.
> PERSON A: Thank you. Yes, it does.
> PERSON B: And how does that make you feel?
> PERSON A: Very good.

So what does happiness give us? I would suggest the following: a stronger sense of well-being, increased optimism, greater personal energy, enhanced creative flow, the ability to spot the potential in situations and improved relationships, and it may even increase our chances of spotting advantageous opportunities. Shawn Achor (2010) puts forward the provocation 'that success orbits around happiness, not the other way round' and that 'in business as in life, the reasonable optimist will win every time'. In addition to happiness, as if that were not enough, praise is also part of feedback, which we discussed above. It is the affirmation of something that is good and working and that we could/should do more of. It is an arrow in the direction of further improvement and development. And the three P's mentioned above apply:

- *personal* – the praise is specific to the individual and their behaviour and contribution;
- *prompt* – as close in time to the subject of the praise as possible (if you save praise up for special occasions like annual reviews, it will lose its impact);
- *precise* – the praise should accurately identify the things that made something good or great. So, in the case of teaching delivery, highlighting that the individual delivered a great teaching session is not enough. Only when what made it good and why are identified will the praise become productive. This detail could, though, be explored in discussion through self-appraisal.

Recognition can take many forms, from letters of commendation and awards through to special mention during a meeting. It rewards the individual and should amplify a point (or points) of praise made previously. But it should not be regarded as a leader only function. One feature of a high-performing team is that it has an appreciative spirit, which means that recognition is free-flowing between individuals in the group. And the recognition goes hand-in-hand with collective learning as the group looks to progress and develop both what it does and how it does it, including the interpersonal dynamic.

Returning to level one modelling (leadership and learning), a culture of praise and recognition within the course delivery team should mirror the qualities important to the facilitation of student learning. A similar appreciative spirit cultivated within the student group, and modelled by tutors, will enhance the quality of the learning environment and strengthen student engagement.

9   *Taming tigers* – a leader knows that there may be tigers in their midst. Tigers are magnificent and powerful, can perform in wonderful ways and, whilst not always as dangerous as they seem, can sometimes be frightening to work with. We are thinking here of colleagues in the team who may be tigers in the sense of their high experience, their reputation, their standing and also their manner. This is by no means a given, of course, and many people who have achieved great reputations have done so by being generous, open collaborators and an asset to any team (these are not your tigers). Tigers can be tremendous contributors to teaching programmes, for all sorts of good reasons, and they can be popular with students, but they can also be challenging to work with and difficult for aspects of team cohesion. So, adopting an expedient, pragmatic approach may be the way to both get things done and gradually build a relationship. A lot will, of course, depend on your personality and confidence, but as a generality, in order to lead teaching delivery effectively in these

situations, it will be advisable to avoid confrontation. However, simple clarity regarding needs and expectations is something that should be appreciated, particularly when there are changes to be made, and the more you can involve them at an early stage, the better. This provides time for their voice to be heard, for the ideas to gain momentum, and it is also good diplomacy. People can feel valued and included in teams, projects and programmes for a range of different reasons. A recent study by Prime and Salib (2014) isolated two separate underlying sentiments that make people feel included: 'uniqueness and belongingness'. Their contention is that these two factors work in combination and that the challenge for leaders is to get the balance right with different individuals and in different situations. It may be that for tigers, therefore, it is important to emphasise uniqueness before opening up belongingness. Prime and Salib go on to suggest that this balancing act requires that 'leaders should embrace a selfless leadership style'. In the case of leading course delivery in higher education, it is certainly important for leaders to be humble so that they can enable and empower others, in all their unique and different ways, to achieve successful outcomes for themselves and the teaching programme. But humble doesn't mean allowing yourself to be devoured:

> The one sure way to conciliate a tiger is to allow oneself to be devoured.
>
> (Konrad Adenauer, 1876–1967,
> West German Chancellor)

10 *Leading from in front and leading from behind* – a good leader will know when to set the pace and walk the talk, and they will also know when to sit back, listen with a friendly ear, praise and encourage. In the nine points above on leading individuals, we have explored a variety of ways in which leadership can be modelled in the context of course delivery. Most of the modelling I would characterise as leading alongside people or leading from behind. It is about enabling and mentoring, the two people-focused attributes in the Programme Leadership Model. The passion of the champion has its place, and that is in-front leadership, but the leadership of individuals is best facilitated with the compassion of leading from behind (unless, of course, a critical situation requires urgent action). One could be crude and suggest an 80/20 split, with the higher proportion being leadership that is alongside and behind – leadership that is about enabling and empowering:

> A leader is not an administrator who loves to run others, but someone who carries water for his people so that they can get on with their jobs.
>
> (Robert Townsend, 1920–98)

This quote brings to mind the idea of a servant leader and, linked to this, the cautionary words of Robert Greenleaf (1977) on the role of ego in leadership: 'Ego can't sleep. It micro-manages. It disempowers. It reduces our capability. It excels in control.'

The danger of leading from in front is that you can never be entirely sure that anyone is following you. And a leader without followers . . . is just someone going for a walk.

QUESTIONS FOR ACTION AND REFLECTION

1   What specific qualities do you bring to facilitating student learning? Are these qualities seen and shared by others in the team?
2   What does your module/programme team associate with the notion of 'delivering' the course?
3   In what ways does your leadership mirror or model the way in which you would like the team to lead/facilitate student learning?
4   On a scale of 1–10, with 1 being very reluctant compliance and 10 being fully empowered, active participation, where would you: a. place your team as a whole?; b. place different individuals?
5   Which do you do the most of as a leader: Telling? Consulting? Involving? Empowering? Which would you like to do more of and what steps could you take right now to increase this by five per cent?
6   What self-limiting belief stands between you and your potential as a leader or a teacher (or both)? What is the most powerful and incisive question you could ask yourself to challenge this belief? In a similar way, what question(s) could you ask to individuals in your team to challenge self-limiting beliefs and foster a *climate of possibility*?
7   When did you last openly seek feedback regarding your performance and impact as a leader? How could you enhance the culture of feedback within the team?
8   Which individuals within your programme/module team are you supporting most closely? What does your support look, sound and feel like? Are there others you should be supporting in a similar way?
9   Think of an example of where you shared feedback really effectively with a colleague? What made the feedback so effective? How could you build on this and share feedback in a similar way with others?
10 In your leadership, what is the proportion of leading from in front (passion and direction) compared with leading from behind (compassion and empowerment)? What could you do right now to cause a five per cent shift towards leading from behind?

Chapter 9

Leading engagement

THE CHALLENGE IN THIS CHAPTER

In universities today there are three major leadership frontiers:

- leading innovation;
- leading enterprise;
- leading engagement.

There are all sorts of other leadership challenges, of course, from the light-footed strategic to the heavily operational, but these three frontiers are the current areas for what might be termed breakthrough leadership in higher education. 'Breakthrough' because these are the arenas in which institutions are striving to develop new potential, distinctiveness and even competitive edge, and in some contexts this is even becoming regarded as critical to future success and sustainability. The breakthrough dimension is also related to the disruptive nature of the transformation which may result and the need to embrace such change nonetheless: speaking specifically about higher education, Clayton Christensen (cited in Roscorla, 2014) observed that 'the big takeaway is that change is hard, failure is much harder, and would you rather be sick or would you rather be dead?' Innovation and enterprise each have their own powerful narrative as regards leadership, change and strategy, distinct from leading engagement, but all three share breakthrough challenges concerned with vision, direction and connecting people with purpose. And in some cases the new purpose can feel very alien and at odds with long-established cultural values: for example, marrying new business goals linked to enterprise with deeply rooted principles to do with academic freedom and knowledge creation. All three frontiers challenge leaders to develop a vision, generate new collaborative energy within the organisation, establish direction and align goals, systems and structures.

Our focus is on the third of these leadership frontiers, leading engagement. Student engagement lies at the heart of this, but a fully engaged environment will also include staff and other stakeholders. The possibilities of engagement are transformational at many levels, from individual student learning right through to the character 'of the institution and its performance. And as has been highlighted before, there is an important relationship to be explored and understood between student expectations, the student experience and student engagement: the 3 Es.

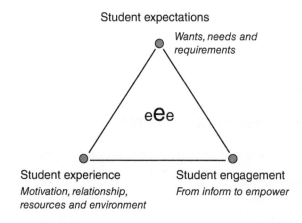

Student expectations
Wants, needs and requirements

eΘe

Student experience
Motivation, relationship, resources and environment

Student engagement
From inform to empower

FIGURE 9.1 The 3 Es

A key part of the discussion regarding leading engagement will therefore involve exploring a model which considers the fundamental elements that make up the optimal student experience. This will be the main focus in this chapter.

LINKS TO THE PROGRAMME LEADERSHIP MODEL

The complacent response to more elusive human challenges is often to turn the question around. So, 'how can we lead engagement?' quickly becomes 'can you lead engagement?' And the implied futility of the proposition is then further elaborated with a statement along the lines of 'surely people are either engaged or they're not – it's up to them in the end'. In the context of learning and teaching, this vein of thought can be amplified by invoking the spectre of the 'good student'. You may well have come across this. 'A good student will learn very effectively from a lecture without the need for questions or interaction', or 'a good student will know what a mark means without reams of explanation' (feedback, as it is otherwise known), or, perhaps most concerning, 'the course requirements will be self-evident to a good student'. This kind of thinking is fundamentally an evasion of responsibility. And the key responsibility is the responsibility to lead. The overriding responsibility to lead and enable an environment where there is no false hierarchy around engagement based on the ability to comprehend oblique messages, conform to poorly expressed requirements or have the confidence to challenge inadequate systems and structures.

Leading engagement is fundamentally transformational. It is about enhancing relationships and re-focusing both interaction and intent. There is a huge amount of listening involved, and the theme of collaborative engagement as the nexus for change, which has been a central theme throughout this book, takes centre stage. There are transactional aspects, too, around the 'give and get' interplay of needs as players with different interests work together: *what's in it for me? – what's in it for you?* The champion attribute will be valuable to promote and highlight these transactional elements to leverage both team commitment and strategic buy-in at a faculty or organisational level. Any business case, for example, should clearly articulate the 'give and get' of needs that sits alongside the transformative 'why' presented in the vision for change. John Kotter (1990) observed that transactional mechanisms can sometimes have a transformational impact, particularly if they sit alongside transformational leadership strategies, and that certainly applies as regards leading student engagement. This observation also lifts the transactional/transformational model out of being seen as a strict or inflexible dichotomy where the transactional leader 'approaches followers with an eye to exchanging one thing for another' (Burns, 1978) – the 'give and get' relationship of needs – whilst the transformational leader seeks to 'arouse and satisfy higher needs, to engage the full person of the follower' (Bass, 1985) – a relationship which connects people with purpose. So, the core theme of collaborative engagement, with the shared commitment and sense of purpose that this potentially creates, draws on many of the enabling skills in the Programme Leadership Model, and happily intertwined with this are skills relating to the more goal/task-focused attributes of champion and organiser.

In Table 9.1 below, the key leadership skills and attributes associated with leading engagement are highlighted (note: this is purely indicative – none of the leadership skills should be regarded as exclusive or restricted to just one area):

TABLE 9.1 Programme Leadership Model – leading engagement

Leadership skills

CHAMPION	ORGANISER	ENABLER	MENTOR
Enthuse	Plan	Encourage	Listen
Promote	Organise	Shield	Invest
Model	Monitor	Support	Praise
Challenge	Control	Share/Convene	Review
Negotiate	Evaluate	Mediate	Relate

THE OPTIMAL STUDENT EXPERIENCE

This model proposes that there are four foundations or dimensions that help to optimise the student learning experience. They are not directly about the learning itself – that is the subject territory, the content, the study level, the pedagogy or the intended outcomes – but they do interact powerfully with all aspects of student learning. As shown in Figure 9.2 below, the four foundations are motivation, relationship, environment and resources.

The quality of the student experience essentially consists of the balance and interplay between these four dimensions, as well as the standard of each independently: understanding and engaging with students' motivation to learn; establishing relationships that enable learning and personal growth to flourish; creating a welcoming and supportive environment in which people can develop and succeed; and providing open and timely access to rich and relevant resources. Even as these four foundations are briefly described here, you can start to see the interconnectedness that is a natural part of this model. A supportive environment will help a student to explore and express their motivation to learn, enhanced through encountering well-designed resources, and out of this learning relationships can flourish, to give just one example. Figure 9.3 below presents an elaboration of the model and starts to suggest the interplay between the four dimensions.

Each of the four headings in this model connects with a very rich literature in both the educational domain and beyond, and it would not be realistic to attempt to cover or summarise this here. They will also trigger a variety of opinions, views and perspectives linked to a context, and that can be a fruitful basis for collaboratively engaging a team or even a whole institution regarding opportunities for enhancement. It is also a model that is eminently scalable as it could be related to the sphere of influence of a single programme, taking in all related aspects of student support, or it could be used as the basis for a wider mapping of the factors that 'help or hinder' the achievement of the optimal student experience in a department, faculty or institution. It goes beyond the programme-based academic experience, if you wish it to, and can take in the wider institutional environment, the resources of every kind that students can enjoy, in the broadest sense, and relationships ranging from key individuals through to the cultural climate of the institution itself. Let us now look at each of the four foundations, beginning with motivation.

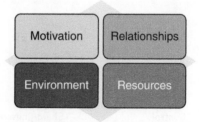

FIGURE 9.2 The student experience: what do students need?

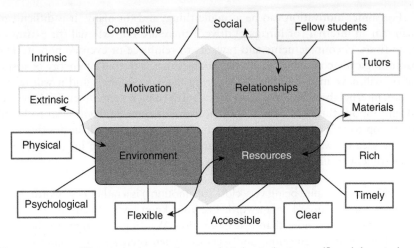

FIGURE 9.3 The student experience: what do students need? – elaborated

MOTIVATION

In other aspects of our life where we help someone to learn something, however informally, there are a handful of obvious yet powerful questions that come to us quite naturally:

- What is your interest in . . . ?
- How do you want to use it . . . ?
- How much will you use it . . . ?
- Have you used one before . . . ?
- What do you know already . . . ?

All of these questions centre around establishing three things: why the person wants to learn, what they need to learn and how much should be invested in helping them learn. This is then a strong basis for engaging them as a learner so long, that is, as we keep the door open to fresh discovery. Some people who start 'vague' (and the questions above will elicit different levels of clarity, of course, from different individuals) achieve a strong focus, some who express clear and specific desires can change or lose direction, and most excitingly the achievement of learning in one area can excite an individual to want to learn new things in another.

These questions equally belong in an academic context, however they are phrased. And it is as important for students to have the reflective space to explore and express their motivation to learn, as something ongoing throughout their studies, as it is for tutors to interact with students on this basis. So it is not just about gaining intelligence to help develop and refine the programme offering (a transactional response), it is an intrinsic part of the learning relationship that helps to focus the energy and commitment of the learner (a transformational engagement).

For some, motivation can be a fragile thing, and for many, it is difficult to maintain an internal (or intrinsic) drive if there are not external (or extrinsic) conditions, encouragements and rewards to reinforce or even amplify it. The psychologically cold climate of a lecture hall that is devoid of energy or inspiration will have many students wondering 'why am I here?' and it will take a strong internal drive or a new external impetus to pick them up again. One way to think about this is as a cascade of motivations running from 'want to learn' at the top to 'can't learn' at the bottom. Figure 9.4 below illustrates this.

The idea of 'want' is beautifully expressed by Phil Race in his discussion of 'how students really learn' in *The Lecturer's Toolkit*:

> Motivation (despite being very close to 'emotion') is a rather cold word: *wanting* is a much more human word. Everyone knows what 'want' means. Also, *wanting* implies more than just motivation. Wanting goes right to the heart of human urges, emotions and feelings. When there's such a powerful factor at work helping learning to happen, little wonder that the results can be spectacular.
>
> (Race, 2015: 11)

If learning is to not only 'add to' but also 'act upon' existing knowledge (in many ways the key assertion in both constructivist and more recent neurocognitive ideas on adult learning), then the energy and vitality required to self-direct, explore, discover and reconstruct understanding needs to draw on an equally well-constructed sense of both personal and social motivation.

RELATIONSHIP

There is a big difference between 'I think' and 'we think'. The former is a lonely but, perhaps, courageous assertion that others may contest, compete against or occasionally admire. The latter is a construction developed through a process of

- Want to learn
  - Need to learn
    - Have to learn
      - Should learn
        - Could learn
          - May learn
            - Won't learn
              - Can't learn

FIGURE 9.4 Cascade of learner motivations

social exchange and debate that reflects the diversity of backgrounds, perspectives and problem-solving skills that the participants share (even if the 'we' is only two). This is a simplification, of course. Both scenarios reflect skills that are admirable and valuable, and interestingly both will often need a high level of relational support to flourish.

In a well-supported learning environment, students will have the opportunity to enjoy three fundamental relationships:

- with tutors;
- with fellow students;
- with course materials.

Michael Moore (1989) put forward a similar typology of learner interactions: learner–content interaction, learner–instructor interaction and learner–learner interaction.

The list could be expanded, of course, to take in particularly the relationship with the institution, or a key department within it, and that would link well with current notions of students as partners, but there is something enticing about this list of three and the suggestion of balance that comes with it. The model might be seen as a game of compensation – for example, considering an early form of distance-based study with a high dependency on asynchronous methods of engagement, the thinking could be to make the materials as rich and immersive as possible to compensate for the infrequency (or absence) of direct relationships with tutors and fellow students (this takes us into the realms of interaction equivalency; Miyazoe and Anderson, 2010). But this is to diminish the truth that lies at the heart of this model. It is the progressive interplay between the three relationships, and the richness of the experience that results, that is an essential aspect of student engagement.

Relationship also plays a huge part in the dynamics of belonging and inclusion that are for many prerequisites for deeper levels of learning and engagement. Acceptance, support, friendship, encouragement, listening, mutual respect and an acknowledgement of values are all key elements of this very human dynamic. Character strengths can flourish within a learning community that both values and respects the distinctiveness of individuals and enjoys the mutuality of the group. Positive relationships are key to well-being in all situations, and well-being, confidence and high self-regard are strong platforms for learning:

> Very little that is positive is solitary. When was the last time you laughed uproariously? The last time you felt indescribable joy? The last time you sensed profound meaning and purpose? The last time you felt enormously proud of an achievement? Even without knowing the particulars of these high points of your life, I know their form: all of them took place around other people.
>
> (Seligman, 2011: 20)

Another aspect of relationship is the process of 'becoming' that helps to build and shape professional and/or disciplinary identities. Student–faculty interactions, with varying levels of formality, are fundamental to the legitimacy that Etienne Wenger describes in his discourse on Communities of Practice as so crucial to being on an 'inbound trajectory':

> Newcomers must be granted enough legitimacy to be treated as potential members . . . Only with legitimacy can all their inevitable stumbling and violations become opportunities for learning rather than cause for dismissal, neglect or exclusion.
>
> (Wenger, 1998: 101)

ENVIRONMENT

I recently asked a colleague what makes an excellent learning environment for students. Their answer was simply 'somewhere people can concentrate'. This caused me to reflect that expectations and aspirations are very much governed by circumstances. If I tell you that this person's department has been relegated to 'temporary accommodation' whilst a new building is constructed in the adjoining field, with all the noise, dust and disruption that inevitably comes with this (a not uncommon scenario in educational establishments), then you will readily understand her perspective. She began by saying 'well, there are whiteboards and all of that nonsense' before going on to observe that none of that matters if students struggle to listen and are surrounded by distractions. For learning, all of this boils down to *being happily present*. If you are, then you are ready to learn – you have the personal freedom to learn.

Maslow's Hierarchy of Needs (1954), a needs-based theory of motivation, is a useful tool for considering the environmental factors influencing learner engagement: the things that help us *to be happily present*. Physiological factors sit at the base of the hierarchy, or the base of the pyramid as it is often depicted. At the top is self-fulfilment or self-actualisation, the desire to become the best you can be. So, if you are wet, cold or hungry, then no matter how good the PowerPoint or how fancy the whiteboards (to come back to my colleague's example), you are unlikely to overcome these fundamental environmental preoccupations to engage at a higher level, or 'concentrate'. A range of social and psychological factors are at work in the middle range of the hierarchy concerned with safety, social belonging and feelings of esteem and self-worth. Figure 9.5 below shows an illustration based on Maslow's Hierarchy of Needs with suggestions as to how it may translate to student learning.

As a humorous footnote, it has been suggested that for the modern student 'Wi-Fi' should be added as the new base of the pyramid to reflect the survival-like yearning these digital natives have for Internet access and online social networks. Like most humour, it carries a strong element of truth . . .

Good learning design looks to progressively introduce elements of conceptual and cognitive discomfort. In other words, the learner is challenged with ideas, problems, contradictions and alternative methodologies that stretch them to

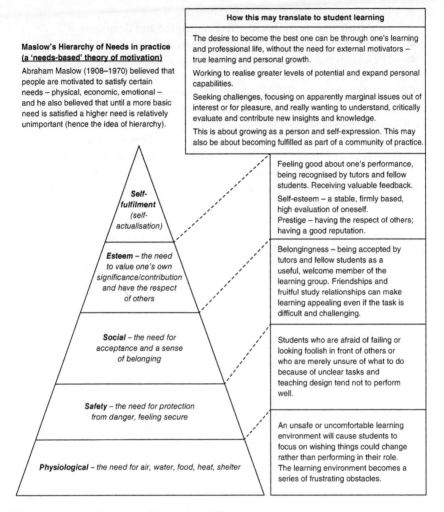

How this may translate to student learning

The desire to become the best one can be through one's learning and professional life, without the need for external motivators – true learning and personal growth.

Working to realise greater levels of potential and expand personal capabilities.

Seeking challenges, focusing on apparently marginal issues out of interest or for pleasure, and really wanting to understand, critically evaluate and contribute new insights and knowledge.

This is about growing as a person and self-expression. This may also be about becoming fulfilled as part of a community of practice.

Maslow's Hierarchy of Needs in practice (a 'needs-based' theory of motivation)

Abraham Maslow (1908–1970) believed that people are motivated to satisfy certain needs – physical, economic, emotional – and he also believed that until a more basic need is satisfied a higher need is relatively unimportant (hence the idea of hierarchy).

Self-fulfilment (self-actualisation)

Feeling good about one's performance, being recognised by tutors and fellow students. Receiving valuable feedback.

Self-esteem – a stable, firmly based, high evaluation of oneself.

Prestige – having the respect of others; having a good reputation.

Esteem – *the need to value one's own significance/contribution and have the respect of others*

Belongingness – being accepted by tutors and fellow students as a useful, welcome member of the learning group. Friendships and fruitful study relationships can make learning appealing even if the task is difficult and challenging.

Social – *the need for acceptance and a sense of belonging*

Students who are afraid of failing or looking foolish in front of others or who are merely unsure of what to do because of unclear tasks and teaching design tend not to perform well.

Safety – *the need for protection from danger, feeling secure*

An unsafe or uncomfortable learning environment will cause students to focus on wishing things could change rather than performing in their role. The learning environment becomes a series of frustrating obstacles.

Physiological – *the need for air, water, food, heat, shelter*

FIGURE 9.5 Maslow's Hierarchy of Needs in practice

learn, unlearn and relearn. The art is to combine this with a range of instruction, support and resources (including online) that will sustain the needs of different students in a flexible way as the curriculum unfolds. Doing less well in an assessment, particularly a formative assignment, need not threaten esteem and security if the relationships are strong, the resources work well, the feedback is useful and timely, and the motivation of individual students is considered (the other dimensions of the model). The psychological environment is of equal importance to the physical environment and both need constant attention and management if learning is to flourish. The idea of a high-challenge, low-threat learning environment, and the way in which such environments generally help us in our learning, is summarised in a neat and compelling way by Bill Lucas (2005):

- Low challenge, low threat – 'feel bored'.
- Low challenge, high threat – 'feel controlled and demotivated'.
- High challenge, high threat – 'feel controlled and compelled'.
- High challenge, low threat – 'feel engaged'.

In Chapter 3 the acronym PRAISE was introduced as a tool to identify and summarise the various responsibilities that together make up a manager's role (*what the manager manages*). Whilst managing people and resources are categories most managers would readily identify as key areas of responsibility, they might be slower to acknowledge the role they have in managing or even leading the environment, and all that that means. However, for the leadership of learning and teaching, a clear focus on managing and facilitating the learning environment is critical. Creating an environment where people can succeed is almost a proxy for leading learning and teaching at its most stripped-back level. And institutions need to move beyond thinking that learning takes place in certain arenas or behind certain doors, and start to conceive of themselves as learning organisations overall (Senge, 1990). This includes the creative and flexible blending of online or virtual learning environments with the fabric of learning and research that is the life of most universities.

RESOURCES

The American author and historian Shelby Foote (1916–2005) is quoted as having said that 'a university is just a group of buildings gathered around a library' (Foote, 1993). Whilst we would certainly see this as a distorted emphasis today, there is something about the centrality of learning resources and the importance of access to them that is nevertheless resonant. As we look at the situation today, technology has provided three fundamental developments: firstly, it has enabled the format of learning resources to have been considerably expanded and diversified; secondly, through the Internet, it has made access to them far more open in terms of time, distance and location; and thirdly, perhaps most significantly, it has challenged what might be considered privileged perceptions of who creates, brokers and validates knowledge. There are merits and potential pitfalls to all three of these developments provided by technology, but the truth is that these changes cannot be ignored and have to be embraced as part of modern education and scholarship. Indeed, a reactive 'catch-up' approach is unlikely to be successful (certainly in terms of responding to competitive pressures) and a more generative strategy will better serve programme teams and institutions, even given high levels of unpredictability.

Returning to the 3 Es, at the top of the triangle we have student expectations. As regards learning resources, a common expectation will be that they are rich and relevant, timely, clear and, above all, accessible. Negotiating and fulfilling this expectation at the same time as preserving the structure, inspiration and integrity of the learning process is another key dimension of the optimal student experience. This 'anytime, anyplace, anywhere' expectation has been termed

Martini information literacy (Walsh, 2011), and considering how this expectation changes or challenges what information literacy means will be an increasingly important issue.

But information is only information, and in this *information age* there is an awful lot of it . . . Instructional technology pioneer David Merrill tells us emphatically that 'information is not instruction' (cited in Zemke, 1998) and without ruling out self-instruction or autonomous learning (and increasingly online resources can be well designed to support this for some areas of study), this keeps in focus the importance of learning as an experience, of learning through doing and of learning as a relationship. And in terms of the skills and attributes needed by many professions and valued by many employers, collaborative qualities are ranked at least equally alongside autonomous thinking and problem solving. In whatever way or in whatever context, information and resources need to be brought to life if they are to effectively support learning, even if this is with just one simple, well-chosen question that stimulates a learning conversation.

The resources dimension illustrates powerfully the integrated nature of this four-box model. It can be readily seen that accessible and timely resources are a key part of what enables an excellent learning environment, and strong relationships and interactions inspire students to not only engage with the 'set' resources, but also go on to explore and discover others and even develop resources of their own. And linking all three is the motivation of individual students, the want or need to learn, that is energised and enhanced when a range of relevant, inspiring and appropriately challenging resources are encountered.

CONCLUSION

Does your programme team have a shared understanding of what student engagement means for you in your context? And does that shared understanding work as a vision that guides decisions, inspires action and forms part of your team identity (and the course identity too)? If not, or if this could be further enhanced, then a piece of collaborative engagement working with the team, involving students, using the format of a model such as this, could be more valuable than a further content review or validation.

There are other models and approaches for considering, exploring and even surveying student engagement, and this is rightly becoming a central consideration in assuring and enhancing higher education quality and also, more tangibly perhaps, in recruiting and retaining students. In Chapter 7 we noted that in June 2012, the Quality Assurance Agency for Higher Education in the UK published a chapter (B5) specifically on Student Engagement as part of the UK Quality Code (Quality Assurance Agency, 2012a). Another model that has been effectively adapted for considering levels or types of student engagement, or student voice, is based on Sherry Arnstein's ladder of citizen participation (1969). The levels of participation can be expressed in various ways, but the poles run

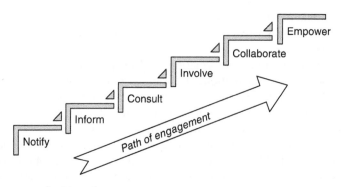

FIGURE 9.6 Ladder of engagement

from inform (making information available) through to citizen control or empowerment (self-direction and agenda setting): note that the Arnstein model also has two levels of nonparticipation. The Technology-Supported Process for Agile and Responsive Curricula (T-SPARC, n.d.) project at Birmingham City University in the UK uses the progression notify, inform, consult, involve, collaborate and empower (adapted from Rudd, Colligan and Naik, 2006) as shown in Figure 9.6 above.

The National Survey of Student Engagement (NSSE, n.d.), launched in 2000 and used in both Canada and the USA (and subsequently in other countries including Australia and South Africa), is an instrument originally structured around five benchmark categories:

- level of academic challenge;
- enriching educational experiences;
- active and collaborative learning;
- supportive campus environment;
- student–faculty interaction.

In 2013 these benchmark categories were expanded to ten engagement indicators: higher-order learning, reflective and integrative learning, quantitative reasoning, learning strategies, collaborative learning, discussions with diverse others, student–faculty interaction, effective teaching practices, quality of interactions and supportive environment. The core purpose of the survey is to measure the degree to which students are engaged in their academic and other educationally purposeful activities. In the UK, the Higher Education Academy (2013) piloted the United Kingdom Engagement Survey (UKES) based on the NSSE and this is now available for institutions to participate in with regard to undergraduate students.

QUESTIONS FOR ACTION AND REFLECTION

1 How would you describe the current understanding of student engagement in your team/department/institution?

2 What steps could you take to work towards a stronger shared understanding of student engagement in your team/department/institution? How could you involve both staff colleagues and students in this process?

3 What opportunities are there for students to discuss, explore and reflect upon their motivation to learn within your module/course/suite of programmes? How could this be further integrated?

4 On your module/course/suite of programmes, what is the balance between learner–content interaction, learner–tutor interaction and learner–learner interaction? How could you enhance the balance and interplay between these three fundamental learning relationships?

5 Which aspects of your current learning environment do you feel work best for strengthening student engagement? How could you build upon these further?

6 In terms of student engagement, which aspects of your learning environment would you most like to change and why? Who else do you need to involve in considering this?

7 Applying the idea of a high-challenge, low-threat learning environment, are there opportunities for either increasing 'challenge' or reducing 'threat' with regard to the student learning experience on your module/course/suite of programmes? If so, what steps could you and/or others take?

8 Which resources do students enjoy and appreciate the most on your module/course/suite of programmes? What makes them special? How could other resources be enhanced to emulate these?

9 How well do you describe your approach to engagement to new and prospective students? What more could you do to make this a central feature of the educational experience?

10 What excites you most about the opportunities for developing and enhancing student engagement over: a) the next year; and b) the next three years?

Chapter 10

Leading yourself

You cannot be true to others until you are true to yourself.

THE CHALLENGE IN THIS CHAPTER

The primary focus in this short chapter will be on *you*. You as a person and you as a leader of change. You as someone with a beating heart, a unique history and a set of values and character strengths that yearn to be fulfilled. And leadership is one of the greatest opportunities to express the values that define us as individuals through the goals we set, the drives we exhibit, the empathy we display and the relationships we form with others. At the very same time, though, the greatest challenge of leadership can be preserving yourself, your true self, in the face of turbulent change, organisational priorities that you may sometimes struggle to connect with, and similarly when you encounter a culture of leadership behaviours either locally or across the organisation that feel at odds with the values that matter to you.

In Chapter 3 the acronym PRAISE was introduced as a tool to identify and summarise the various responsibilities that together make up a manager's role (*what the manager manages*). The 'S' in PRAISE stands for self-management and in Chapter 3 a list was provided of the variety of things that would come under this heading, which extends considerably further than just managing time and task:

- own objectives – work contribution and development;
- time and task management;
- image and impact – how you are perceived by others;
- modelling and inspiration – the behaviours and values you model;
- setting standards – your focus, energy and effectiveness;

218

- personal resilience;
- personal inspiration – what inspires you?;
- work/life balance – your own well-being;
- outlook and happiness.

Self is also the strand that runs through the centre of the Programme Leadership Model. Linked to this, the model articulates six leadership qualities ('the indispensable six') that can be regarded as fundamental because without them, trust will quickly evaporate:

- honest;
- humble;
- reliable;
- respectful;
- committed;
- courageous.

Chapter 2 includes a brief narrative elaborating on each of these.

Self-awareness, self-management and self-reflection are really the underlying themes in this chapter. And having compassion for yourself is the key message:

> If your compassion does not include yourself, it is incomplete.
>
> (Siddhārtha Gautama Buddha)

Perhaps the greatest challenge for any leader is self-awareness: a refined understanding of what drives us, what makes us who we are, the strengths that enable us to flourish and, very importantly, the impact we have on others. We are neither chameleons nor automatons, and if we approach leadership as though we were, our effectiveness will be reduced and we may also suffer personally in terms of our health, well-being and happiness. Within Daniel Goleman's model of emotional intelligence, self-awareness is the foundation, which he defines as:

> Knowing one's emotions, strengths, weaknesses, drives, values and goals – and their impact on others.
>
> (Goleman, 1996)

Figure 2.3 in Chapter 2 provides an illustration of the five components of emotional intelligence.

To 'know thyself' (a variously attributed maxim from ancient Greece) is a lifelong quest as we rediscover ourselves anew in different situations and as latent values and qualities find their expression. For this reason, you will observe that emotionally intelligent leaders seek feedback all the time, both formally and informally, because they appreciate the mirror this holds up for them and the productive self-reflection that it triggers. And the stronger the self-awareness, the greater the foundation for self-management. Self-management in leadership particularly involves the ability to control or redirect 'disruptive emotions' (Goleman, 1996) for the benefit of the group or collective: the way in which the leader reacts will often set the tone for the team or organisation. If self-awareness is detached from self-management, it becomes a kind of hollow indulgence that can result in us leading in a particular way or conforming to some sort of 'house style', without our own drives, strengths and values being authentically engaged. If prolonged, this can be damaging; at the very least, it will be the cause of dissatisfaction and fatigue.

Self-leadership involves engaging with three powerful questions (see Figure 10.1).

PERSONAL LEADERSHIP – WHAT SORT OF LEADER DO YOU WANT TO BE?

It is amazing how few leaders have consciously asked themselves this question. For many, of course, the spirit of this question has been part of their personal journey of development, and they can reflect back on twists and choices (mini- and major moments of epiphany) that shaped the leader they have become. But how wonderful to be invited to consider this question as a development intervention at a reasonably early stage! What a difference it could make as an opportunity and encouragement to consider and consciously mould a personal vision of leadership that flows from drives and values that feel both natural and native. Leadership development activities should be reflective opportunities to contemplate a personal vision of leadership as much as they are about exploring things like teams, performance and strategies for change. But seldom in life can you have it all your own way, even in an ostensibly powerful role, and this brings us to the second question.

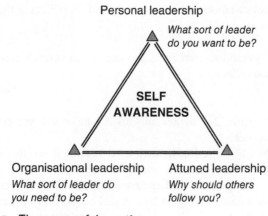

FIGURE 10.1 Three powerful questions

ORGANISATIONAL LEADERSHIP – WHAT SORT OF LEADER DO YOU NEED TO BE?

This question invites you to consider what sort of leader the organisation 'apparently' needs you to be. The culture of leadership in an organisation, or surrounding an endeavour, will have been shaped by a range of factors:

1   history (narrative factors);
2   key players (past and present);
3   professional or disciplinary norms (tribal factors);
4   customer/client expectations (however that is defined);
5   the pressure to produce (the imperatives of the task or goal);
6   levels of social exchange (community factors);
7   internal structures and systems (organisational factors); and
8   the sometimes hard-to-discern map of prevailing cultural assumptions currently in place.

All of this leads to what Marvin Bower (1966) memorably described as 'the way we do things around here' and however strange or alien this might initially seem to a new entrant (a new leader), the 'gradual process of taking things for granted' (Schein, 1984) can easily take hold of any of us. This is why it is so powerful to be invited to consider the first question on personal leadership. We do have a choice, at least to some extent, and the first question encourages us to consider our personal reference point, our personal vision. This is a healthier position than merely being swept along by a way of engaging with others that feels wrong and causes a kind of spiritual tension, an internal conflict that we cannot properly define or address because our personal vision of leadership is poorly understood. Sometimes, though, as leaders we discover our true voice 'after the event' and have to live with a sense of regret that we did not influence the organisational leadership in some small but perhaps important way. Depending on the circumstances, and the scale and nature of the impact on others, these can sometimes be uncomfortable reflections.

At the end of a long list of sound and memorable advice, Polonius, with rich paternal intent, advises Laertes: 'This above all: to thine own self be true' (*Hamlet*, Act 1, Scene 3). Never let it be said that emotional intelligence is a modern invention; this is a line that deserves to belong in every leadership manual, whether ancient or modern.

ATTUNED LEADERSHIP – WHY SHOULD OTHERS FOLLOW YOU?

It is easy for this to seem, on the surface, a question driven by insecurity. But actually it takes a good measure of inner confidence to really consider the needs of followers and to put them first. As discussed previously, there are no leaders without followers, and ultimately power comes from the engaged consent

221

of those that follow: *a leader without followers is just someone going for a walk* . . . And this is nowhere more true than in situations where the power lines are hazy and the challenge is to lead with influence rather than authority, as is often the reality when leading learning and teaching. Attuned leadership is a form of authentic engagement that looks to close that gap and make connections between the values of the leader and the values of followers, both individually and collectively. In 2006 Rob Goffee and Gareth Jones produced a book called *Why Should Anyone Be Led by YOU?*, which explored what it takes to be an authentic leader:

> At the beginning of the new millennium, our research was driven by this single, simple question. It had an impact . . . Rooms fell silent as people pondered their right to lead and the willingness of their followers to be led by them.
>
> (Goffee and Jones, 2006: 1)

In this attuned leadership the leader looks to achieve a level of deep influence that is as much about 'being' as it is 'doing' (we are, after all, human beings, not 'human doings'). The emotional and interpersonal environment will figure highly in the leader's focus and priorities, and the emphasis will be on the climate of the group and liberating potential rather than on giving strong direction. This very much links with the model of liberating leadership discussed in Chapter 8.

Completing the three sides of the triangle, there is also the tension which may exist – and which invariably does exist to some extent – between the needs of followers and the prevailing organisational leadership. There are a multitude of reasons for this, and in large, complex organisations there will be pockets where the tension is high and other areas where the organisational leadership is more attuned. One factor in this tension will be the degree to which leadership is distributed, and it is a growing proposition in public service leadership, certainly in the UK, that the key to creating a high sense of mutual accountability for collective results, and thereby improved service standards and quality, is the flattening of structures and allowing leadership to find its own level, as it were: leadership moves to those most closely involved in carrying out an activity, delivering a service or creating/supporting an experience. In the UK, for example, collective leadership has become the current proposition in health services (West et al., 2014) and shared leadership is gaining prominence as a proposition in higher education (Bolden et al., 2015).

The following provides some important insights into what is meant by collective leadership:

> Collective leadership represents a new way of sharing power, ensuring that leadership and expertise are correlated at every level in relation to every task. It also represents a strategy for integrating leadership collectively across the organisation . . . Collective leadership means the distribution and allocation

of leadership power to wherever expertise, capability and motivation sit within the organisation.

(West et al., 2014: 7)

The following provides a flavour of the challenges that arise from the notion of shared leadership:

In moving forward, we urge you to take an open yet critical approach to shared leadership in which you become alert to the wider dynamics of leadership and the social, political and cultural context in which it takes place. We encourage you to ask the inconvenient questions about power, purpose and privilege in order to gain genuine insight into what enables and constrains active leadership and followership from all quarters.

(Bolden et al., 2015: 38)

COMPASSION FOR YOURSELF

Self-awareness is the basis of self-management, the ability to redirect 'disruptive emotions' (Goleman, 1996) and transform situations in a positive way. It is also about understanding the impact you have on others, not just in terms of controlling difficult emotions, but also in terms of enhancing the motivational climate through optimism and positivity:

Leaders who can stay optimistic and upbeat, even under intense pressure, radiate the positive feelings that create resonance. By staying in control of their feelings and impulses, they craft an environment of trust, comfort and fairness. And that self-management has a trickle-down effect from the leader.

(Goleman et al., 2002: 47)

Another manifestation of self-management is humility. One of the great outcomes that flows from the ability to monitor effectively our inner world is confidence. This inner confidence reduces the insecurity that comes from always feeling you need to prove yourself to others in the outer world, to be invulnerable and a leader that is 'in the lead'. And with this humility and confidence, the potential to share leadership with others, to distribute leadership power and to be a leader who 'enables leadership' really starts to come into play.

In Chapter 3, POMCE (plan, organise, monitor, control and evaluate) was introduced based on the model of functional management originally proposed by Henri Fayol, and this is what sits at the heart of the organiser attribute in the Programme Leadership Model (the five associated leadership skills). As a brief summary of a lot that has been discussed in this book, could a similar model be put forward to capture the essence, or the art, of leadership? Well, leadership develops with others a shared *vision*, it models and inspires the *energy* for change, it builds commitment through collaborative *engagement* and powerful communication,

223

VEEDA – Five Leadership Arts

Vision – *'Aligning the energies of the organization (others) behind an attractive goal'* (Bennis and Nanus, 1985)
'Start with why' (Sinek, 2009)

Energy – modelling and inspiring the energy for change: *away from, moving towards or generative*

Engagement – powerful communication, collaborative engagement and *collective commitment*

Direction – building consensus, clarifying decisions, showing commitment and *modelling the way*

Alignment – vertical and horizontal – structures, systems and contributions – *line of sight* to the vision

FIGURE 10.2 VEEDA

it creates *direction* through building consensus and clear decisions, and it works to achieve an *alignment* of contributions that links clearly with the vision and connects people with purpose. So, there are five compelling leadership arts: vision, energy, engagement, direction and alignment (VEEDA – see Figure 10.2 above).

And leaders can be passionate – sometimes very passionate – about their purpose and achieving the five arts in VEEDA in a way that is both goal/task-focused and people-focused, working right across the spectrum of personal characteristics in the Programme Leadership Model, from passion to compassion, but with one exception . . . themselves. In the heat of it all and in our admirable and courageous efforts to support others, we can sometimes fail to show ourselves the care and compassion necessary for our own well-being. Compassion for yourself should not be an awkward concept because if you do not sustain yourself in your leadership, then it will be impossible for you to sustain others. The following are ten questions based on self-reflection and mindfulness that encourage leaders to find peace and balance in an often frantic world:

1 What is good about the current moment? Setting aside past events and plans for the future, what is good about now?
2 Which three values currently matter most to you? Think of examples large or small where you have expressed those values in your recent work with others.
3 If you had to praise one achievement of you and your team right now, what would it be?
4 What helps you to feel centred? What things in any aspect of your life help you to feel peaceful and centred?

5 What inspires you? How could you carry that inspiration with you?
6 Who gives you energy and support in your professional role? How can you find time to have quality conversations with them?
7 Who gives you energy and support in your wider life? How can you find time to have quality conversations with them?
8 What is the personal goal that sits behind your current work and leadership? Try to express this to yourself in both a new and a familiar way.
9 How does your role and your work benefit others, near or far? What is your current focus on serving others?
10 What is good about the current moment? What is good about now?

Mindfulness is about observation without criticism: being compassionate with yourself . . . In essence, mindfulness allows you to catch negative thought patterns before they tip you into a downward spiral. It begins the process of putting you back in control of your life.

(Williams and Penman, 2011: 5)

As my final message, let me share with you what I regard as leadership value number one:

Love others and be kind to yourself.

The Programme Leadership Model: self-assessment questionnaire

In the listings below, the statements in the questionnaire are linked to the four key leadership attributes in the Programme Leadership Model and also the critical skills associated with each of the attributes.

In the statements below:

- 'Project' (or initiative, if you prefer) can be taken to refer to new course or module development/design, the redevelopment of a significant part of a course/module, or refreshing a course/module with, perhaps, a new course team and a fresh sense of purpose.
- The terms 'course', 'programme' and 'module' are used fairly interchangeably and should be interpreted widely to encompass the blocks of curricula that tend to be the focus of design, development and delivery in your institution.

CHAMPION

1   (C1) People are likely to lose interest in a project if they are not given full credit for their ideas (PROMOTE)

5   (C2) Spotting the links between apparently diverse ideas and viewpoints is often the key to identifying course design opportunities (NEGOTIATE)

9   (C3) Sticking power counts for more than flair during the early stages of a new project (MODEL)

13   (C4) The needs of people with strong influence must be addressed or satisfied (NEGOTIATE)

17   (C5) Very outspoken people with strong influence must be kept energetically on-side (ENTHUSE)

21   (C6) The most infectious quality in any sales pitch is enthusiasm (ENTHUSE)

25   (C7) It is easy to find reasons not to do something, and so negative viewpoints need to be openly explored (CHALLENGE)

29   (C8) Highlighting the learning benefits to students is more persuasive when seeking support for a course than talking about design features (PROMOTE)

33   (C9) Saying what you believe and value about a project creates an important sense of conviction (MODEL)

37   (C10) Presenting a balanced view of risks and benefits from the outset of a project helps to keep obstacles in perspective (CHALLENGE)

41   (*C11) If people don't see the project as a priority, then you need to sell it to them again (PROMOTE)

45   (*C12) During the early stages of the project, you must inject energy into every piece of communication (ENTHUSE)

ORGANISER

2   (*O1) Thinking through the pathway of logical steps and their timings is the first real management action in the course development process (PLAN)

6   (O2) Progress should be checked regularly, if not constantly, if a complex course development project is going to succeed (MONITOR)

10   (O3) Deciding who does what is the central role of the leader (ORGANISE)

14   (O4) A gentle hand on the tiller is the answer to keeping a project on course (CONTROL)

18   (*O5) We should be learning at every step in the course development process and making adjustments accordingly (CONTROL)

22   (O6) Consulting on ideas is fine, but ultimately one person has to take responsibility for deciding what needs to be done, in what order and by when (PLAN)

26   (O7) Each new module/programme development team should successively learn from the experiences of previous teams (EVALUATE)

30   (O8) Milestones should be created in the project plan for the team to take stock, review progress and make adjustments if necessary (MONITOR)

34   (O9) I enjoy the process of bringing people and resources together to achieve goals (ORGANISE)

38   (O10) If we don't look back and review progress against the goals we set ourselves, then we will never learn how to make better choices in the future (EVALUATE)

42   (O11) Whilst I sometimes admire managers who improvise what to do next, this is not the approach for me (PLAN)

46   (O12) I'm happy to make bold decisions to change the project plan if new circumstances arise (CONTROL)

ENABLER

3   (E1) I am happy to field difficult questions and challenges if it leaves others free to stay focused on the task and make progress (SHIELD)

227

7   (*E2) The role of the leader is to create an environment in which others can succeed (SUPPORT)

11   (E3) Team performance always improves when people are told they are doing well (ENCOURAGE)

15   (E4) People need to be free to express different views, but in a climate of respect (MEDIATE)

19   (E5) Getting people to meet can be hard work, but it is always worthwhile (SHARE/CONVENE)

23   (E6) I always aim to settle differences between people before larger problems arise (MEDIATE)

27   (E7) If anyone must take criticism, it should be the leader rather than the follower (SHIELD)

31   (E8) When difficulties arise, the leader needs to go on showing belief in the team (SUPPORT)

35   (*E9) If someone if too self-critical, then the leader's role is to balance this with praise and positive energy (ENCOURAGE)

39   (E10) If people are protective of their ideas and materials, then the team will not succeed (SHARE/CONVENE)

43   (E11) The most demanding aspect of leadership is showing confidence in a team during periods of uncertainty (SUPPORT)

47   (E12) People in a team should not have to wait to learn they are doing a good job (ENCOURAGE)

MENTOR

4   (M1) Even if I disagree with someone, I will always work hard to understand their point of view (LISTEN)

8   (M2) I believe that it is more important to praise small achievements than it is larger ones (PRAISE)

12   (M3) People don't always realise what they are good at, and it is the leader's role to spend time remedying this (INVEST)

16   (M4) Helping people to assess their own performance is generally the key to improved performance in the future (REVIEW)

20   (M5) I like to talk about situations I've experienced myself to help colleagues explore their own difficulties and challenges (RELATE)

24   (*M6) The most important thing to do when team members have problems is to listen and understand (LISTEN)

28   (M7) In management, providing feedback on individual performance is the key to strengthening outcomes (PRAISE)

32   (*M8) I would rather spend time helping a team member find a solution than give them a ready-made solution (INVEST)

36   (M9) When working on a problem, I always work hard to see things from the other person's point of view (RELATE)

40   (M10) Supporting a colleague to reflect on their work before making changes is key to personal development (REVIEW)

44   (M11) Management is more about listening than telling (LISTEN)

48   (M12) It pays off in the end if you spend time building a colleague's confidence (INVEST)

* Star boxes: the questionnaire includes eight statements that are given additional weighting in the scoring as star boxes. If selected, the star indicates that you feel the statement concerned reflects something essential for achieving excellence in programme leadership.

The change journey: emotional responses to change

Response	Some possible leadership actions
Immobilisation (caused by shock, surprise or disorientation)	• (Prior consultation – to gain involvement, share information, and ask for ideas, etc.) Draw upon the prior consultation – the 'shock' should be less because of this • Acknowledge concerns and fears • Accept that things may slow down • Give people time to talk about it • Listen – listen – listen • Allow or facilitate discussion • Highlight opportunities and benefits of the change • Plan further communication – open and honest (build trust) • Counselling
Denial (disbelief, ignoring the change, looking for ways to reject it)	• Give people space • Don't conclude that *all's well* and that everything has been accepted • Remain watchful and attentive • Maintain communication – the issue has not gone away • Listen • Let people know that when they need to talk they *can* talk – the door is still open • Be clear about what's fixed and what's flexible
Anger (frustration, hurt, a sense of injustice or loss)	• Remain professional yourself – set the example • Be aware of the impact of the change on your own capabilities and behaviour – empathise with others • Make time to listen and discuss the issues • Repeat the positive messages – keep the vision alive • Maintain normal workplace standards • Try not to be personally critical of people's feelings and concerns

Response	Some possible leadership actions
Bargaining (looking to minimise the impact or manoeuvre for position)	• Listen • Be clear about objectives, demands and constraints • Repeat the facts • Emphasise the stabilities – points of continuity • Allow positive ideas through – pass them on – but manage expectations carefully • Be reasonable but realistic • Maintain feedback
Depression (a low mood, lack of energy, a sense of helplessness)	• Listen • Keep people focused on the day-to-day work • Value people – highlight the skills and qualities that individuals have • Reinforce positive messages • Look for natural opportunities to energise the team • Celebrate short-term benefits, victories and achievements • Keep out, about, informed and in touch
Testing (initial engagement, experimenting, checking the boundaries)	• Allow people to test the boundaries • Allow people to learn and discover things for themselves about the new situation (accept some mistakes) • Give people time • Acknowledge all positive actions, contributions and efforts • Be tolerant of mistakes and confusion • Listen • Clarify and share feedback • Identify and communicate clear objectives
Acceptance (engagement, positivity, and discovering a new orientation)	• Ensure clarity of goals • Ensure clarity of roles • Review progress against initial concerns – look back over the 'change journey' and give recognition to all on the achievement • Accept small quality compromises (at least initially) • Encourage positive thinking and new insights • Celebrate the transition • Burn bridges if necessary (*no going back*) • This is the new norm, the new 'status quo'

Bibliography

Achor, S. (2010) *The Happiness Advantage: The Seven Principles that Fuel Success and Performance at Work*. New York: Crown Business

Adair, J. (1973) *Action-Centred Leadership*. New York: McGraw-Hill

——. (1983) *Effective Leadership: A Self-Development Manual*. Aldershot: Gower

Anderson, L. (2003) A Leadership Approach to Managing People in Education. In L. Kydd, L. Anderson and W. Newton (eds), *Leading People and Teams in Education*, London: Sage Publications

Anderson, L. W. and Krathwohl, D. R. (eds) (2001) *A Taxonomy for Learning, Teaching and Assessing*. Boston, MA: Addison Wesley Longman

Archer, D. and Cameron, A. (2013) *Collaborative Leadership: Building Relationships, Handling Conflict and Sharing Control*, 2nd edn. London: Routledge

Arnstein, S. R. (1969) A Ladder of Citizen Participation. *Journal of the American Planning Association*, 35(4): 216–24

Bandura, A. (1977) *Social Learning Theory*. Upper Saddle River, NJ: Prentice Hall

Barnett, R. and Coate, K. (2005) *Engaging the Curriculum in Higher Education*. Maidenhead: SRHE and Open University Press

Bass, B. M. (1985) *Leadership and Performance Beyond Expectations*. New York: Free Press

Bass, B. M. and Avolio, B. J. (eds) (1994) *Improving Organizational Effectiveness through Transformational Leadership*. Newbury Park, CA: Sage Publications

Bateson, G. (1972) *Steps to an Ecology of Mind*. Chicago: University of Chicago Press

Becher, T. and Trowler, P. R. (2001) *Academic Tribes and Territories*, 2nd edn. Maidenhead: SRHE and Open University Press

Bee, R. and Bee, F. (1996) *Constructive Feedback*. London: Institute of Personnel and Development

Belbin, R. M. (1981) *Management Teams: Why They Succeed or Fail*. London: Heinemann

Bennis, W. (2003) *On Becoming a Leader: The Leadership Classic Updated and Expanded*. New York: Perseus Publishing

Bennis, W. and Nanus, B. (1985) *Leaders: The Strategies for Taking Charge*. New York: Harper & Row

Bessant, J., Hughes, T. and Richards, S. (2010) *Beyond Light Bulbs and Pipelines: Leading and Nurturing Innovation in the Public Sector*. Sunningdale: National School of Government, Sunningdale Institute

Biggs, J. and Tang, C. (2007) *Teaching for Quality Learning at University*, 3rd edn. Maidenhead: SRHE and Open University Press

Black, P. (2006) *Assessment for Learning: Where Is It Now? Where Is It Going? Improving Student Learning through Assessment.* Oxford: Oxford Centre for Staff and Learning Development

Bloom, B. S. (ed.) (1956) *Taxonomy of Educational Objectives: Handbook 1 – The Cognitive Domain.* New York: Longman

Bolden, R., Gosling, J., O'Brien, A., Peters, K., Ryan, M. and Haslam, A., with Longsworth, L., Davidovic, A. and Winklemann, K. (2012) *Academic Leadership: Changing Conceptions, Identities and Experiences in UK Higher Education.* Final Report for the Leadership Foundation for Higher Education.

Bolden, R., Jones, S., Davis, H. and Gentle, P. (2015) *Developing and Sustaining Shared Leadership in Higher Education.* London: Leadership Foundation for Higher Education

Bolden, R., Petrov, G. and Gosling, J. (2008) *Developing Collective Leadership in Higher Education.* Leadership Foundation for Higher Education

Bolton, R. and Bolton, D. G. (1996) *People Styles at Work: Making Bad Relationship Good and Good Relationships Better.* New York: AMACOM

Bolton, R. and Bolton, D. G. (2009) *People Styles at Work and Beyond: Making Bad Relationship Good and Good Relationships Better,* 2nd edn. New York: AMACOM

Bower, J. L. and Christensen, C. M. (1995) Disruptive Technologies: Catching the Wave. *Harvard Business Review,* January–February

Bower, M. (1966) *The Will to Manage.* New York: McGraw-Hill

Bradley, D., Noonan, P., Nugent, H. and Scales, B. (2008) *Review of Australian Higher Education.* Canberra: Department of Education Employment and Workplace Relations

Brent, M. and Dent, F. E. (2010) *The Leader's Guide to Influence: How to Use Soft Skills to Get Hard Results.* Upper Saddle River, NJ: Prentice Hall

Browne, J. (2010) *Securing a Sustainable Future for Higher Education: An Independent Review of Higher Education Funding and Student Finance.* London: HMSO

Bryman, A. (2009) *Effective Leadership in Higher Education.* London: Leadership Foundation for Higher Education

Buckley, A., Soilemetzidis, I. and Hillman, N. (2015) The 2015 Student Academic Experience Survey, www.hepi.ac.uk/wp-content/uploads/2015/06/AS-PRINTED-HEA_HEPI_report_print4.pdf

Burchard, B. (2009) *The Student Leadership Guide,* 4th edn. New York: Experts Academy Press

Burns, J. M. (1978) *Leadership.* New York: Harper & Row

Bush, T. (2003) *Educational Leadership and Management,* 3rd edn, London: Sage Publications

Butcher, C., Davies, C. and Highton, M. (2006) *Designing Learning: From Module Outline to Effective Teaching.* Abingdon: Routledge

Calvin, S. (2012) *Quiet: The Power of Introverts in a World That Can't Stop Talking.* London: Penguin

Camgoz, S. M., Mehmet, B. K. and Ergeneli, A. (2011) Relationship between the Big-five Personality and the Financial Performance of Fund Managers. In M. A. Rahmin (ed.), *Diversity, Conflict and Leadership.* Piscataway, NJ: Transaction Publishers

Campbell, S. (2009) The Truth about Trust, Index of Leadership Trust Special Report. *Edge Magazine,* September: 20–25

Carless, D. (2015) What's in a Grade? *Times Higher Education,* April, https://www.timeshighereducation.co.uk/comment/opinion/whats-in-a-grade/2019504.article

Caruso, D. R. and Salovey, P. (2004) *The Emotionally Intelligent Manager: How to Develop and Use the Four Key Emotional Skills of Leadership.* New York: Jossey-Bass

233

Chamorro-Premuzic, T. (2012) The Dark Side of Charisma. *Harvard Business Review*, https://hbr.org/2012/11/the-dark-side-of-charisma

Change Style Indicator, Discovery Learning Inc., https://www.discoverylearning.com/products-services/change-style-indicator-1b

Chickering, A. W. and Reisser, L. (1993) *Education and Identity*, 2nd edn. New York: Jossey-Bass

Clutterbuck, D. (2001) *Everyone Needs a Mentor, Fostering Talent at Work*, 3rd edn. London: CIPD

Commonwealth of Australia (2009) *Transforming Australia's Higher Education System*. Canberra: Department of Education Employment and Workplace Relations

Conger, J. A. (1998) The Necessary Art of Persuasion. *Harvard Business Review*, May–June

Covey, S. R. (1992) *The Seven Habits of Highly Effective People: Powerful Lessons in Personal Change*. New York: Simon & Schuster

Cuban, L. (1988) *The Managerial Imperative and the Practice of Leadership in Schools*. Albany, NY: State University of New York Press

Dearing, R. (1997) *Higher Education in the Learning Society: Report of the National Committee of Enquiry into Higher Education*. London: HMSO

Denham, Rt. Hon. John (2008) Higher Education. Speech delivered by the Secretary of State for Innovation, Universities and Skills, 29 February

Department for Business Innovation and Skills (2013) *The Benefits of Higher Education Participation for Individuals and Society: Key Findings and Reports, 'The Quadrants'*. BIS Research Paper No. 146, https://www.gov.uk/government/uploads/system/uploads/attachment_data/file/254101

Downey, M. (1999) *Effective Coaching*. London: Orion Business

Drucker, P. F. (1955) *The Practice of Management*. Oxford: Elsevier

Duarte, N. and Sanchez, P. (2016) *Illuminate: Ignite Change through Speeches, Stories, Ceremonies and Symbols*. New York: Portfolio Books

Dweck, C. S. (2008) *Mindset, the New Psychology of Success: How We Can Learn to Fulfill Our Potential*. New York: Ballantine Books

Eiser, B. J. A. (2008) Meeting the Challenge of Moving from Technical Expert to Leader. *Leadership in Action*, 8(5): 13–14

Ernst, C. and Chrobot-Mason, D. (2010) *Boundary Spanning Leadership: Six Practices for Solving Problems, Driving Innovation, and Transforming Organizations*. New York: McGraw-Hill Professional

Exley, K. and Dennick, R. (2004) *Small Group Teaching: Tutorials, Seminars and Beyond*. London: RoutledgeFalmer

——. (2009) *Giving a Lecture: From Presenting to Teaching*, 2nd edn. Abingdon: Routledge

Fayol, H. (1913) The Basic Tools of Administration. Address given to the Second International Congress for the Administrative Sciences

——. (1949), *General and Industrial Management*. London: Pitman

Foote, S. (1993) *North Carolina Libraries*, 51–4: 162

Freedman, J. (2002) Emotional What? Definitions and History of Emotional Intelligence. *Six Seconds Magazine: EQ Today*, www.6seconds.org/2010/01/26/emotional-intelligence-definition-history

French, J. R. P. and Raven, B. (1959) The Bases of Social Power. In D. Cartwright and A. Zander (eds), *Group Dynamics*. New York: Harper & Row

Gallo, A. (2012) How to Get Feedback When You're the Boss. *Harvard Business Review*, https://hbr.org/2012/05/how-to-get-feedback-when-youre

Gallwey, W. T. (1975) *The Inner Game of Tennis.* London: Pan Books

Gandhi, M. K. (1957) *An Autobiography: The Story of My Experiments with Truth.* Boston, MA: Beacon Press

Gardner, J. W. (1990) *On Leadership.* New York: Free Press

Garrett, G. and Davies, G. (2010) *Herding Cats: Being Advice to Aspiring Academic and Research Leaders.* Axminster: Triarchy Press

Gentle, P. and Forman, D. (2014) *Engaging Leaders: The Challenge of Inspiring Collective Commitment in Universities.* Abingdon: Routledge

Gibbs, G., Knapper, C. and Piccinin, S. (2009) *Departmental Leadership of Teaching in Research-Intensive Environments.* London: Leadership Foundation for Higher Education

Gill, R. (2011) *Theory and Practice of Leadership,* 2nd edn. London: Sage Publications

Godin, S. (2008) *Tribes: We Need You to Lead Us.* London: Piatkus

Goffee, R. and Jones, G. (2006) *Why Should Anyone Be Led by YOU? What it Takes to Be an Authentic Leader.* Cambridge, MA: Harvard Business Review Press

Goffee, R. and Jones, G. (2009) *Clever: Leading Your Smartest, Most Creative People.* Cambridge, MA: Harvard Business Press

Goleman, D. (1996) What Makes a Leader? *Harvard Business Review,* June

Goleman, D., Boyatzis, R. and McKee, A. (2002) *Primal Leadership: Learning to Lead with Emotional Intelligence.* Cambridge, MA: Harvard Business School Press

Gosling, D. (2010) Professional Development for New Staff: How Mandatory is Your Post-Graduate Certificate? *Educational Developments,* 11(2): 1–4

Greenleaf, R. K. (1970) *The Servant as Leader.* Atlanta: Robert K. Greenleaf Center for Servant Leadership

——. (1977) *Servant Leadership: A Journey into the Nature of Legitimate Power and Greatness.* Mahwah, NJ: Paulist Press

Grundy, T and Brown, L. (2002) *Be Your Own Strategy Consultant: Demystifying Strategic Thinking – The Cunning Plan.* London: Thomson Learning

Hamelink, C. J. (1994) *Trends in World Communication: On Disempowerment and Self-empowerment.* Penang, Malaysia: Southbound World Network

Handy, C. (1993) *Understanding Organizations,* 4th edn. London: Penguin

Harden, R. M., Crosby, J. R. and Davis, M. H. (1999) An introduction to outcome-based education. *Medical Teacher* 21(1): 7–14

Harrison, K. (2014) Institutional Approaches to HEA Accreditation. Higher Education Academy, https://www.heacademy.ac.uk/download/institutional-approaches-hea-accreditation

Haslam, A., Reicher, S. D. and Platow, M. J. (2011) *The New Psychology of Leadership: Identity, Influence and Power.* New York: Psychology Press

Haughton, J. (2015) Business Leaders in Call for Soft Skills Boost, www.managers.org.uk/insights/news/2015/january/business-leaders-in-call-for-soft-skills-boost

Healey, M., Flint, A. and Harrington, K. (2014) Engagement through Partnership: Students as Partners in Learning and Teaching in Higher Education. Higher Education Academy, https://www.heacademy.ac.uk/sites/default/files/resources/engagement_through_partnership.pdf

Heider, J. (1985) *The Tao of Leadership: Lao Tzu's Tao Te Ching Adapted for a New Age.* Atlanta: Humanics New Age

Hein, G. E. (1991) Constructivist Learning Theory. Paper presented at The Museum and the Needs of People, CECA (International Committee of Museum Educators) Conference, Jerusalem, Israel, 15–22 October

Heron, J. (1999) *The Complete Facilitator's Handbook*. London: Kogan Page

Higher Education Academy (2011) The UK Professional Standards Framework for Teaching and Supporting Learning in Higher Education, https://www.heacademy.ac.uk/recognition-accreditation/uk-professional-standards-framework-ukpsf

——. (2012) A Handbook for External Examining, https://www.heacademy.ac.uk/sites/default/files/downloads/HE_Academy_External_Examiners_Handbook_2012.pdf

——. (2013) United Kingdom Engagement Survey, https://www.heacademy.ac.uk/research/surveys/united-kingdom-engagement-survey-ukes

Holt, J. (1991) *Never Too Late: My Musical Life Story*. New York: Perseus Publishing

ITU (2015) ICT Fact and Figures: The World in 2015, 26 May, https://www.itu.int/net/pressoffice/press_releases/2015/17.aspx

Jackson, N. (2002) Principles to Support the Enhancement of Teaching and Student Learning: Implications for Educational Developers. *Educational Developments*, 3(1): 1–7

Jackson, N. J. (2003) Introduction to Brokering in Higher Education. In N. J. Jackson (ed.), *Engaging and Changing Higher Education through Brokerage*. Aldershot: Ashgate

Jenkins, A., Healey, M. and Zetter, R. (2007) Linking Research and Teaching in Disciplines and Departments. Higher Education Academy, https://www.heacademy.ac.uk/resource/linking-teaching-and-research-disciplines-and-departments

Johns, C. (2004) *Becoming a Reflective Practitioner*, 2nd edn. Oxford: Blackwell

Jung, C. G. (1971 [1921]) *Psychological Types*. London: Routledge & Kegan Paul

Kellerman, B. (2008) *Followership: How Followers Are Creating Change and Changing Leaders*. Boston, MA: Harvard Business Press

Kelley, R. E. (1992) *The Power of Followership: How to Create Leaders People Want to Follow, and Followers Who Lead Themselves*. New York: Bantam Doubleday Dell

Kennedy, J. F. (1961) Special Message to the Congress on Urgent National Needs. Delivered in person before a joint session of the US Congress, 25 May

Kline, N. (1999) *Time to Think: Listening to Ignite the Human Mind*. London: Cassell Illustrated

Knowles, M. S. (1980) *The Modern Practice of Adult Education: From Pedagogy to Andragogy*. Upper Saddle River, NJ: Prentice Hall

Kolb, D. (1984) *Experiential Learning: Experience as the Source of Learning and Development*. Upper Saddle River, NJ:: Prentice Hall

Koontz, H. (1962) Making Sense of Management Theory. *Harvard Business Review*, 40(4): 24–46

Koontz, H. and O'Donnell, C. (1972) *Principles of Management*, 5th edn. New York: McGraw-Hill

Kotter, J. P. (1990) *A Force for Change: How Leadership Differs from Management*. New York: Free Press

——. (1996) *Leading Change*. Cambridge, MA: Harvard Business School Press

Kotter, J. P. and Cohen, D. S. (2002) *The Heart of Change: Real Life Stories of How People Change their Organizations*. Cambridge, MA: Harvard Business Review Press

Kouzes, J. M. and Posner, B. (2002) *The Leadership Challenge*, 3rd edn. New York: Jossey-Bass

——. (2007) *The Leadership Challenge*, 4th edn. New York: Jossey-Bass

——. (2009) To Lead, Create a Shared Vision. *Harvard Business Review*, January

Kübler-Ross, E. (1969) *On Death and Dying*. London: Routledge

Kydd, L., Anderson, L. and Newton, W. (eds) (2003) *Leading People and Teams in Education*. London: Sage Publications

Laurillard, D. (2014) Five Myths about MOOCs. *Time Higher Education Magazine*, January

Lave, J. and Wenger E. (1991) *Situated Learning: Legitimate Peripheral Participation*. Cambridge: Cambridge University Press

Lawton, W., Ahmed, M., Angulo, T., Axel-Berg, A., Burrows, A. and Katsomitros, A. (2013) *Horizon Scanning: What Will Higher Education Look Like in 2020?* London: UK HE International Unit

Lee, S. and Ditko, S. (1962) *Amazing Fantasy #15, Introducing Spider Man*. New York: Marvel Comics

Lencioni, P. (2002) *The Five Dysfunctions of a Team: A Leadership Fable*. New York: Jossey-Bass

Lewin, K., Lippit, R. and White, R. K. (1939) Patterns of Aggressive Behavior in Experimentally Created Social Climates. *Journal of Social Psychology*, 10: 271–301

Lewis, S., Passmore, J. and Cantore, S. (2011) *Appreciative Inquiry for Change Management: Using AI to Facilitate Organizational Development*. London: Kogan Page

Light, G. and Cox, R. (2001) *Learning and Teaching in Higher Education: The Reflective Professional*. London: Sage Publications

Linden, R. M. (2010) *Leading Across Boundaries: Creating Collaborative Agencies in a Networked World*. New York: Jossey-Bass

Linstead, S., Fulop, L. and Lilley, S. (2009) *Management and Organization: A Critical Text*, 2nd edn. Basingstoke: Palgrave Macmillan

Lucas, B. (2005) *Discover Your Hidden Talents: The Essential Guide to Lifelong Learning*. Stafford: Network Educational Press

Macfarlane, B. (2012) *Intellectual Leadership in Higher Education: Reviewing the Role of the University Professor*. Abingdon: Routledge

Marshall, S., Adams, M. and Cameron, A. (2000) In Search of Academic Leadership. Paper presented at the ASET-HERDSA Conference, University of Southern Queensland, Toowoomba, 2–5 July. Available at: www.ascilite.org.au/aset-archives/confs/aset-herdsa2000/procs/marshall.html

Marshall, S. J., Adams, M. J., Cameron, A. and Sullivan, G. (2003) Leading Academics: Learning about their Professional Needs. In L. Kydd, L. Anderson and W. Newton (eds), *Leading People and Teams in Education*. London: Sage Publications

Maslow, A. (1954) *Motivation and Personality*. New York: Harper

Maslow, A. H. (1943) A Theory of Human Motivation. *Psychological Review*, 50(4): 370–96

Maxwell, J. C. (2007) *The 21 Irrefutable Laws of Leadership*, revised edn. Nashville: Thomas Nelson

Mayer, J. D. and Salovey, P. (1997) What Is Emotional Intelligence? In P. Salovey and D. J. Sluyter (eds), *Emotional Development and Emotional Intelligence: Educational Implications*. New York: Basic Books

McCrae, R. R. and Costa, P. T. Jr. (1996) Toward a New Generation of Personality Theories: Theoretical Contexts for the Five-Factor model. In J. S. Wiggins (ed.), *The Five-Factor Model of Personality: Theoretical Perspectives*. New York: Guilford

Mead, G. (2014) *Telling the Story: The Heart and Soul of Successful Leadership*. New York: Jossey-Bass

Merrill, D. W. and Reid, R.H. (1981) *Personal Styles and Effective Performance: Make Your Style Work for You*. Boca Raton, FL: CRC Press

Meyer, H. F., Land, R. and Baillie, C. (eds) (2010) *Threshold Concepts and Transformational Learning*. Rotterdam: Sense Publishers

Middlehurst, R. (1997) Enhancing Quality. In F. Coffield and B. Williamson (eds), *Repositioning Higher Education*. Maidenhead: SRHE and Open University Press

237

Milne, A. A. with decorations by Shepard, E. H. (1926) *Winnie-the-Pooh*. New York: Dutton Children's Books, Penguin Young Readers Group

Mintzberg, H. (1973) *The Nature of Managerial Work*. New York: Harper & Row

Miyazoe, T. and Anderson, T. (2010) Empirical Research on Learners' Perceptions: Interaction Equivalency Theorem in Blended Learning. *European Journal of Open, Distance and E-Learning*, 4(7). Available at: www.eurodl.org/?p=archives&year=2010&halfyear=1&article=397

Moore, M. (1989) Editorial: Three Types of Interaction. *American Journal of Distance Education*, 3(2): 1–7.

Moore, M. R. and Diamond, M. A. (2000) *Academic Leadership, Turning Vision into Reality*. New York: Ernst & Young

Myers, I. B., McCaulley, M. H., Quenk, N. L. and Hammer, A. L. (2003) *MBTI Manual: A Guide to the Development and Use of the Myers-Briggs Type Indicator*, 3rd edn. Hanover, NH: Mountain View

Norton, P. and King, R. (2013) *Regulating Higher Education: Protecting Students, Encouraging Innovation, Enhancing Excellence*. London: Higher Education Commission

NSSE (n.d.) http://nsse.indiana.edu

Obeng, E. (1996) *Putting Strategy to Work: The Blueprint for Transforming Ideas into Action*. London: Pitman Publishing

Parkin, D. (2013) Winning the Inner Game: Imagine Being the Best You Could Possibly Be. Leadership Foundation for Higher Education website blog, http://lfheblog.com/2013/07/22/winning-the-inner-game

——. (2015) No More Heroes . . . ? Leading Engagement. Leadership Foundation for Higher Education blog, http://lfheblog.com/2015/05/29/no-more-heroes-leading-engagement

Pfeffer, J. and Sutton, R. (2006) Evidence-Based Management. *Harvard Business Review*, https://hbr.org/2006/01/evidence-based-management

Pink, D. H. (2011) *Drive: The Surprising Truth about What Motivates Us*. Edinburgh: Canongate Books

Porter, M. E. (1979) How Competitive Forces Shape Strategy. *Harvard Business Review*, March–April

Pratt, D. D. (2005) Personal Philosophies of Teaching: A False Promise? *Academe*, 91(1): 32–5

Prensky, M. (2001) Digital Natives, Digital Immigrants. *On the Horizon*, 9(5): 1–6

Prime, J. and Salib, E. (2014) The Best Leaders Are Humble Leaders. *Harvard Business Review*, https://hbr.org/2014/05/the-best-leaders-are-humble-leaders

Quality Assurance Agency (2012a) The UK Quality Code for Higher Education, Part B, Chapter B5: Student Engagement, www.qaa.ac.uk/assuring-standards-and-quality/the-quality-code/quality-code-part-b

Quality Assurance Agency (2012b) The UK Quality Code for Higher Education, Part B, Chapter B10: Managing Higher Education Provision with Others, www.qaa.ac.uk/assuring-standards-and-quality/the-quality-code/quality-code-part-b

Race, P. (2015) *The Lecturer's Toolkit: A Practical Guide to Assessment, Learning and Teaching*, 4th edn. Abingdon: Routledge

Ramsden, P. (1998) *Learning to Lead in Higher Education*. London: Routledge

Reid, A., Dahlgren, M. A. and Dahlgren, L. O. (2011) *From Expert Student to Novice Professional, Professional Learning and Development in Schools and Higher Education*. New York: Springer

Rittel, H. W. and Webber, M. M. (1973) Dilemmas in a General Theory of Planning. *Policy Sciences*, 4(2): 155–69

Robinson, K. (2013) How to Escape Education's Death Valley. *TED Talks Education*, April, www.ted.com/talks/ken_robinson_how_to_escape_education_s_death_valley? language=en#t-86929

Rogers, C. R. (1969) *Freedom to Learn: A View of What Education Might Become.* Columbus, OH, Charles E. Merrill

———. (1983) *Freedom to Learn for the 80s.* New York: Merrill Publishing

Rogers, E. M. (1962) *Diffusion of Innovations.* New York: Free Press

Roscorla, T. (2014) 3 Things Higher Education Should Know about Disruptive Innovation. EDUCAUSE higher education conference keynote speech, www.govtech. com/education/3-Things-Higher-Education-Should-Know-about-Disruptive-Innovation-.html

Rowland, D. and Higgs, M. (2008) *Sustaining Change, Leadership That Works.* Chichester: John Wiley & Sons

Rudd, T., Colligan, F. and Naik, R. (2006) *Learner Voice: A Handbook from FutureLab.* Bristol: FutureLab

Ryde, R., and Sofianos, L. (2014) *Creating Authentic Organizations: Bringing Engagement Back to Work.* London: Kogan Page

Salmi, J. (2009) *The Challenge of Establishing World-Class Universities.* Washington DC: World Bank

Salovey, P. and Mayer, J. D. (1990) Emotional Intelligence. *Imagination, Cognition, and Personality,* 9: 185–211

Sandel, M. J. (2005) Episode 1, What's The Right Thing to Do? The Moral Side of Murder. *Justice,* Online Harvard Course, www.justiceharvard.org/2011/03/episode-01/#watch

Scase, R. and Goffe, R. (1989) *Reluctant Managers: Their Work and Lifestyles.* London: Unwin Hyman

Schein, E. H. (1984) Coming to a New Awareness of Organizational Culture. *Sloan Management Review,* 25(2): 3–16

Seligman, M. (2011) *Flourish: A New Understanding of Happiness and Well-Being – And How to Achieve Them.* London: Nicholas Brealey Publishing

Senge, P. M. (1990) *The Fifth Discipline: The Art and Practice of the Learning Organisation.* New York: Doubleday

Shuell, T. J. (1986) Cognitive Conceptions of Learning. *Review of Educational Research,* 56: 411–36

Shulman, L. (1987) Knowledge and Teaching: Foundations of the New Reform. *Harvard Educational Review,* 57(1): 1–22

Sinek, S. (2009) *Start with Why: How Great Leaders Inspire Everyone to Take Action.* New York: Portfolio

Skills CFA (2012) Management and Leadership, National Occupational Standards, March, www.skillscfa.org/standards-qualifications/management-leadership.html

Skinner, B. F. (1968) *The Technology of Teaching.* New York: Appleton-Century-Croft

Smith, R. (2010) Feed Forward, http://jiscdesignstudio.pbworks.com/w/page/ 52947129/Feed%20forward

Spielberg, S. (2011) The Adventures of Spielberg: An Interview. *New York Times,* http:// carpetbagger.blogs.nytimes.com/2011/12/20/the-adventures-of-spielberg-an-interview/?_r=0

Stogdill, R. (1948) Personal Factors Associated with Leadership: A Survey of the Literature. *Journal of Psychology,* 25: 35–71

Summerfield, J. and Smith, C. C. (eds) (2011) *Making Teaching and Learning Matter: Transformative Spaces in Higher Education.* New York: Springer

Swain, H. (2013) What Universities Need: Regulation, Regulation, Regulation. *The Guardian*, 7 October, www.theguardian.com/education/2013/oct/07/higher-education-regulation-report-legislation

Tannenbaum, R. and Schmidt, W. H. (1958) How to Choose a Leadership Pattern. *Harvard Business Review*, March–April

——. (1973) How to Choose a Leadership Pattern, Original Article (1958) with a Retrospective Commentary. *Harvard Business Review*, May–June

Taylor, B. (2014) The Best Leaders 'Talk the Walk'. *Harvard Business Review*, https://hbr.org/2014/08/the-best-leaders-talk-the-walk

Taylor, F. W. (1947) *Scientific Management*. London: Harper & Row

Thompson, M. (2009) *The Organizational Champion: How to Develop Passionate Change Agents at Every Level*. New York: McGraw-Hill

Tomasi di Lampedusa, G. (1961) *The Leopard* (translated from the Italian by Archibald Colquhoun). London: Collins and Harvill Press

Trowler, V. (2010) Student Engagement Literature Review. Higher Education Academy, https://www.heacademy.ac.uk/studentengagement/Research_and_evidence_base_for_student_engagement

T-SPARC blog (n.d.) Project Overview, http://blogs.bcu.ac.uk/tsparc/what-is-t-sparc

Tuckman, B. (1965) Development Sequence in Small Groups. *Psychological Bulletin*, 63(6): 384–99

Tysome, T. (2014) *Leading Academic Talent to a Successful Future: Interviews with Leaders, Managers and Academics*. London: Leadership Foundation for Higher Education

University of Lincoln (2013) Student as Producer. Higher Education Academy, https://www.heacademy.ac.uk/sites/default/files/studnet_producer_lincoln_1.pdf

US Department of Education (2006) A Test of Leadership: Charting the Future of US Higher Education, www.ed.gov/about/bdscomm/list/hiedfuture/index.html

Vieru, S. (2015) NUS Vice-President Blames University Teaching for Struggles of Poorer Students. *Times Higher Education*, August

Vygotsky, L. S. (1978) *Mind in Society: Development of Higher Psychological Processes*. Cambridge, MA: Harvard University Press

Walsh, A. (2011) Martini Information Literacy: How Does 'Anytime, Anyplace, Anywhere' Access to Information Change What Information Literacy Means? LILAC Conference 2011, UK, 18–20 April, http://eprints.hud.ac.uk/9936

Warawa, J. (2014) Nine Attributes of Highly Effective Collaborators, www.virgin.com/entrepreneur/nine-attributes-of-highly-effective-collaborators

Watkins, M. (2007) Do You Work for a Sink-or-Swim Organization? *Harvard Business Review*, https://hbr.org/2007/07/do-you-work-for-a-sinkorswim-o-1

Wenger, E. (1998) *Communities of Practice: Learning, Meaning, and Identity*. Cambridge: Cambridge University Press

West, M., Eckert, R., Steward, K. and Pasmore, B. (2014) *Developing Collective Leadership for Health Care*. London: The King's Fund

Whitchurch, C. (2013) *Reconstructing Identities in Higher Education: The Rise of Third Space Professionals*. Abingdon: Routledge

Williams, M. and Penman, D. (2011) *Mindfulness: A Practical Guide to Finding Peace in a Frantic World*. London: Piatkus

Zemke, R. (1998) Wake Up! (And Reclaim Instructional Design). *Training*, 35(6): 36–42

Index

ability 32
academic leadership 52, 61
academics 20–1, 50–1, 121; *see also* colleagues; lecturers; staff engagement
access 8, 141
accountability: collaborative engagement 114; collective commitment 182; management/leadership distinction 58; mutual 4, 11, 26, 113, 115, 166, 182, 222; plans 69; transformational leadership 60
accreditation 140, 163
achievement-focused leadership 36, 44, 45
Achor, Shawn 201
action-centred leadership 25–6
activists 88–9, 90, 92, 95–6, 98, 104–7, 114
activities 66
Adair, John 25–6, 77
adaptive leadership 78
Adenauer, Konrad 203
administration 30
administrative leadership 52
agreement 115–16
Alexander, Graham 193
alignment 94, 120, 140, 142, 171, 191; assessment 148, 164–7; curriculum 109, 110, 135; leadership frontiers 205; management/leadership distinction 58; review process 200; VEEDA 224
Altbach, Philip 14–15
Anderson, L. 54–5
Anderson, T. 211
Anglund, Joan Walsh 78

Archer, D. 120
Aristotle 28
Arnstein, Sherry 215–16
ART grid 143
art of leadership 48, 223
'ask don't tell' habit 194, 195
asserting 79, 80
assertiveness 83–4
assessment 147–68; alignment 164–7; authenticity 167–8; course design 140, 142; giving and receiving 149–50; leadership challenge 151–5; for learning 147, 152; level 162–4; load 161–2; Programme Leadership Model 148–9, 151; purpose of 155–60; types of 160–1
assessment tasks (ATs) 164–5, 166, 191
attracting 79, 80, 83
attributes 29–31, 34–5, 46, 64; assessment and feedback 148–9; briefs 89–90; collaborative 119; course delivery 171–2; course design 113–14; push/pull model 81; self-assessment questionnaire 41, 42–3
attuned leadership 221–2
Australia 14, 216
authentic assessment 148, 167–8
authentic leadership 78, 222
authority 71, 72, 102
autonomy 175, 177, 183
Avolio, B. J. 63
awareness 29, 31, 43

Barnett, R. 128
Bass, Bernard 60, 63, 207

Bee, Roland and Frances 198
behaviour 72, 75–6
being 2, 126–7, 129, 130, 132, 186
Belbin, Meredith 189
belonging 211
benchmarks 140, 161, 162
benefits of higher education participation 7
Bennis, Warren 32, 62, 78, 183
Biggs, J. 18, 164, 167
Blake, Robert R. 26–7
Bloom's Taxonomy 128, 140, 165–6
Bolden, R. 62, 223
Bolton, Robert and Dorothy 83–4
boundary-spanning 5, 119–20, 190, 200
Bower, Marvin 221
Bradley Review (2008) 14
brainstorming 134
breakthrough leadership 205
Brent, M. 73
bridging 79, 80, 81
briefs 88–111; activists 104–7; clarity
    90–1, 104; mandating yourself
    91–2; originators 96–9; Programme
    Leadership Model 89–90; stakeholders
    99–104
brokerage 141
Brown, L. 103
Browne Review (2010) 5
Bryman, A. 50
Buckley, A. 14
Buddha 219
Burchard, B. 187
Burns, James MacGregor 59, 61, 76, 207

Cameron, A. 120
Camgoz, S. M. 92
Campbell, S. 32
Canada 216
Cantore, S. 159
Carless, D. 154
Caruso, David 27, 112, 135
Chamorro-Premuzic, T. 74
champion leadership attribute 29–30,
    31, 35, 43, 53; achievement-focused
    leadership 36, 45; assessment and
    feedback 148, 149; briefs 89, 90;
    course delivery 171, 172; course design
    114; divergent and convergent phases
    135; enthusiasm and modelling 105;

inspirational motivation and idealised
    influence 64; leading engagement 207;
    modelling 170; passion 203; push/pull
    model 81; self-assessment questionnaire
    41, 226–7
change 5–11, 34, 43; achievement-
    focused leadership 44; brokerage 141;
    change journey 84–6, 230–1; course
    design 114; 'high magnitude' 124;
    management/leadership distinction 55,
    56, 58; modelling values and behaviour
    186; understanding and articulating
    107–10
Change Style Indicator 116–17
charisma 60, 74
Chartered Management Institute (CMI)
    15
choice 10
Christensen, Clayton 205
Chrobot-Mason, D. 120
climate 169, 173, 174, 185
Clutterbuck, D. 18
CMI see Chartered Management
    Institute
co-creation 30, 94, 122, 148; Fully
    Engaged Curriculum 131; growth
    mindset 160; openness to 159
co-management 17–18
coaching-focused leadership 36, 44, 46
Coate, K. 128
codes of practice 8
Cohen, D. S. 106, 156
collaboration 5, 160, 179
collaborative engagement 2, 11, 192,
    215; assessment and feedback 151;
    collective commitment 182; course
    design 113, 114–15, 124, 126, 132,
    140; empowerment 179–80; enabler
    leadership attribute 30; Fully Engaged
    Curriculum 130; innovation 118;
    modelling values and behaviour 185;
    opportunities for 160; stakeholder
    analysis 101; VEEDA 223–4; see also
    engagement
collaborative leadership 10, 17, 62, 78,
    119–20
colleagues 120–1, 124–5, 174; see also
    academics; staff engagement
collective commitment 182, 184

collective leadership 222–3
collegiality 201
command 55, 72, 175, 184
commitment 34, 179, 192, 219; collective 182, 184; course delivery 171; course design 114, 115; management/ leadership distinction 58; plans 69
communication 139
compassion 22, 71, 203; course design 132; liberating leadership 76, 181; Programme Leadership Model 29, 31; self-assessment questionnaire 43; soft skills 82; for yourself 223–5
competence 192
competitive pressures 6
complexity 10, 124
compromise 97–8
confidence 188–9, 192, 211, 223
conflict 113, 135, 136
Conger, Jay 86
connectedness 49, 200–1
consistency 32, 33, 183
constructive alignment 140, 164–7, 171, 191
constructivism 128, 164
consumerism 150
context 1, 5, 18, 21
contingency theory of leadership 177
continuing professional development (CPD) 19, 21; see also professional development
Continuum of Leadership Behaviour 177
convergent thinking 113, 133–4, 135, 136–8, 139, 140
conviction 183
Costa, P. T. Jr. 92
courage 28–9, 34, 183, 219
course delivery 169–204; empowerment 179–80; leading individuals 192–204; liberating leadership 180–4; modelling values and behaviour 184–7; Programme Leadership Model 171–2; team-level modelling 187–92; terminological issues 172–4
course design 112–46; divergent and convergent thinking 132–9; educational philosophy 123–6; Fully Engaged Curriculum 126–32; outcomes-based education 92; planning 139–45;

Programme Leadership Model 113–14; student workload 150
Covey, Stephen 97, 195
Cox, R. 173
CPD see continuing professional development
creating 126–7, 129, 130, 131–2
credibility 86, 186
Crosby, J. R. 93
Cuban, L. 57
curriculum: course design 140; curriculum alignment 109, 110, 164–7; Fully Engaged Curriculum 113, 126–32, 135, 186; large-scale reviews 168

Dahlgren, L. O. 128
Dahlgren, M. A. 128
Davies, G. 160
Davis, M. H. 93
Dearing Report (1997) 13
debate 190
decision making 175–6
Denham, John 14
Dennick, R. 3, 173
Dent, F. E. 73
Department for Business Innovation and Skills 7
determination 29, 30, 89
dialogue 147, 153, 154, 158, 173, 181
DICE 103–4
diplomacy 29, 203
direction 223–4
direction-focused leadership 36, 44, 45
distance education 7
distributed leadership 62, 120, 222
divergent thinking 113, 132–3, 134–5, 140
diversity 18–19, 141, 189
doing 2, 126–7, 128, 129, 130, 131, 186
Downey, M. 46
drivers for change 5–11, 114
Drucker, Peter 55
Dweck, Carole 159–60

educational leadership 52
educational philosophy 113, 123–6, 186
Eiser, B. J. A. 4
emotional connection 86

emotional intelligence 5, 22, 27–8, 107, 135, 177; Caruso on 112; influence 74, 76, 78; Programme Leadership Model 28; self-awareness 191, 219–20

emotions 106–7, 135–6; change journey 230–1; control over 223; feedback 198–9

empathy: emotional intelligence 28; empathic listening 195; liberating leadership 76, 181, 183; Programme Leadership Model 29, 31; self-assessment questionnaire 43; soft skills 4, 82

empowerment 179–80; definition of 180; facilitation 176; liberating leadership 170, 181, 183, 184; management/leadership distinction 58; mentor leadership attribute 31; transformational leadership 49

enabler leadership attribute 30–1, 35, 43, 74; assessment and feedback 148, 149, 151; briefs 90; course delivery 172; course design 114; divergent and convergent phases 135, 138; engagement-focused leadership 36, 46; intellectual stimulation 64; leading engagement 207; mediation and shielding 190; modelling 170, 203; push/pull model 81; self-assessment questionnaire 41, 227–8

energy 132, 152, 154, 197, 210, 223

engagement 5, 205–17; assessment and feedback 151, 156; briefs 89; collaborative leadership 120; divergent and convergent phases 138; Fully Engaged Curriculum 113, 126–32, 135, 186; head and heart 106; innovation 118; liberating leadership 181; mentor leadership attribute 31; optimal student experience 208–9; planning 93–4, 103–4; Programme Leadership Model 206–7; review process 200; student 9, 10–11, 21, 93–4, 122–3, 137, 206; transformational leadership 49; VEEDA 223–4; see also collaborative engagement

engagement-focused leadership 36, 44, 46

enhancement 117, 118, 148, 182

enthusiasm 105

environment 67, 132, 208–9, 212–14

equality 8, 141

Ergeneli, A. 92

Ernst, C. 120

evidence-based management 108

Exley, K. 3, 173

expectations 9, 21, 104, 109, 160, 206, 214–15

experience: as source of power 72, 73–4; student 9, 21, 208–9

expert power 3, 73–74

facilitation 169, 172, 174, 176–7

fairness 7–8, 32

Fayol, Henri 54, 55, 68, 69, 72, 138, 223

feedback 147, 198–200; course design 140; giving and receiving 149–50; leadership challenge 151–5; planning and implementation 144–5; praise 201–2; Programme Leadership Model 31, 148–9, 151; purpose of 152, 155–60; teams 191–2; types of 160–1

feedforward 147, 152–3

FHEQ see Framework for Higher Education Qualifications

Fine, Alan 193

Fishbone Analysis 134

five forces model 107

5 Whys' technique 125

Flint, A. 94

followership 49, 62–3, 78, 221–2

Foote, Shelby 214

Force Field Analysis 134

Ford, Henry 105

Forman, D. 155

Four-Branch Model 135

four I's 60, 64

Framework for Higher Education Qualifications (FHEQ) 162

French, John 72

frontiers 205

Fully Engaged Curriculum 113, 126–32, 135, 186

Fulop, L. 53

functional management 36, 48, 55, 223

funding 5–6

Gallwey, Timothy 180

Gandhi, Mahatma 74, 119, 184

Garrett, G. 160

Gentle, Paul 155, 182
Gibbs, G. 61, 180, 183, 186
Gill, R. 3
global changes 6–7
goals 56, 57, 58, 86, 91, 119; *see also* objectives
Goffee, Rob 222
Goleman, Daniel 27–8, 78, 219, 223
Gosling, J. 13–14, 62
great man theory 77
Greenleaf, Robert 77, 204
Group Development Model 187, 188
group processes 133, 135, 136
GROW model 193–4, 200
growth mindset 159–60
Grundy, T 103

Hamelink, C. J. 180, 182
Handy, Charles 57
happiness 201, 219
Harden, R. M. 93
Harrington, K. 94
Haslam, A. 190
HEA *see* Higher Education Academy
Healey, M. 94
Heider, John 76, 81
Hein, G. E. 128
Heron, John 176, 177, 178
Hierarchy of Needs 212–13
Higgs, Malcolm 124
high-challenge, low-threat learning environments 213–14
Higher Education Academy (HEA) 8, 13, 15, 162
Holt, John 95
honesty 33, 178, 219
hope 197–8
humanist school 4
humility 33, 203, 219, 223

idealised influence 60, 64
identity: collective 179; Fully Engaged Curriculum 128, 129; social identity theory 190; teams 30
ILM *see* Institute of Leadership and Management
ILOs *see* intended learning outcomes
implementation planning 142–3, 171
inclusion 8, 141, 211

inclusive leadership 51, 62
individualised consideration 60, 64
influence 29, 52, 70; briefs 89; change journey 84–6; collaborative leadership 120; idealised 60, 64; impactful 71; open and hidden 81–2; people styles 82–4; 'push' and 'pull' influencing styles 71, 78–81; stakeholder analysis 100–1, 102, 103; *see also* persuasion
information: Fully Engaged Curriculum 127, 129, 131; information literacy 214–15; PRAISE 66–7
innovation 51, 52, 74, 179, 205; collective commitment 182; course design 112, 116; diffusion of 189; six dimensions of 117–18
inspiration 29, 64, 178, 218; course design 112; liberating leadership 180–1, 183, 184; modelling values and behaviour 187; personal 219; personality 74; transformational leadership 49, 59
inspirational motivation 60, 64
Institute of Leadership and Management (ILM) 16
institutional standards 163–4
integrity 32, 36
intellectual leadership 52–3, 61
intellectual stimulation 60, 64
intended learning outcomes (ILOs) 164–5, 166, 171, 191
intention 112
interest 100, 102, 152
international standards 163
international students 6–7
Internet 8–9, 212, 214
intuition 116

Jackson, Norman 84, 117, 141
Jenkins, A. 21
Jones, Gareth 222
Jung, Carl 83, 116

Kellerman, Barbara 62
Kelley, Robert Earl 62
Kennedy, John F. 59–60, 82
Kline, N. 188
Knapper, C. 61, 180, 183, 186
knowing 126–7, 129, 130, 131
knowing-your-stuff fallacy 2–3

knowledge 3, 4, 52; Bloom's Taxonomy 166; Dearing Report 13; Fully Engaged Curriculum 129; institutional 163–4; as source of power 72, 73–4
Kolb, David 193
Koontz, Harold 54, 55, 57, 62
Kotter, John 61, 106, 138, 139, 155, 156, 193, 207
Kouzes, J. M. 33, 124, 178–9, 180, 183, 184
Kübler-Ross, Elisabeth 85
Kydd, L. 54–5

ladder of citizen participation 215–16
Lampedusa, Tomasi di 117
language 158, 181, 183, 184
Lao Tzu 75–6, 81
Laurillard, Diana 8
leadership 1–2, 19–20; assessment and feedback 151–5; climate control 169; collective 222–3; conceptions of 43–4; decision making 175–6; followership 62–3; gradual steps approach 5, 16–17; learning-focused 4, 76; liberating leadership 76, 170, 180–4, 222; management distinction 43, 48, 55–9; modelling values and behaviour 170, 184–7, 192; models of 25–8; myths about 78; purpose 22; responsibility 11–12; self-leadership 218–25; shared 51, 62, 78, 120, 222, 223; 'sink-or-swim' approach 4; standards 15–16; style 32, 36, 65, 177; UKPSF 15; see also Programme Leadership Model; transformational leadership
leadership development 15–18, 19, 82, 220
Leadership Foundation for Higher Education 51, 60, 180, 197
leadership frontiers 205
learner interactions 211, 212, 216
learning: assessment and feedback 150; assessment for 147, 152; challenge and threat 213–14; collective 30, 58, 192, 202; course design 140, 142; Dearing Report 13; educational philosophy 125; experiential 193; facilitation of 169, 172, 173, 176; Fully Engaged Curriculum 127, 130,

131–2; information and resources 215; learning practice spiral 194; modelling 170; modelling values and behaviour 185–6, 192; outcomes-based education 92, 140; responsibility for 11; student-centred 11–12, 94–5, 140, 173, 185; teaching and 149, 172–3; transformational leadership 61
learning-focused teaching and leadership 4, 76
lecturers 3, 8, 21; see also academics; colleagues
Lencioni, Patrick 32, 183
Lennon, John 143
level 148, 162–4
Lewin, Kurt 175, 177, 178
Lewis, S. 159
liberating leadership 76, 170, 180–4, 222
Light, G. 173
Lilley, S. 53
Linden, Russell 119
Linstead, S. 53
listening 2, 46, 89, 136, 187–8; to activists 106; change journey 230, 231; collaborative leadership 119; course delivery 171; emotional intelligence 135; leading engagement 207; leading individuals 192, 195–6; liberating leadership 183; mentor leadership attribute 31; relationships 211; soft skills 4, 82
load 148, 161–2
Lucas, Bill 213–14

McCrae, R. R. 92
Macfarlane, B. 53
management 3, 48–69; assessment and feedback 151; definitions of 53–5; evidence-based 108; followership 62–3; high-challenge, low-threat learning environments 214; leadership distinction 43, 48, 55–9; models of 25–8; planning 143–4; POMCE 65, 68; PRAISE 65–8; Programme Leadership Model 63–4
Managerial Grid 26–7
mandating yourself 91–2, 99
Marlowe, Christopher 77
Marshall, S. 61
Maslow, Abraham 212–13

massive open online courses (MOOCs) 7, 8
mastery 183
Maxwell, John 52
Mayer, J. D. 135
Mead, G. 197
mediation 120, 135, 190
Mehmet, B. K. 92
mentor leadership attribute 31, 35, 43; assessment and feedback 149; briefs 89, 90; coaching-focused leadership 36, 46; course delivery 171, 172; course design 114; individualised consideration 64; leading engagement 207; leading individuals 192; push/pull model 81; self-assessment questionnaire 41, 228–9
mentoring 18, 19, 170, 180, 193, 203
Merrill, David 83, 215
Middlehurst, R. 118
Milne, A. A. 16
mindfulness 224–5
Mintzberg, Henry 57
Miyazoe, T. 211
modelling 16, 30, 75, 105, 203, 218; praise and recognition 202; team-level 187–92; values and behaviour 170, 171, 175, 179, 184–7
MOOCs see massive open online courses
Moore, Michael 211
moral authority 72, 74–5
motivation 10, 182–3, 209–10, 215; course design 140; emotional intelligence 27; Hierarchy of Needs 212–13; inspirational 60, 64; management/leadership distinction 58; optimal student experience 208–9
Mouton, Jane 26–7
moving away 80
mutual accountability 4, 11, 26, 113, 115, 166, 182, 222

Nanus, Burt 32, 62, 78, 183
narrative 30, 58, 80, 106, 117, 123, 124, 181
NASA 59–60
National Committee of Inquiry into Higher Education 13
National Student Survey (NSS) 153, 154
National Survey of Student Engagement (NSSE) 216

negativity 185
Newton, W. 54–5
Norton, P. 13
NSS see National Student Survey
NSSE see National Survey of Student Engagement

Obeng, Eddie 115
objectives 55, 138, 140, 141; see also goals
O'Donnell, C. 57
open and hidden influence 81–2
openness 32
optimal student experience 208–9
optimism 60, 156, 197, 201, 223
organisational champions 105
organiser leadership attribute 30, 31, 35, 43, 69; assessment and feedback 149, 151; briefs 90; course delivery 172; course design 114; direction-focused leadership 36, 45; divergent and convergent phases 135, 138; leading engagement 207; push/pull model 81; self-assessment questionnaire 41, 227; transactional leadership 64
originators 88–9, 90, 95, 96–9, 101, 117
outcomes-based education 92–3, 94, 140

pain language 181
participation 2, 169–70, 175, 178; course design 121, 122; empowerment 179–80; ladder of 215–16
partnership 2, 10, 94, 122, 123
passion 22, 71, 203, 224; briefs 89; course design 132; liberating leadership 76, 181; Programme Leadership Model 29, 30, 31; self-assessment questionnaire 43
Passmore, J. 159
pedagogy 34, 170, 186
peer assessment 147, 154
Penman, D. 225
people styles 82–4
personal characteristics 31–2
personal leadership 220, 221
personality 72, 74, 92, 116
persuasion: necessary art of 86; people styles 83; Programme Leadership Model 29, 32; push/pull model 79–80, 81; see also influence

PESTLE analysis 108
Petrov, G. 62
Pfeffer, J. 108
Piccinin, S. 61, 180, 183, 186
Pink, Daniel 182–3
planning 30; convergent phase 136; course design 139–45; engagement 93–4, 103–4; management/leadership distinction 58; POMCE 68; Programme Leadership Model 69
Platow, M. J. 190
politics 98
Pollack, Sydney 36
POMCE 49, 65, 68, 142, 223
Porter, Michael 107
positional authority 72–3, 77
positivity 223
Posner, B. 33, 124, 178–9, 180, 183, 184
potential 169, 173, 180, 181, 183, 185, 188–9
power 11–12, 70, 221–2; language 181; sources of 71–8; stakeholder analysis 100–1, 102
praise 201–2
PRAISE 49, 65–8, 214, 218
Pratt, D. D. 187
precision 29, 30
Prime, J. 203
professional development 13, 19, 81
professional standards 163
Programme Leadership Model 24–5, 28–47, 53, 74, 219; assessment and feedback 148–9, 151; briefs 89–90; courage 183; course delivery 171–2; course design 113–14; divergent and convergent phases 135; engagement 206–7; guidance notes for workshops 43–6; leading individuals 192; management 63–4; plans 69; push/pull model 81; self-assessment questionnaire 37–43, 46, 226–9
purpose 2, 22, 183, 207; of feedback 152, 155–60; shared 59, 152
'push' and 'pull' influencing styles 71, 78–81, 119

qualities 32–4, 35–6, 219
quality 7, 8, 11, 34, 52, 118, 182

Quality Assurance Agency for Higher Education (QAA) 13, 122, 162, 163, 215

Race, Phil 210
Ramsden, Paul 21
Raven, Bertram 72
recognition 21, 53, 201–2
reform 13
regulation 12, 13–14
Reicher, S. D. 190
Reid, A. 128
relationships 2, 4, 76–7, 89, 210–12; assessment and feedback 153; building 5; collegiality 201; liberating leadership 181, 183, 184; optimal student experience 208–9; voice of relationship 72
reliability 33, 219
'reluctant managers' 50
renovation 116, 118
reputation 12, 13, 193, 202
research 20–1
resilience 29, 30, 89, 219
resources 66, 200, 208–9, 214–15
respect 33–4, 219; liberating leadership 76, 181; modelling the pedagogy 186; mutual 211
responsibility 2, 11–12, 206–7; coaching-focused leadership 44; course design 140; PRAISE 65–8; transformational leadership 60
responsiveness 83–4
review process 200
rewards 21, 53, 59, 182
Robinson, Ken 169, 173, 174
Rogers, Carl 4, 94, 155, 172
role rotation 53
'roving' line of sight 182, 184
Rowland, Deborah 124
Ryde, R, 183, 196

Salib, E. 203
Salovey, P 27, 135
Sandel, Michael 142
satisfaction 154
Schmidt, Warren 177, 178
self 32, 35–6, 67, 219
self-appraisal 31, 199–200, 202

self-assessment 147, 154–5

self-assessment questionnaire 24–5, 37–43, 46, 226–9

self-awareness 36, 223; emotional intelligence 27, 74, 191, 219–20; People Styles at Work model 84; Programme Leadership Model 28

self-determination 55, 176

self-direction 182, 184, 185, 197

self-empowerment 92

self-leadership 218–25

self-limiting beliefs 181, 183

self-management 218, 220, 223

self-reflection 128, 219–20, 224

self-regulation 27

Seligman, M. 211

senior sponsors 101–2

sensing 116

servant leadership 62, 77, 78, 204

shadowing 18

Shakespeare, William 78, 221

shared leadership 51, 62, 78, 120, 222, 223

shared purpose 59, 152

shared vision 34, 58, 60, 112, 179, 223

Shepard, E. H. 16–17

Shuell, T. J. 164

Sinek, Simon 156

'sink-or-swim' approach 4

skills: assessment and feedback 148–9; briefs 89–90; course delivery 171–2; course design 113–14; Dearing Report 13; engagement 207; influence 71; Programme Leadership Model 31–2, 34–5, 43, 46; self-assessment questionnaire 24–5; social skills 28; soft skills 4, 82

Skinner, B. F. 59

social capital 200–1

social development theory 149

social identity theory 190

social skills 28

Sofianos, L. 183, 196

soft skills 4, 82

South Africa 216

spectrum of personal characteristics 24, 28–29, 31, 34–35, 244

Spielberg, S. 118

staff engagement 120–1, 156, 206; see also academics; colleagues; lecturers

stakeholder analysis 100–4, 134

stakeholders 88–9, 95–6, 99–104

standards 8, 12, 13; academic 162–3; assessment 162; institutional 163–4; international 163; occupational 15–16; professional 163; setting 218

Stogdill, Ralph 77

stories 86, 196–7

strengths 189

student-centred approach 2, 9, 11–12, 94–5, 140, 173, 183, 185

student engagement 9, 10–11, 21, 93–4, 122–3, 137, 156, 206, 215–16; see also engagement

student expectations 9, 21, 206, 214–15; see also expectations

student experience 9, 21, 206, 208–9

student satisfaction 154

student voice 10, 21, 153–4, 157, 188

students as partners 2, 10, 93–4, 122, 123, 154, 211

supporting individuals 192–204

Sutton, R. 108

SWOT analysis 134

taking stock 133, 134, 136

'taking turns' 51, 53

'talking the walk' 193

Tang, C. 18, 164, 167

Tannenbaum, Robert 177, 178

targets 151

Taylor, B. 193

teaching 3, 15, 174, 192–3; autonomy and freedom 183; course design 140; Dearing Report 13; learning and 149, 172–3; learning-focused teaching and leadership 4, 76; research and 21; student satisfaction 154; transformational leadership 60–1

teaching and learning activities (TLAs) 164–5, 191

teams: action-centred leadership model 25–6; empowerment 180; engagement-focused leadership 44; identity 30; leadership modelling 187–92; PRAISE 66; recognition 202; 'team charters' 180, 191; trust 32

technology 8–9, 214; see also internet

Thompson, Mike 90, 105

3 Es 9, 206, 214
'tigers' 202–3
TLAs *see* teaching and learning activities
Townsend, Robert 203
Toyoda, Sakichi 125
training 13, 19, 170
trait theories 77
transactional leadership 59, 61, 64, 78, 207
transferability 8, 10
transformation 10–11, 49, 84–5, 108; course design 112, 124–5, 132, 137, 141; curriculum alignment 110; learning 180; modelling values and behaviour 186; *see also* change
transformational feedback 147, 156
transformational leadership 4, 48–9, 59–61, 78; intellectual leadership 53; leading engagement 207; organisational champions 105; Programme Leadership Model 43, 63
transnational education 6–7
transparency 8
trust 2, 36, 160, 179; climate of 173; engagement-focused leadership 44; leadership qualities 219; liberating leadership 76, 181, 183, 184; mentors 31; modelling the pedagogy 186; respect and 34; team management 32; transformational leadership 49, 60
Tuckman, B. 187
tuition fees 5, 10

UK Professional Standards Framework for Teaching and Supporting Learning in Higher Education (UKPSF) 15
understanding 32

United Kingdom Engagement Survey (UKES) 216
United States 14, 216

value for money 10
values 52, 175; briefs 89; commitment to 34, 182; modelling 170, 171, 184–7, 192; mutual 90; 'team charters' 180
VEEDA 223–4
verbs 158, 164–5
Vieru, S. 174
vision 29–31, 43, 44, 64, 175; assessment and feedback 156, 157, 158; attracting with 80; briefs 89, 98; collaborative leadership 119; commitment to 34; communication of 139; liberating leadership 181; management/leadership distinction 58, 59; modelling values and behaviour 187; shared 34, 58, 60, 112, 179, 223
voice 10, 21, 153–4, 157, 188
Vygotsky, Lev 149

'walking the talk' 192–3
warmth 76
Watkins, M. 4
well-being 67, 201, 211, 219, 224
Wenger, Etienne 212
West, M. 222–3
Whitchurch, C. 121
Whitmore, John 193
Wilde, Oscar 75
Williams, M. 225
Wilton, Petra 82
Winnie-the-Pooh 16, 17
work/life balance 219
workload 150, 151
World Wide Web 9; *see also* internet